Quick Degunking Sheet!

The Degunking 12-Step Program

Here is the basic 12-step degunking process that you should follow to fully degunk your PC:

1. Get rid of the files you don't really need (Chapter 3).

2. Uninstall programs you don't need (Chapter 4).

3. Organize your files and folders (Chapter 5).

4. Clean up your Desktop and Start menu (Chapter 6).

5. Reduce your e-mail spam, and sort through and organize your Outlook mail (Chapters 7 & 8).

6. Clean and fine-tune the Registry (Chapter 9).

7. Optimize your hard drive (Chapter 10).

8. Install the latest upgrades (Chapter 11).

9. Incorporate PowerToys and good shareware to help keep your machine clean and running efficiently (Chapter 13).

10. Improve security and set up a good firewall (Chapter 14).

11. Back up your system on a regular basis (Chapter 15).

12. Use a smart approach if you think your machine is ready to be retired (Chapter 16).

Degunking with Time Limitations

To get the full benefits of degunking, we highly recommend that you complete all of the main degunking tasks in the order that they are presented. Performing all of these tasks will require a bit of time. If your time is limited, here are some suggestions for valuable degunking tasks you can perform in the time you *do* have—whether it's ten minutes, three hours, or a half day.

Ten-Minute Degunking

If you have a very short amount of time—less than half an hour, say— you should focus on archiving, deleting, and compressing some of your e-mail:

1. Move a large group of old e-mails to an archived folder and delete the e-mails from your current inbox (Page 126).

2. Empty the deleted bin of your emails.

3. If you have any more time, look for large blocks of e-mails that you no longer need and delete them. A good place to look is any folder that contains e-mail more than six months old.

4. Look in the Sent folder and delete all sent e-mails with attachments.

5. Empty the Recycle Bin to free up space on your hard drive (Page 70).

Thirty-Minute Degunking

If you only have thirty minutes or so, we recommend you perform the ten-minute degunking plan listed above and then the following tasks to get rid of files and programs stored on your hard drive that you no longer use:

1. Remove the excessive junk in your default folders: My Documents, My Music, My Videos, and so on (Page 24).

2. Remove the temporary files on your system (Page 37).

3. Try to remove the programs you no longer use by utilizing the programs' uninstall options (Page 44). Because deleting a program might take a few minutes, you might need to focus on deleting five or so programs.

4. Remove unwanted programs that don't have an uninstall option with the Control Panel (Page 47).

5. Empty the Recycle Bin to free up space on your hard drive (Page 70).

One-Hour Degunking

If you have an hour to degunk your PC, you can go a little deeper and remove more e-mails, files and folders, and programs you no longer need. Here are the tasks to focus on:

1. Perform the thirty-minute degunking plan.

2. Delete more unnecessary files by focusing on the following:

    *   Remove the files you don't need from your root directory on your main drive (C:\) (Page 31).

- Search for files you don't need on your default drive and remove them (Page 34).
- Remove unused unzipped files and other duplicate files (Page 36).
3. Uninstall more unnecessary programs by focusing on the following:
   - Remove extraneous Windows components from Control Panel (Page 48).
   - Search for programs you didn't know you had and remove them (Page 50).
   - Remove programs for hardware you no longer own or don't use any more (Page 54).
4. Empty the Recycle Bin to free up space on your hard drive (Page 70).

Three-Hour Degunking

Because you now have a little more time to degunk your PC, with this plan you'll be able to:

1. Perform the one-hour degunking tasks.
2. Fine-tune the programs you regularly use to improve their performance (Page 55).
3. Organize the default folders by creating additional, embedded folders and moving files into them (Page 64).
4. Use the File and Folders tasks pane in Windows XP to rename, move, copy, or delete folders (Page 68).
5. Use Disk Cleanup and Disk Defragmenter to really complete the cleansing process (Page 73).

Half-Day Degunking

When you have limited time to degunk, your focus should be on cleaning up e-mails, files and folders, and unused programs. Having a half day to degunk allows you to clean up and tweak your Desktop and Start menu, as well as perform some additional e-mail degunking tasks:

1. Perform the three-hour degunking tasks.
2. Clean up and personalize the Taskbar so you can work faster and smarter (Page 78).
3. Remove items from the System Tray that use valuable system resources (Page 79)
4. Limit the programs that start when Windows starts (Page 85).
5. Personalize the Start menu by adding or deleting programs, reordering the list, and more (Page 86).
6. Personalize the Desktop with your favorite folders and shortcuts, and remove unused icons (Page 89).
7. Set-up a separate spam filtering utility to help you reduce the amount of spam you receive (Page 108).

Spare Moment Degunking

There may be times when you are doing something with your computer and you discover that you have a few minutes to spare. To this end, we've created our top twenty list of degunking tasks that you can perform. These tasks do not need to be performed in any specific order. Simply select a task and perform it to help clean your machine.

Twenty Useful Degunking Tasks

1. Delete five icons off of your Desktop (Page 90).

2. Get rid of annoying pop-up messages with a useful utility (Page 217).

3. Empty the Recycle Bin (Page 70).

4. Uninstall one or more programs you no longer use (Page 44).

5. Remove annoying Spyware (Page 52).

6. Delete 10 of your top 30 largest e-mails (Chapter 8).

7. Setup Internet Explorer to better manage cookies (Page 230).

8. Remove extraneous Windows components from Control Panel (Page 48).

9. Add or remove default icons on your Desktop (Page 90).

10. Remove a program from your Start menu that you really don't need (Page 85).

11. Check your e-mail outbox and drafts folders to make sure gunk isn't accumulating there (Page 132).

12. Locate five one megabyte or larger files that you no longer need and delete them.

13. Empty your Deleted Items in your e-mail (Chapter 8).

14. Use the Windows Backup utility to back up important files and folders (Page 244).

15. Download and use the TweakUI PowerToy to customize Windows settings (Page 211).

16. Personalize the Windows default folders with folders of your own (Page 68).

17. Configure your virtual memory settings to fully utilize the memory you have (Page 193).

18. Unsubscribe from an e-mail newsletter you no longer read (Chapter 7).

19. Configure Internet options to protect, secure, and keep your private information private (Page 225).

20. Physically clean your screen or keyboard (Page 200).

Joli Ballew

Jeff Duntemann

President
Keith Weiskamp

Editor-at-Large
Jeff Duntemann

Vice President, Sales, Marketing, and Distribution
Steve Sayre

Vice President, International Sales and Marketing
Cynthia Caldwell

Production Manager
Kim Eoff

Cover Designers
Kris Sotelo and Jesse Dunn

Degunking Windows™

Limits of Liability and Disclaimer of Warranty

The author and publisher of this book have used their best efforts in preparing the book and the programs contained in it. These efforts include the development, research, and testing of the theories and programs to determine their effectiveness. The author and publisher make no warranty of any kind, expressed or implied, with regard to these programs or the documentation contained in this book.

The author and publisher shall not be liable in the event of incidental or consequential damages in connection with, or arising out of, the furnishing, performance, or use of the programs, associated instructions, and/or claims of productivity gains.

Trademarks

Trademarked names appear throughout this book. Rather than list the names and entities that own the trademarks or insert a trademark symbol with each mention of the trademarked name, the publisher states that it is using the names for editorial purposes only and to the benefit of the trademark owner, with no intention of infringing upon that trademark.

Paraglyph Press, Inc.
4015 N. 78th Street, #115
Scottsdale, Arizona 85251
Phone: 602-749-8787
www.paraglyphpress.com

Paraglyph Press ISBN: 1-932111-84-0

Printed in the United States of America
10 9 8 7 6 5

PARAGLYPH
P R E S S

The Paraglyph Mission

This book you've purchased is a collaborative creation involving the work of many hands, from authors to editors to designers and to technical reviewers. At Paraglyph Press, we like to think that everything we create, develop, and publish is the result of one form creating another. And as this cycle continues on, we believe that your suggestions, ideas, feedback, and comments on how you've used our books is an important part of the process for us and our authors.

We've created Paraglyph Press with the sole mission of producing and publishing books that make a difference. The last thing we all need is yet another tech book on the same tired, old topic. So we ask our authors and all of the many creative hands who touch our publications to do a little extra, dig a little deeper, think a little harder, and create a better book. The founders of Paraglyph are dedicated to finding the best authors, developing the best books, and helping you find the solutions you need.

As you use this book, please take a moment to drop us a line at **feedback@paraglyphpress.com** and let us know how we are doing—and how we can keep producing and publishing the kinds of books that you can't live without.

Sincerely,

Keith Weiskamp & Jeff Duntemann
Paraglyph Press Founders
4015 N. 78th Street, #115
Scottsdale, Arizona 85251
email: **feedback@paraglyphpress.com**
Web: **www.paraglyphpress.com**

As always, I'd like to dedicate this book to my family, for all their help and support.

—Joli Ballew

In memory of Chewy, 1982-1998, who chose the long life rather than the glorious one!

—Jeff Duntemann

&

About the Authors

Joli Ballew, MCSE, A+, is a full time writer and digital enthusiast who also teaches, creates Web sites, and consults from her home base of Dallas, Texas. Joli has written almost a dozen books on subjects ranging from digital photography to network administration. Two of her books, *Windows XP—The Ultimate Users Guide 2nd Ed.* and *Windows 2000 Server On Site*, are also available from Paraglyph Press.

Jeff Duntemann is an author, editor, programmer, lecturer, and technology columnist, with over a dozen books under his belt, including *Jeff Duntemann's Drive-By Wi-Fi Guide* and *Assembly Language Step-by-Step*. Jeff is the former editor-in-chief of *PC Techniques Magazine* and *Visual Developer*.

Acknowledgments

Quite a few people made our latest book together a success. First, a special thanks to Keith Weiskamp and Steven Sayre for giving me the opportunity to help with this book. I'd also like to thank team members Ben Sawyer, Jeff Duntemann, Cynthia Caldwell, and Kim Eoff for their help in producing this book in record time.

I'd also like to thank my agent Neil Salkind, who always finds something for me to do, and who always has a project up his sleeve. It's always a pleasure working with you.

Finally, I'd like to thank my family for all of their support and encouragement. First, my parents, who are the most wonderful and supportive people in the world; without you I wouldn't be who I am today. Also my daughter Jennifer, who is so beautiful, patient, and smart; how I wish I could be half as good a person as you. Finally, Cosmo, who is always there with words of encouragement, a laugh and smile, and who drags me out to the golf course when I get too stressed. I could not be surrounded by more beautiful and wonderful people.

—Joli Ballew

Many thanks to the whole Paraglyph crew, Keith, Cynthia, Steve, and Ben, for getting the project off the ground and keeping it going!

—Jeff Duntemann

Contents at a Glance

Chapter 1   Why Is My Computer All Gunked Up? 1

Chapter 2   Degunking Your PC 13

Chapter 3   Getting Rid of Files that Shouldn't Be There 23

Chapter 4   Uninstalling Programs You Don't Need
              and Tweaking Those You Do 43

Chapter 5   Organizing Your Remaining Files and Folders 63

Chapter 6   Tweaking Your Desktop and Start Menu 77

Chapter 7   Preventing Spam Gunk 97

Chapter 8   Cleaning Up E-Mail Gunk 122

Chapter 9   Cleaning and Tweaking the Registry 139

Chapter 10   Optimizing Your Hard Drive and Startup System 159

Chapter 11   Installing Upgrades for Your System 175

Chapter 12   The Best Hardware for PC Degunking 189

Chapter 13   PowerToys and Awesome Shareware 207

Chapter 14   Improving Security 221

Chapter 15   Backing Up Precious Files 243

Chapter 16   Last Resort Degunking Techniques 261

Contents

Introduction xxiii

Chapter 1
Why Is My Computer All Gunked Up? 1

What the Experts Know   3
Understanding How You Got So Gunked Up   3
   Files Are Saved All over the Hard Drive   4
   Temporary Files Aren't Always So Temporary   4
   Spam, Spam, Eggs, Bacon, and Spam!   4
   Installing Too Many Programs   5
   Your Menu System Is Overrun   5
   Your Desktop Is Overrun with Icons   6
   Segmented Hard Drive   7
   Low Hard Drive Space   7
   Unorganized Data Files   8
   Unorganized Web Favorites   9
   Spyware Boogieman   9
   The Dreaded Cookie Monster   10
   You're Gunked Up!   10
Ready for Degunking?   11

Chapter 2
Degunking Your PC 13

The Strategy Behind Degunking   14
   Important Questions to Ask Yourself   15
   File Management 101   16
   Desktop and Start Menu   17
   E-Mail Degunking   17
   Clean Up Those Program Remnants   18
   Hard Drive Optimization   18
   Patch Things Up   18

     Security 19
     Backups 20
     Doing a Clean Start 20
   The Degunking 12-Step Program 20
   Summing Up 21

Chapter 3
Getting Rid of Files that Shouldn't Be There 23

   Clean Up the Default Folders 24
     Documents 25
     Media Files 26
     Shared Folders 30
   Clean Up Your Main Drive 31
     Delete Files from the Root Directory (C:) 32
     Delete Unused Files in Other Locations 34
     Clean Up the "Unzipped" Folder 36
     Locating Duplicate Files 37
   Get Rid of Those Pesky Temp Files 37
     Use Disk Cleanup 38
     Cleaning Up What Disk Cleanup Has Missed 39
   Deleting User Files from Unused User Accounts 41
   Summing Up 42

Chapter 4
Uninstalling Programs You Don't Need
and Tweaking Those You Do 43

   Remove Programs You Don't Use 44
     Using a Program's Uninstall Command 46
     Using the Control Panel to Remove Programs 47
     Extraneous Windows Components 48
     Cleaning Up the Start Menu 49
   Find Programs You Don't Even Know You Have 50
     Check Out the Program Files Folder 50
     Remove Spyware 52
   Remove Programs for Hardware You No Longer Own 54
   Tweaking Programs You Do Need 55
     Right-Click Your Program Icons 55
     Program Compatibility Mode 55
     Make Multimedia and Games Run Better 56
     Performance Options 57
     System Restore 59
   Summing Up 61

Chapter 5
Organizing Your Remaining Files and Folders 63
Better Organize the Default Folders   64
Where Should You Put Your Data?   65
Personalize the Default Folders with Folders of Your Own   68
Empty the Recycle Bin   70
Restart the Computer   71
Make a Final Pass   72
Ready? Empty!   72
Use Disk Defragmenter   73
Summing Up   76

Chapter 6
Tweaking Your Desktop and Start Menu 77
Clean Up and Personalize the Taskbar   78
Managing the Taskbar's System Tray   79
Add Quick Launch Icons   83
Lock, AutoHide, and Group Options in the Taskbar   84
Customizing with TweakUI   85
Personalize the Start Menu   85
XP Start Menu   86
Classic Menu   87
Clean Up and Personalize the Desktop   89
Get Your Desktop Organized   89
Add or Remove Default Icons   90
Create Folders and Program Shortcuts   91
Removing Folders and Shortcuts   92
Run the Desktop Cleanup Wizard   92
Choose Non-System-Intensive Screensavers   93
About Themes   93
Explore Folder Options   94
Summing Up   96

Chapter 7
Preventing Spam Gunk 97
Choose the Best E-Mail Addresses   98
Set Up Your Primary E-Mail Address   99
Set Up Your Backup and Disposable
E-Mail Addresses   99
Avoid Spammer Dictionary Attacks   100
Choose Your E-Mail Client Carefully   101
Be Careful with Outlook   101

Watch Out for Spam Beacons   102
Use Alternative E-Mail Clients   103
Use Your E-Mail Address Carefully   104
Never "Unsubscribe" from a Spammer Mailing List   105
*Never Post (or Let Others Post) Your
E-Mail Address on the Web*   105
*Obfuscate Your E-Mail Address on Newsgroups and
Discussion Boards*   106
Use Disposable E-Mail Addresses for E-Commerce   107
Services That Manage Disposable E-Mail Addresses   108
Use a Separate Spam Filtering Utility   108
A Short Spam Filtering Glossary   109
Filtering Within Your E-Mail Client Is Not Enough   110
How Mail Proxies Work   111
POPFile and Its Buckets   113
Configuring Your E-Mail Client to Use POPFile   113
Using and Training POPFile   114
Creating POPFile Magnets   116
Avoid Triggering Other People's Spam Filters   118
Summing Up   119

Chapter 8
Cleaning Up E-Mail Gunk 122

Keep, Hold, or Pitch?   122
The 100-Message Rule   123
Is Autosorting a Good Idea?   123
It's Psychology, not Technology!   124
Create a One-Screen Folder Hierarchy   124
Keep Your Folder List to One Screen   125
Keep Time-Delimited Mail in Separate Folders   126
Use Nested Folders Carefully   127
Don't Accumulate Attachments   128
Miscellaneous E-Mail Housecleaning Pointers   131
Watch Out for Abandoned Drafts   132
Delete Duplicate Copies of Your Mailbase   132
Outlook Express E-Mail Gunk in the Windows Registry   133
Use a File Shredder for Messages with Personal or Financial Data   135
Summing Up   137

Chapter 9
Cleaning and Tweaking the Registry 139

Inside the Registry   140
A Quick Note about Windows Versions   141
REGEDT32 Is Your Gateway to the Registry   142

Back Up and Restore the Registry   144

Clean the Registry   149

Use Registry Cleaning Software   150

*Use Microsoft's RegClean to Clean the Registry in Windows 95/98/NT
or Windows 2000   152*

Tweak the Registry   153

Turn My Documents Into a Cascading Folder   155

Display Compressed Files in an Alternate Color   156

Display Hidden Files with Explorer   157

Remove All Icons from Your Desktop   157

Summing Up   158

Chapter 10
Optimizing Your Hard Drive and Startup System 159

Use NTFS   160

Converting to NTFS   160

Resize Your Partitions   161

Degunk the Startup Process   162

Clean Up the Startup Folder   162

Clean Up the Boot Process   163

View Errors with Dr. Watson   168

Running Dr. Watson (Drwtsn32.exe)   168

Get Rid of Unsigned Files and Drivers   168

Using File Signature Verification   169

Updating Unsigned Drivers   172

Error Checking   172

Summing Up   173

Chapter 11
Installing Upgrades for Your System 175

Use Windows Update to Stay Up-to-Date   176

Updates Enhance the Security of Your Computer   178

Get Updates Automatically or Manually   178

Critical Updates and Service Packs   182

Other Updates   182

Upgrade to Windows XP Professional   184

Upgrade the Media Applications   185

Upgrade to MSN Messenger 6.1   186

Summing Up   187

Chapter 12
The Best Hardware for PC Degunking 189

Add Memory   190
   Physical Installation   191
   Tweak Virtual Memory Settings   193
Add a Backup Device   195
   External Hard Drive   195
   USB CD-R, CD-RW, DVD-R, DVD-RW   195
   Zip Drive   196
   Other Storage Options   197
Add a Second Monitor   197
   Purchasing a New Adapter   198
   Physical Installation   199
   Configuring the Display Settings   199
Physically Clean the Machine   200
   Cleaning Keyboards, Mice, and Monitors   201
   Degunking Inside the Case   202
Purchase a New Computer   203
Summing Up   205

Chapter 13
PowerToys and Awesome Shareware 207

Use PowerToys for Degunking   208
   Downloading and Installing   209
   Customize Windows Settings with TweakUI   211
   Organize Your Desktop with Virtual Desktop Manager   213
   Resize Images with the Image Resizer   215
   Alt-Tab Replacement   215
WUGNET'S Shareware Picks   215
   Keep Your Registry Clean with Registry First Aid   216
   Get Rid of Annoying Pop-Up Messages with Pop-Up
     Stopper Professional   217
   Synchronize Your Folders with FolderMatch   219
   Keep Your Computer Running Smoothly with System Mechanic   219
Summing Up   220

Chapter 14
Improving Security 221

How Secure Is Your Computer?   222
Purchase and Configure
  Anti-Virus Software   223
Configure Internet Options   225

Configure Security Zones 225
Privacy Options 228
Understand Your Options 229
Create a Guest Account 232
Enable and Configure a Guest Account 232
A Look at Administrative Tools 233
Local Security Policies 234
Computer Management 236
Firewalls 239
Windows XP's Internet Connection Firewall 239
Home Office and Business Firewalls 240
Get the Best Security for the Buck 241
Summing Up 241

Chapter 15
Backing Up Precious Files **243**
Perform Backups with the Backup Utility 244
Getting Started 245
Creating a Simple Backup 246
Creating a Thorough Backup 247
Use Different Types of Backups 249
Recommendations for the Home User 250
How Often to Back Up 250
About Storing the Backups 251
Scheduling a Backup Using the Backup Utility 252
Schedule Backups with the Windows Scheduled Tasks Utility 253
Configuring a Scheduled Task 254
Using the Restore Utility 255
Copy to CD as a Backup Option 257
Summing Up 260

Chapter 16
Last Resort Degunking Techniques **261**
Locate Incompatible Hardware 262
Fix Problems with Hardware Drivers 264
*Return to Older Versions of Drivers Using the Device Driver Rollback
Utility 265*
Return Your System to an Earlier State with System Restore 266
Configure System Restore 268
Create Restore Points Manually 269
Using System Restore 270
Repair XP with the XP CD-ROM 271
What If I Don't Have an XP CD? 272

How to Boot to the CD 272
Changing the BIOS 272
Repair XP Without Doing a Clean Install 273
Upgrade to Windows XP 274
Do a Clean Install But Only If You Really Have to 274
Gather Your Critical Information 275
Reinstall Everything 277
Summing Up 278

Appendix A
Performing a Clean Windows Install 279

Appendix B
Recovering from a Corrupted Registry 287

Appendix C
Troubleshooting Your PC with Degunking Techniques 295

Index 303

Introduction

You're in heaven with your brand new PC. You tell all your friends how wonderful Windows XP is and how fast your new PC is. With all of the extra time you have, you start fixing up things around the house and catching up with old friends. You think to yourself, "Why did I wait so long to get a new version of Windows?"

Then weird things start to happen. Your PC starts getting a little slower. It starts crashing in situations where it never crashed before. You start to develop problems with your favorite applications and your Web browser. Another month goes by, and your PC gets even slower. The number of spam e-mails you receive is starting to increase dramatically. It seems as if every time you surf the Web, you're bombarded with more and more pop-up ads. It becomes difficult, sometimes impossible, to run your PC for a whole day (or even a few hours) without crashing. Then your PC becomes so slow and so gunked up you wish you had a new computer again.

Of course, you don't really need a new computer. You just need to degunk the one you have! Ideally, a clean install of the operating system would be the best thing to do, but this could take hours. You could spend days backing up all of your files, reinstalling Windows, and reinstalling all of your important applications (and you probably can't even locate the master installation CD-ROMs for a lot of them). If you're feeling rich, you could hire one of those high-priced consultants to clean the gunk out of your machine. But who are you kidding? You've got kids to put through college; bills are pilling up; Visa is calling. Besides, you just spent a bundle on this fast, new machine—why should you spend even more money degunking it?

There is a much better solution. You can degunk your computer in just a few hours using a set of tried-and-true techniques. With this step-by-step guide, *Degunking Windows,* you can quickly clean your machine, speed it up, secure it from dangerous hackers, clean up your e-mail, reduce spam, and make your computer work as fast and reliably as the day you brought it home. (Do you still remember that day? That's when you promised your spouse that your new machine would save you so much time that you'd have time to get all the stuff done around the house that's been pilling up!)

Degunking Windows is not just another book on how to use Windows. This book is an easy-to-read and concise guide showing you, step-by-step and in plain English, how to improve the performance of your computer after you've gunked it up. We'll show you how to reorganize files that are stored all over the place, how to reduce or eliminate spam, what to do with a fragmented hard drive, how to fix improperly installed and uninstalled programs, and how to handle a host of other problems you don't want to discuss with your closest friends.

Why You Need This Book

We've talked with scores of Windows users, and the common problem they *all* had was what we call a gunked-up machine. Although Windows is an excellent operating system, it has some peculiarities that cause it to slow down over time. Without regular maintenance, *all* PCs running Windows will get gunked up. The goal of this book is to show you how to degunk your own PC.

Degunking Windows is a unique guide that can save you hundreds of hours of valuable time, and a bundle of money. Here are some of the unique features of this book:

- An easy-to-follow 12-step degunking process that you can put to work immediately.

- Explanations, in everyday terms, of how to easily fix common problems that create gunk on your PC.

- Information on how to save money with free degunking tools that are easily found on the Internet.

- A unique "GunkBuster's Notebook" feature in every chapter to help you reduce the clutter on your PC.

- Degunking maintenance tasks that you can perform on a regular basis to keep your machine in top form.

- Instructions on how to degunk your e-mail and reduce the amount of spam you receive.

- Advice on how to keep your PC gunk-free so you don't have to reinstall the operating system.

- How to know when you have to do a clean install, or buy a new computer.

How to Use This Book

Degunking Windows is structured around the order of the degunking process that you should follow. The book starts off by explaining the importance of degunking and why operating systems like Windows XP require degunking.

Each subsequent chapter describes an important degunking task, explained in plain English with step-by-step instructions.

TIP: *This book is designed around a 12-step program (outlined in Chapter 2) that we recommend you follow, starting with Chapter 3 and continuing through the end of the book. We highly recommend that you follow the process in the order that it is presented here. This will result in the most benefit from the time you spend degunking your PC.*

Once you've completely degunked your PC, you can perform different degunking operations at different times, depending on your needs. We expect that *Degunking Windows* will become one of your most-used computer books, and we'll bet that it will end up on your bookshelf right next to your computer.

A Note on Windows Versions

The degunking tasks presented in this book were written to work with the current version of Windows XP Home Edition and Windows XP Professional Edition. Some of the operations presented, such as backing up Windows, are very specific to Windows XP. If you are using an older version of Windows, such as Windows 98, Windows NT, or Windows 2000, you can still benefit from many of the degunking routines presented here. Many of our degunking tasks involve general operations—such as removing files you don't need, organizing your hard drive, and cleaning up your e-mail—that you can easily adapt to the version of Windows you are using. Here are some of the more general (less version-specific) tasks you can perform, regardless of the version of Windows you have:

- Getting Rid of Files That Shouldn't Be There (Chapter 3)
- Uninstalling Programs You Don't Need and Tweaking Those You Do (Chapter 4)
- Organizing Your Remaining Files and Folders (Chapter 5)
- Tweaking Your Desktop and Start Menus (Chapter 6)
- Preventing Spam Gunk (Chapter 7)
- Cleaning Up E-Mail Gunk (Chapter 8)
- Optimizing Your Hard Drive and Startup System (Chapter 10)

You can also perform the tasks that are more version specific (such as cleaning the Registry) by using the appropriate software. For example, if you are using Windows 98 and you want to clean the Registry, you can follow the general discussions presented in Chapter 9, but to actually clean the Registry, you'll need to use a Registry cleaning tool designed for Windows 98.

The Degunking Mindset

The more you learn about degunking your PC, the more you'll realize that degunking is a mindset, not just a set of technical skills. We view degunking as mostly psychology, not just technology. Rather than simply being a process that you follow when your computer gets really gunked up, degunking involves a disciplined approach to managing your computer. If you follow the basic steps outlined in this book on a regular basis, you'll give yourself an insurance policy and save yourself from encountering aggravation down the road. We also believe that *Degunking Windows* will make your time on your computer more time-efficient, more productive, and maybe even more enjoyable.

Why Is My Computer All Gunked Up?

Degunking Checklist:

√ Make sure you understand the four basic processes involved in degunking Windows.

√ Learn how files saved on your hard drive can gunk up your machine.

√ Understand why you need a strategy for dealing with pesky temporary files.

√ Learn that you can develop a plan to combat spam.

√ Understand why installing too many programs can really gunk up your machine.

√ See how your Desktop and menu system are two places where gunk can build up if you are not careful.

√ Learn how hard drive segmentation and limited drive space can impact the performance of your drive.

√ Understand how unorganized data files and Web favorites can gunk up your machine.

B ecause you've picked up this book, chances are you fall into one of three categories: You're a person with a Windows machine that is struggling to stay afloat; you're a person whose dad or mom just asked why his or her machine has run out of hard-drive space and can't seem to function properly; or you're a help-desk clerk trying to show people how to save their machines from oblivion. Whatever the case, you're the victim of a fairly common problem—you have a gunked-up computer that you need to keep from falling apart. The hard drive works overtime just to send out a two-line e-mail. The start-up process takes three times longer than it did the day you first bought your computer. When you shut down your PC, you can run down the street to get your latte and get back home before the machine finishes winding down. When you feel that your computer is ready to be put out to pasture, you're likely to ask yourself: What the heck happened? Where did I go wrong?

Don't let hardware vendors convince you that your hard drive has suddenly gone bad or that your computer processing chip has gotten too old and cranky. They want you to buy a new machine every year. You can probably see the magazine ads now: "You need the latest whiz-bang RX43210-75 chip" or "Our new micro-woofer, repeater, wireless, sub-atomic, low-heat hard drive will run circles around the competition."

The truth is, you probably don't need what these guys are selling. You just need a little experience, some degunking insight, and a copy of this book.

Our PCs are like our houses: benign neglect usually leads to problems like leaky roofs and clogged drains. Through a combination of internal factors (forgetting to back up your hard drive, not closely watching what gets installed, subscribing to too many e-mail newsletters, and so on) and external factors (spam, viruses, and poorly programmed software), our PCs get really gunked up. Files get plastered all over like clothes in a teenager's bedroom, the Registry (the place where information about your files is stored) starts to go south, and your hard drive can barely support what's currently installed on it (let alone that new road atlas CD-ROM you got for your birthday that you want to install).

It's hard to pinpoint exactly why your computer has gotten so gunked up. After all, every user's experience is a little different. "Getting gunked" involves a combination of many factors. After a while, with normal wear and tear, every computer will start to slow down. The hard drive spins longer, programs take longer to load, programs crash more frequently, and in general a PC becomes harder to use.

The good news is, there are common factors that create gunk on every PC. In this book, we'll identify common PC gunk creators and how to manage them so your computer keeps running quickly and efficiently.

What the Experts Know

Hardcore Windows users and those geeky guys you hear on Sunday afternoon radio shows know how to keep their machines working well. And the good news is that most people can learn to do this, too. The problem is, until now, no one has put all this degunking information into an easy-to-follow book. What we're about to show you is really not that hard. By following these sequential steps, you can improve the operation of your machine considerably.

Our process is divided into four key areas:

1. *Basic computer housekeeping 101:* Here we'll focus on how to get everything back in its place and rid yourself of all the gunk. (Just think about how good it feels to clean out your closet and throw away all of the stuff you don't need.) We'll also concentrate on how you can optimize your files for the best performance.

2. *Repairing common problems:* Once you've culled down the programs and files on your machine, it's time to repair some basic and common problems. You can think of this as a basic tune-up of your system, and it can be the capstone to a core cleaning and improvement process.

3. *Total reinstall:* In the most extreme cases, some Windows users will need a clean wipe of their system and a reinstallation. Fortunately, you don't always have to do this. But as many savvy users will tell you, this is the tried-and-true way to get back to the good old days of when your computer was cranked up for the first time.

4. *Improving preferences and settings to maintain things better:* Once you've officially degunked your machine, you'll want to tweak the operating system and key programs to improve the chances that you don't end up back where you started. You can make improvements by setting preferences to improve the chances files go where they should, scheduling automated tasks such as hard drive optimizations, and creating simple shortcuts that make it easy to remove unwanted files. Another final set of improvements involves incorporating some programs that improve security, virus protection, and overall optimization of system performance. Consider this step as putting the wax on a newly cleaned car.

Understanding How You Got So Gunked Up

You understand now that it is common for your system to not be running as fast as it once did, and that you haven't done anything wrong. Things in your computer might be, well, a bit disorganized. Let's review how most users end up in this predicament.

Files Are Saved All over the Hard Drive

Novice users, and even some savvy ones, will have document files, downloaded files, and other programs saved in many different places on their hard drive. This happens all the time. For example, the program used to open an attachment from Outlook or Outlook Express stores a copy of the file in a temporary directory in your Windows directory system. If you don't resave the file in your My Documents or other designated document folder, the document will remain in the temporary directory. This is an example of gunk.

Other users will also casually save stuff to their desktop or the C: root directory of their drive without giving it any further thought. Files received from IM (Instant Message) services usually end up in completely different directories. The point to all of this is that, if you don't pay attention to where your files are going, you could end up with a situation in which you easily jam up your hard drive with a lot of data you don't need or even know how to find again.

Temporary Files Aren't Always So Temporary

Windows has a fascination with temporary files. The problem is that when computers crash or files are improperly saved, temp files like to stay around and gunk up your system. It's like temporary tax hikes—they somehow become permanent fixtures. The result is that you can find hundreds, if not thousands, of files stuck in obscure places, with obscure filenames, throughout your hard drive. To make matters worse, some of these files can't even be located unless you really understand how to find them. Getting these files off your hard drive is not always easy.

Of course, there are automated utilities that locate and delete your temporary files, but they don't typically clean out all of the files. In some cases, you have to resort to some hand-cleaning to get rid of all of the temporary files you don't need on your hard drive. Thus, it helps to know where they hide and how they get there in the first place.

Spam, Spam, Eggs, Bacon, and Spam!

Spam is the bane of anyone with an e-mail account. We all hate spam. Spam is like weeds in our gardens. The more we try to get rid of it, the faster it comes back. Eventually, it overwhelms us one way or the other. We end up with e-mail repositories teaming with irrelevant files, adding to a bloated hard drive, one that is slow to respond to searches, deletions, sorts, and more.

You might have convinced yourself that there is nothing you can do about spam. But as you'll learn in this book, there are strategies you can put to work right away to greatly reduce your exposure to spam. Many users we talk to simply throw in the towel when it comes to spam, and some spend up to 30 minutes or more per day sorting through their e-mail and deleting their spam. If you take a more proactive approach by using different e-mail addresses, setting up spam filters, using different e-mail clients, and avoiding activities that trigger spam in the first place, you could save a lot of time.

Installing Too Many Programs

We are all guilty of this sin. You hear about some cool utility or you need a neat game to keep the kids occupied. Worse yet, your kids find 18 games to keep themselves occupied. You download a couple of media programs, 5 instant messaging systems, and more. You install the gardening CD-ROM in the spring, use it once, and then forget about it. And what about the genealogy CD you put in last Christmas and totally forgot about until we just brought it up? Caught you! Remember the 50 screensavers you're downloaded over the last four years? Maybe, if you're lucky, you uninstalled some of them. The problem is, your idea of uninstalling them was to drag them into the trash and ignore the warnings that these were *installed* programs. Windows technically still thinks you have them.

When you install a program, you're doing more than just copying files to the hard drive. Programs can make physical changes to the Windows operating system, including something called the Registry, which is sort of like a street map or rulebook on how programs work in Windows. Gum up your Registry and it can be like driving in New York City without the traffic lights working.

We've done this before and believe us, it's not fun.

Your Menu System Is Overrun

As you add and remove programs, they each tend to add program icons to your Start menu. Eventually, given enough time and lack of upkeep, you'll end up with tons of separate folder entries on the Start menu (like the one Figure 1-1), making it unmanageable. Worse yet, some of the icons might not even work anymore. Your system is probably still functional, but you can make Windows quicker to load and easier to use by cleaning up the Start menu. If your Start menu looks like the one in Figure 1-1, you picked up the right book.

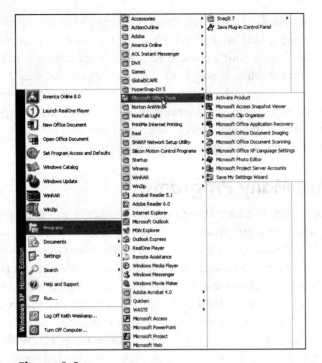

Figure 1-1
Does your Start menu look like this, with a bloated set of program folders you probably don't even use anymore?

Your Desktop Is Overrun with Icons

Does your Desktop look like the one shown in Figure 1-2? Okay, we admit it. This is a screen capture from one of our computers once upon a time. We saved it to show you that even the most experienced geek needs some degunking help from time to time. A bloated Desktop is similar to the Start menu problem just discussed, and it can be even worse because not only are some program icons put on the Desktop when programs are installed, but users often put other junk on their Desktop as well. The result is a Desktop that looks like it contains the contents of your entire drive. Every piece of junk that you found while using your computer is out there for the world to see. It's like a closet without doors. The background image on Windows is so obscured you probably don't even recognize it anymore. Your friends walk by and think you are a power user because you have all these icons on your Desktop, when in fact, you just never thought about cleaning it up.

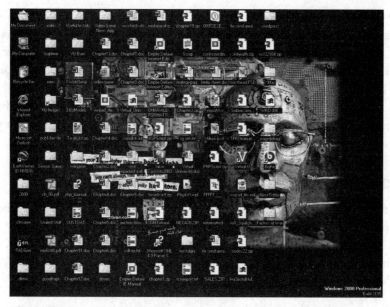

Figure 1-2
Does your Desktop look like this, a sea of program icons? If it does, you need to degunk.

Segmented Hard Drive

As a computer utilizes its hard drive, it stores programs and files in bits and pieces all over the place. Big data files and large programs aren't stored in one contiguous stretch; they are stored hopscotch style, with a piece here and a piece there. As a result, the reader on your hard drive has to physically move back and forth multiple times to read the data in one file. This slows down the hard drive and causes more wear and tear on it. And the more wear and tear on your hard drive, the higher the likelihood that it will crash, misbehave, or wear out more quickly.

Users who install and uninstall lots of programs, create and delete lots of files, and construct large e-mail files (and don't delete them when they should) can suffer from this disk access problem. By optimizing the hard drive correctly, you can speed things up and keep your machine running better and longer.

Low Hard Drive Space

Windows often utilizes the hard drive to keep it running and perform basic tasks—not just for temporary files that speed Web surfing. Windows also uses the hard drive to serve as an extension of working memory and to perform other core operating system functions. Thus, if your hard drive runs very low on disk space, you can create a problem that causes Windows to crash more frequently or slow waaaaay down. This is less of a problem nowadays because more people have machines with gigantic hard drives and loads of memory. However, by increasing the number of video files, music files, big Internet downloads, and digital photographs they store, people are filling up their hard drives much faster and they aren't keeping up with their cleaning and organization tasks. Laptops and subnotebooks fall victim to this a lot because they tend to have smaller hard drives. By learning to keep only what you need on your drive, organize what you do keep, and clear out files expertly, you can ensure that you don't fall victim to the dreaded "low hard drive space" syndrome.

Unorganized Data Files

Some people put their files all over the place. There are a few people who at least put files in a few core folders. But wouldn't it be nice if you not only had your data files in the right folders, but you also named them correctly? While you are at it, you could even get rid of duplicate files, making folders easier to search, and get rid of files you don't need anymore.

Here's a pop quiz: How many digital photos do you have on your computer that have a thumb in front of the lens and you've failed to delete them? How easy is it for you to find that great sunset photo from two years ago when most of your photos have filenames like SNR062500b.jpg? Look at the file directory in Figure 1-3 and tell me it doesn't look like one of yours. Consider how hard it is to locate files when they are stored in a directory with tons of ambiguous filenames.

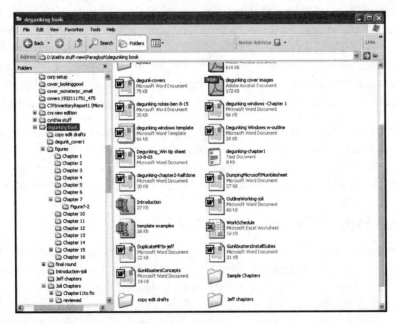

Figure 1-3

Now where did I stick that nice sunset photo?

Our computers get gunked up because we're flooded with new files all the time. We're not just dealing with word processing documents and a few spreadsheets anymore. We're downloading MP3 files for music; we're ripping our CD collection to the hard drive; we're taking hundreds of digital photos and videos; we're adding PDFs and PowerPoint slides, JPEGs and GIFs, and Photoshop collages. Somehow, we need to do more than just dump this stuff in folders without having some type of organization.

Unorganized Web Favorites

If you surf the Web a lot, you probably have a long list of bookmarks or Web Favorites. Chances are that you've discovered a quick-key for saving Web Favorites (Ctrl+D in Internet Explorer), so you may have a long list of Web Favorites (see Figure 1-4) that is almost useless unless the Favorite you want is in the top 25. Don't worry, we'll show you how to clean all of that up!

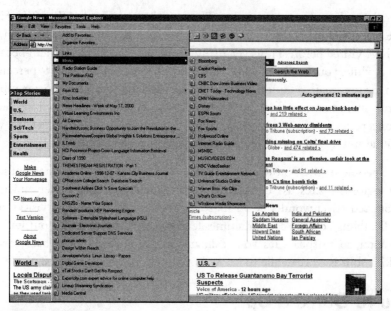

Figure 1-4
Does it take you five minutes to get to the last item on your Web Favorites list? If so, you need to degunk!

Spyware Boogieman

Spyware is a catchall name for products that, once installed, essentially report back information on your Web surfing habits or help bombard you with pop-up ads and other advertising. Spyware has also become synonymous with installed programs that don't show up in your installed programs directory. This makes them hard to find, hard to deal with, and, worst of all, hard to uninstall. In truth, some spyware is pretty harmless—it won't raid your hard drive or report the balance of your bank account to hackers. However, these programs can sometimes eat up available memory or resources and slow down your machine. They can also interfere with other programs. Therefore, you might want to get rid of them.

The Dreaded Cookie Monster

Cookies are not programs. They're basically tiny pieces of text data that Web sites place in a special directory on your machine. For example, a site like Yahoo! might place a small cookie on your machine with the contents "xu44$@dncsdlk3," which is a unique string of characters that it uses to recognize your computer. Unless you log in to Yahoo!, that string doesn't serve any purpose; it is used only by Yahoo! to recognize you when you visit their site. Cookies can also store more specific data, such as the date of your last visit.

Overall, Cookies are fairly harmless. They usually eat up only 1K to 2K of hard drive space, and they usually don't give a site much information other than that you have visited before. However, many people like to get rid of them because, after a while, you can have a few thousand of them, and about 99 percent of them are useless. In addition, if you ever accidentally stumble onto a gambling or porn site, you might find cookies from them on your machine, which can be disconcerting for some people. Imagine searching for all text files on your machine and seeing a small 1K file named cookie:www.tripleXfunland.net.txt.

Some people set their browsers to avoid accepting cookies altogether, but some very legitimate sites use cookies to make your experience better and more customized. (Ever wonder how Amazon recognizes you when you visit? Cookies.) Disabling cookies can sometimes lead you to throw the baby out with the bathwater, so to speak. It's your call, and in the end, you'll probably accept cookies, so it is worthwhile to know how to clean them out by hand.

You're Gunked Up!

Chances are that if one of these things is happening on your computer, nearly all of them are. But if you commit yourself to degunking, you can get most or all of your computer back running the way it used to. The problems we just discussed above will only get worse with time, and that's why your entire computer can get so bogged down.

Ready for Degunking?

The most difficult part of getting your machine back to where it should be involves dedicating a little time. As we move on and look at the different degunking techniques, we'll arrange the tasks in the order that will likely get you the most results in the shortest amount of time. Our approach will be to show you not only how to fix things, but how to get yourself on a maintenance program so that your computer *always* runs well. If you're new to the world of degunking, don't worry. It's much easier than putting together a barbecue in the backyard with those ridiculous instructions they provide.

Degunking Your PC

Degunking Checklist:

√ Make sure you understand that the best degunking results can be obtained by performing cleanup tasks in a specific order.

√ Understand how you can manage the limited resources in Windows.

√ Learn why good file management is a critical aspect of degunking Windows.

√ Understand why the Desktop and Start menu are two places that attract gunk.

√ See how your e-mail can get really gunked up.

√ Learn degunking procedures such as Registry cleanup, hard drive optimization, and security setup.

√ Understand what you can do when your PC doesn't respond to the standard degunking procedures.

√ Learn the degunking 12-step program.

We could have called this chapter "Degunking: The 12-Step Program to Success" because our final goal is to introduce our proven 12-step program, which can really help you improve the performance of your PC. But to get there, we need to focus on the strategy behind the degunking process and then introduce you to the critical Windows activities that relate to degunking. This chapter is designed to help you get into the mindset for degunking. In the following chapters, we'll show you, step-by-step, how to roll up your sleeves and complete the 12 essential steps of our degunking program. The best part is that even if you have limited time, any step you perform will go a long way in helping you make your machine run better.

The most important thing to understand about the degunking process is that you will get the best results if you just follow the process we outline in this book. For example, defragmenting your hard drive (also known as optimizing the hard drive) is typically worthwhile only after you've deleted the files you no longer need. You shouldn't defrag your hard drive and then delete files because the process of deleting a bunch of files will simply defragment your drive again. Similarly, cleaning out the Registry before you've uninstalled and cleaned out all the installed programs (or uninstalled remnants) that you no longer need doesn't make good sense.

You might feel tempted to skip around in this book. If you do, you probably won't see the best results. Of course, there are some processes that could be performed at any time to solve specific problems. But in our experience, we've found that it's best to have an organized strategy the first time you do a "major degunk" so that you get the best results out of our degunking routines.

The Strategy Behind Degunking

The strategy behind degunking is based on how Windows operates in the first place:

- How Windows stores certain types of files in specific folders (directories)
- How Windows provides default directories, such as My Music and My Pictures, for specific types of files
- How data is stored and retrieved on your hard drive
- How Windows installs and removes programs on your computer
- How main programs and other utilities can be set up to automatically load when you start Windows
- How Windows uses an internal database, called the *Registry,* to store critical information about your computer

- How Windows uses different types of memory (disk space, RAM, virtual memory) to store and process data
- How basic services such as e-mail, security, and backing up data work
- How Windows' built-in tools, such as System Restore, can be used to repair your system when things go wrong.

As you'll learn in this book, the more you understand about the basics of how Windows operates, the better you'll get at degunking and improving the performance of your PC. Of course, you don't need to be an expert on operating systems to make your machine run better. A little bit of knowledge and common sense goes a long way.

Windows has lots of free memory and system resources. Most Windows computers also have ample amounts of free hard drive space. The big challenge with Windows is that there are many components, such as files, programs, and system utilities, that aggressively compete for the available resources. When too many resources get used up, your machine really starts to bog down.

Your basic degunking and ongoing maintenance strategy is to ensure that the resources you have are used wisely. If you have too many files on your hard drive because you never remove any, your computer will slow down. If you have too many programs installed on your computer (or you try to run too many at the same time), your computer will take a long time to start up and will run very slowly. Of course, you can add more memory to your computer (we'll cover this later in this book) and increase the size of your hard drive, but you'll eventually run out of resources unless you monitor the ones you have and regularly get rid of the things you don't need.

Important Questions to Ask Yourself

As you use your computer on a regular basis, you need to ask yourself some of the following questions:

- Does it seem that my computer is running slower and slower with each passing month?
- Do I put a lot of new files on my computer but rarely remove any old ones?
- How often do I look at my personal data directories, such as My Documents, to see if I'm storing files I don't need or keeping my system organized?
- Do I really need all the programs on my computer? (When was the last time you even looked at all the programs you have installed?)
- Do I use all of the programs and utilities that load automatically when Windows starts up?

- When was the last time I went through my e-mail and deleted the messages I no longer need?
- When was the last time I ran a utility, such as PC Cleanup, to remove the temporary files on my hard drive?
- When was the last time I defragmented my hard drive?
- Do I have a firewall set up to keep viruses and other nasty programs from gunking up my machine?
- Do I know what to do if something goes wrong with my machine because it has gotten really gunked up?

Let's continue by putting together a degunking strategy that first explores the important system-level components of Windows. Once you are familiar with how Windows works, you'll be able to see how our 12-step degunking program (which we'll introduce at the end of this chapter) will help improve the speed and performance of your computer.

File Management 101

The biggest initial problem with a gunked-up PC is that it is probably overrun with files. Personal data files and installed programs take up a lot of space, and your computer likely won't have enough free hard drive space for Windows to run well. Degunking a machine for the first time can be a real challenge because it's likely that data files and programs have not been saved in an organized fashion. And you can't just step in there and start deleting files. You should first go through all the directories on the hard drive and take an inventory of what you have. Then you'll need to reorganize the data so that you get a clear picture of what to keep and what to get rid of. In the next chapters, you'll see a set of strategies to help you quickly deal with hard drives that need serious degunking. These chapters will walk you through the beginning of our 12-step degunking program.

Another aspect of file management is that there are often numerous small utilities and Taskbar programs running on your system that really aren't needed. This alone can really gunk up your machine. Often these programs get set up accidentally, and before you know it your system starts to slow down. You'll especially notice this if your system takes a very long time to boot up. In Chapter 6, we'll show you how to eliminate unwanted Taskbar programs and other utilities.

Finally, within the file reorganization process, you'll find a number of programs to uninstall, which will help clean up the Registry. To ensure an even cleaner Registry, we will also run some utilities that automatically clean up the Registry, which in turn makes it run smoother and helps protect it from getting corrupted.

So as part of your overall degunking strategy, the first thing you'll need to do is reorganize your entire file system and in the process delete as much stuff as possible. The best part is that after you complete this work, you'll feel as if you've really accomplished something and you'll notice that your PC runs better than you would have thought possible.

Desktop and Start Menu

Once you've cleaned up the programs and data files on your drive, you will need to turn your attention to the Start menu and Desktop. These components usually need to be cleaned up for a few reasons. First, you may have uninstalled a program but didn't delete its shortcut from your Desktop or Start menu. There are also other data files on your Desktop worth getting rid of. Finally, everyone's Start menu can use some better organization. The fewer programs in your Start menu, the easier it is to find what you want—and the menu will load faster, making your computer more responsive overall. In Chapter 6, we'll show you how to fix your Desktop and Start menu by using some easy-to-follow processes that work wonders.

E-Mail Degunking

After you've completed the file system and Desktop overhaul, you'll need to turn your attention to the next culprit that eats up a lot of hard drive space—your e-mail system. E-mail programs store e-mail in a relatively similar fashion; that is, all e-mail is stored in a database. Unfortunately, each e-mail program stores its data in a different database system, so it's not a one-size-fits-all situation. The good news is that no matter what e-mail program you use, you can apply some general principles to manage your e-mail better, reduce the amount of spam (junk e-mail) you receive, and better organize the e-mail you receive and send out.

The two e-mail programs we're going to focus on in this book are Outlook and Outlook Express, although we will discuss other e-mail programs to provide you with some alternatives to reducing the amount of spam you receive. Both Outlook and Outlook Express store data differently, but the degunking process is the same for both. First, you want to delete as much e-mail as possible, and second, you want to compress the remaining e-mail to reclaim some disk space. At the same time, we'll show you how to set up rules and other filters to make it easier to delete stuff and keep the volume of your e-mail down and more manageable going forward. Because of the importance of e-mail, we've devoted two chapters (Chapters 7 and 8) to it.

Clean Up Those Program Remnants

In an ideal computing world, you could install and remove as many programs on your PC as you wanted without any repercussions. Unfortunately, our PCs operate like our bodies. If we just stuff ourselves with food all of the time, we'll likely pay the price—gain too much weight and slow down. Eating is fine as long as we have a good exercise program to back up our passion for food. With your computer, you can install as many programs as you want and later remove them, but you'll need to perform some important maintenance tasks to keep your internal system from getting too bloated.

Windows is designed around a central database system called the *Registry,* which keeps track of just about everything under the sun related to your computer, including the programs that have been installed and removed. To keep your computer in top shape, the Registry needs to be placed on a regular maintenance program. In Chapter 9, you'll learn how to get out your broom and dustpan and really clean the Registry and maintain it well. As you'll learn, the Registry needs to be cleaned on a regular basis to remove all of the program remnants that can get left behind, which in turn can cause your computer to boot slowly and run inefficiently.

Hard Drive Optimization

With your file system cleaned and organized and your e-mail reclaimed, you'll need to focus on optimizing your hard drive. This process, called *defragmenting your hard drive,* takes all the files on the drive and stores them as close to the center of the drive as possible. It will also organize files in a way that speeds up access and load times for programs. Depending on the size of your drive and the amount of data you deleted during the degunking process, the defragmentation or optimization step could take a while. The good news is that the optimization process is fairly automatic.

Once you've optimized your hard drive, you'll be well down the degunking road. Your machine should be running faster, with better response and fewer problems. Unfortunately, that doesn't mean you're done just yet...

Patch Things Up

Now it's time to upgrade the software on your machine and patch up the programs you use most often. This can benefit you in two ways:

- It reduces exposure to bugs that could crash the machine. Crashes are often indications of the need for degunking, but they can also contribute to adding more gunk.

- It reduces exposure to viruses and security problems (leaks). If your software isn't fully up-to-date, nasty viruses can easily get into your machine and attack your computer when you least expect it. Viruses and security leaks are the bane of diligent degunkers.

CAUTION: *Microsoft releases patches (fixes) for all its programs, including Windows and Office. However, the savviest users, despite wanting to keep their systems up-to-date, usually wait to update their machines. This happens because some newly issued patches and service packs actually do more harm then good. What we recommend is that you upgrade minor patches and security patches quickly, usually within a week. On the other hand, you should wait a month or so to upgrade with larger, all-encompassing service packs.*

With your machine patched and the basic degunking steps completed, you can move on to more preventative tasks. This includes improving how your installed programs run, putting stuff in the right place, setting up e-mail filters, and installing programs that will improve your security.

Security

Security is a key degunking issue, and that's why we've devoted an entire chapter to this topic—Chapter 14. Without proper security on your machine, you're at serious risk of getting viruses and other menacing programs that can be directly harmful or take up power and resources. This could cause your computer to run slower or crash more often. A good security plan has three pieces:

- Anti-virus software: This software will help prevent malicious computer programs from getting installed or otherwise affecting your system.

- Firewall: Installation or activation of a firewall will protect your computer from unwanted intrusion by hackers or programs.

- Pest protection: Installation of a Trojan horse or pest protection system is sometimes built into firewall software. Trojan horses and pest programs may not be malicious, but they could install themselves on your computer and eat up resources. One example is Gator, a small system program that installs itself and shares information about your computer and past browsing history with advertisers. The Gator applet provides little benefit to you. Aside from sending out information about you, it also takes up bandwidth and processor time.

Thankfully, all three types of security software are readily available and easy to install. As part of our plan to secure your computer, we'll show you how to remove unwanted programs and prevent new ones from entering your system.

Backups

Your best electronic friend in the universe is your most recent system backup, which you've stored in a safe place. If you're reading this thinking, "I don't need to back up regularly because I've never lost anything," you're missing an important lesson here. Tempting fate with your computer and all of your valuable data is not a good idea.

Developing a regular backup procedure is a must, not only because it will keep you from losing valuable data but because it will save you from losing all of the setup information and critical programs that are essential to the operation of your computer. As you'll learn in Chapter 15, creating backups on a regular basis using proper procedures will allow you to quickly get your machine back up and running in the event your suffer a major setback, such as a hard drive crash.

Doing a Clean Start

The best part about degunking is that you can easily extend the life of your PC by performing the set of tasks presented in this book. But there may come a time when your PC simply won't respond to the basic degunking operations—the first 11 steps of our 12-step program. So if you're at the end of your rope and you're tempted to throw in the towel, you can first try a few lower-level options such as getting rid of incompatible hardware devices, fixing hardware drivers, and restoring your system to an earlier state using the System Restore feature. You can also use the Repair option on the Windows XP CD-ROM to repair your computer. As a last resort, you can either install a new version of Windows or you can give up completely and get a new machine.

Whatever option turns out to be the best one for your situation, you'll want to proceed carefully and apply a smart approach to help save time and money. For example, if you decide to reinstall Windows or purchase a new machine, there is a set of procedures you should follow to safely move all of your personal data and applications over to your new setup. In Chapter 16, we'll carefully walk you through the decision process and help you solve your critical problems.

The Degunking 12-Step Program

Here is the basic 12-step degunking process that you'll follow in this book:

1. Get rid of the files you don't really need.
2. Uninstall programs you don't need.
3. Organize your files and folders.

4. Clean up your Desktop and Start menu.

5. Reduce your e-mail spam, and sort through and organize your Outlook mail.

6. Clean and fine-tune the Registry.

7. Optimize your hard drive.

8. Install the latest upgrades.

9. Incorporate PowerToys and good shareware to help keep your machine clean and running efficiently.

10. Improve security and set up a good firewall.

11. Back up your system on a regular basis.

12. Use a smart approach if you think your machine is ready to be retired.

These steps are straightforward and easy to follow. If you set aside time to follow them, you'll save yourself a lot of time, money, and aggravation in the long run.

Summing Up

If you follow the degunking process in the way that we've described and you perform certain tasks on a regular basis, you'll be surprised at how your PC will respond. Even though you may think your computer is ready for the trash heap, we'll show you that (in most cases) you can squeeze more life out of it. So don't throw in the towel too soon. Just take the time to perform the tasks that we've outlined and you'll begin to see results.

Getting Rid of Files that Shouldn't Be There

Degunking Checklist:

√ Remove the excessive junk in your default folders: My Documents, My Music, My Videos, and so on.

√ Remove the files you don't need from your root directory on your main drive (C:\).

√ Clean up your root directory by moving files (and folders) to more appropriate locations.

√ Search for files you don't need on your default drive and remove them.

√ Remove unused unzipped files and other duplicate files.

√ Remove the temporary files on your system.

√ Remove the unused files from unused user accounts.

Welcome to Basic Housekeeping 101. You know the drill: *Your mother doesn't live here, so please pick up after yourself!* You have to sweep the floors, put away the laundry, stack the dishes, and vacuum the floor. You have to keep things from getting too cluttered by taking out the trash regularly. You also need to clean out your closets once or twice a year and throw away things you no longer need. These are chores you do to make your home livable, and if you don't do them, your house won't function as well as you'd like.

Just as you take out the trash when you clean your house, you have to clean up the trash you've accumulated on your computer occasionally too. *Therefore, getting rid of unnecessary files is the first step in degunking your computer.* If you're a pack rat, this could be painful, but we'll help you get through it! We'll take a look at what you've accumulated on your computer in the last few months (or years) and get rid all of the gunk you've added and don't need—music files, digital pictures that didn't make the cut, files you unzipped and viewed but never deleted, temporary files, documents you've created and mailed (or e-mailed), and anything else you don't need.

Clean Up the Default Folders

Hopefully you've been saving files to the default folders. You've likely seen them around as you've been using Windows:

• My Documents folder

• My Music folder

• My Videos folder

• My Pictures folder

If you have or haven't been saving to these folders, if you've created folders of your own, or if you've simply saved everything to the C: drive, you should start the cleaning process here. That's because when you first get your new XP computer, XP prompts you to save pictures to the My Pictures folder, documents to the My Documents folder, music to the My Music folder, and videos to the My Videos folder. If you accept the default saving options at any point, you'll have files in these default folders. Deleting superfluous files might not seem necessary if you have an 80 GB hard drive, but it is. When XP looks for a file, it has to search the *full* hard disk for it. The more stuff on your hard disk, the more stuff it has to look through. Additionally, deleting unnecessary files is certainly essential if you've received the dreaded "low on disk space" error. Either way, we'll bet money that you've got some files you can throw out!

Documents

Windows XP provides a My Documents folder where many users store all of the documents they create. This folder serves as the default location until it is changed. Stop reading for a minute and go take a peek in there and see what you can find. If you see something you don't like or you don't need, delete it. Here's how:

1. Double-click the My Documents folder. It should be on the Desktop, but if it isn't, you can find it on the Start menu. See Figure 3-1.

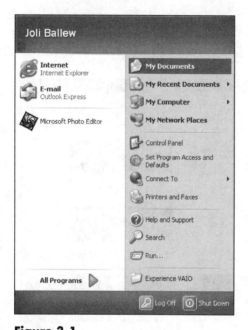

Figure 3-1
Locate the My Documents folder, and then delete unnecessary files.

2. Right-click any file, and choose Delete from the shortcut menu.
3. In the Confirm File Delete dialog box, click Yes to delete the file.

TIP: *You can also delete a file in any folder by hovering the mouse over it to select it and then clicking Delete This File in the File And Folder Tasks pane, or you can drag the file to the Recycle Bin.*

Delete to your heart's content, but don't delete files if you don't know who they belong to or what they are used for. For now, let's just concentrate on taking out a bit of the garbage that *you've* created.

Media Files

Let's now take a look at some other folders. Windows XP also provides default folders called My Pictures, My Videos, and My Music for storing other types of files. If you have a digital camera, for example, you might find that you have a lot of files in the My Pictures folder. If you make a lot of movies with Movie Maker 2, we'll bet you've got some files in the My Videos folder you can delete as well. If you are a music hound, we'll bet your My Music folder is really scary!

My Pictures

Look at Figure 3-2 and you'll see an example of one of our My Pictures folders.

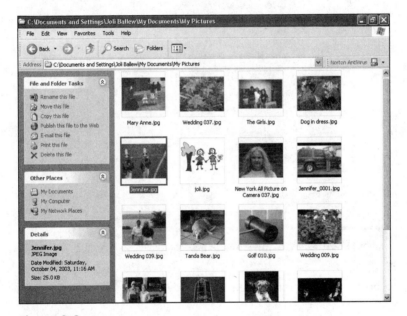

Figure 3-2
Here are the pictures in our My Pictures folder.

The pictures shown here are nice, but we think we can part with the dog in the dress in the top-right corner. Deleting pictures from this folder is just the same as deleting from the My Documents folder. You simply right-click, choose Delete, and be done with it!

TIP: Don't delete any pictures you've used in Movie Maker 2 project files, office documents, or similar applications. When the file or program calls on them and they aren't there, you'll certainly hear about it!

My Videos

Deleting video files is a little trickier. With Movie Maker 2, you capture the video files (raw footage) to your computer, and you create a project using those files. These project files are given a .MSWMM file name extension, as shown in Figure 3-3. You tweak the project file and then you create a movie, and the movie files are given a .wmv extension. The movie is the final product, so if you've turned a particular project file into a movie, you can delete that particular project file. However, if you think you'll need any of those files later, if you want to save the raw footage for posterity, or if you are planning to use those files in another movie, you shouldn't delete them. Figure 3-3 shows an example of a pretty gunked-up My Videos folder.

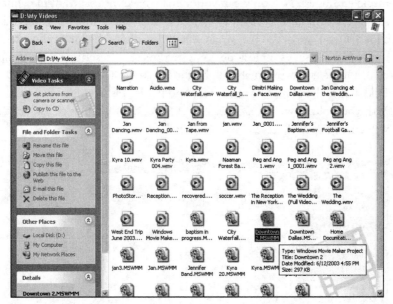

Figure 3-3

A gunked-up My Videos folder contains project files (.MSWMM), movie files (.wmv), audio files (.wma), and more.

In this example, we can delete many of the project files because most have been turned into movies. We can also delete duplicate movie files and any sound files we don't need. As you can see, we have several completed movies that are basically the same, and we only need to keep the final version of the movie we created. In Figure 3-4, you can see that there are multiple files of a friend dancing at a wedding. We'll choose the best one and delete the rest.

Figure 3-4

Delete multiple versions of a movie, but keep the one you like best.

Remember, though, a movie (the final product) is uneditable. So, if you think you might need the project files at another time, don't delete them.

My Music

Ah, your music. We bet that you have quite a lot of files stored here if you're a music enthusiast. Not only can you literally have thousands of files, but if you've subscribed and unsubscribed to various online music sources, you probably have a lot that you can't even play because you don't have the proper licenses. Deleting music files is just as simple as deleting anything else described so far: simply right-click and delete. You can also highlight the song or folder and click Delete This Folder or Delete This File in the File And Folder Tasks pane as shown in Figure 3-5. (If you hold down the CTRL key to select multiple files or folders, the option will change to Delete The Selected items.)

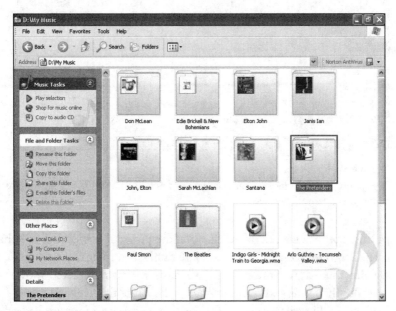

Figure 3-5

Delete any music files that you don't have licenses for, that are corrupt, that you don't like, or that you simply don't want.

GunkBuster's Notebook: Saving Space by Spotting Duplicate MP3s

If you're like most people who collect MP3 music files, you gather them from wherever you can and then toss them into a designated MP3 directory somewhere on your (huge) hard drive. If you do this, chances are excellent that you have duplicate MP3 files in that directory—and since each MP3 file is several megabytes in size, you can waste a *lot* of disk space that way.

Most of the problem stems from inconsistent file-naming conventions. If you get MP3s from newsgroups or file sharing services or your friends, their names may be arranged very differently. Even if they are the very same file, Windows will not catch your duplicates if they have different file names!

Here's an example. The following four files are identical. Only the names are different:

Beatles – If I Fell 3330 KB Winamp Media File 1/5/2003 10:05 AM

If I Fell – Beatles, The 3330 KB Winamp Media File 7/1/2003 10:05 AM

The Beatles – If I Fell 3330 KB Winamp Media File 4/17/2001 11:18 PM

If I Fell – Beatles 3330 KB Winamp Media File 8/29/2003 10:05 AM

It's easy to spot the duplicates, *if they're one after the other in Windows Explorer.* Unfortunately, if they're mixed in with hundreds of other MP3s, you may not know they're all there. Most people sort files in a Windows Explorer window by file name. In this case, the first file would be up with the *B*s, the second and fourth would be with the *I*s, and the third would be down with the *T*s.

The easiest way to spot dupes like this is to click on the Size header in a Windows Explorer display to sort the files by *size.* That will bring all files of identical size together (here, 3330 KB) in the display. As you scroll down through your files in the Windows Explorer pane, look for multiple adjacent lines with the same file size and you'll discover that many of those are dupes with slightly different file names.

This isn't a complete solution, of course. Ultimately, eliminating MP3 file dupes requires that you decide how you will name your MP3 files. Band name first? Album? Or cut? It's good practice to impose a file-naming convention on your MP3 files as you gather them so you don't have to go through 1,000 MP3s and change 1,000 file names. As you rename your files according to your file-naming convention, Windows will object when you try to give a duplicate file the exact same name as an existing file.

Watch out for band names beginning with "The" and either eliminate the word entirely or make sure it's *after* the first significant word in the band name (e.g., "Beatles, The"). A lot of duplicates happen that way. Also, look for underscore characters (which are not obvious at a glance) between words in a file name. Even a few duplicate MP3s can hog 40 or 50 megabytes of disk space. Nuke' em till they glow!

Shared Folders

If you share a computer with another person (or with several people) and you don't belong to a large corporate network, you might have used the Shared Documents folder to pass along information or documents to others who access the computer. You might have also employed the Shared Music or Shared Pictures folder. These shared folders contain files that anyone who logs onto the computer can view (even guests), and they are just as susceptible (if not more) to getting gunked up as any other folder on the computer.

You can locate and clean the Shared Documents folder using Windows Explorer:

1. Log on as an Administrator.

2. Right-click the Start button and click Explore All Users.

3. Locate the Shared Documents folder. It's at C:\Documents And Settings\All Users\Shared Documents. This is shown in Figure 3-6.

4. Browse through each folder, deleting items as needed.

If you take the time to clean out these default folders, you'll be well on your way to getting your machine running smoothly again. This is a good first step. Now, let's take a look at some of the other places you could have saved your files.

CAUTION: *Don't empty the Recycle Bin just yet. Leave the files in there for a week or so, just to make sure you aren't going to miss anything you've deleted.*

Figure 3-6
Shared folders can also contain extraneous or duplicate files.

Clean Up Your Main Drive

Go ahead, admit it. Sometimes you just save files randomly to whatever folder they open in. Sometimes you simply click Local Disk (C:) in the Save In dialog box and save all of your stuff to the root directory on your main hard drive. (We won't make you admit that you sometimes can't find that stuff later.) Saving randomly or leaving the files in a jumbled, disorganized mess in your root directly is just going to make things uglier as time passes; it's time to clean out the garage and do a little organizing. In this section, we'll show you how to both clean and better organize your root directory and remove unwanted files that have been randomly saved on your hard drive.

GunkBuster's Notebook: Be Careful What You Delete

As you begin exploring the C: drive and removing files, you'll notice lots of folders. Windows XP has specific files it needs to function properly, to boot up, and to run effectively, and they are stored on this drive. Windows files are stored in the Windows folder (makes sense), which contains many other folders, including Drivers, Downloaded Installations, Fonts, Profiles, Repair, and Resources. You certainly don't want to delete anything from that folder (at least not yet)!

Another folder you'll notice on the C: drive is the Program Files folder. In this folder, you'll find additional folders as well, and they contain the files for the programs you've installed. We have folders entitled Adobe, Canon, Corel, Emusic Download Manager, Microsoft Plus!

and Lexmark. However, you'll find built-in folders as well, including Internet Explorer, Messenger, Movie Maker, Outlook Express, and Windows Media Player. You certainly don't want to delete any of these folders or their files either.

Tip: If you want to delete a program, you don't do that by right-clicking and deleting the folder that contains the files anyway. Deleting programs is done from Control Panel. We'll talk about that in the next chapter.

So, what can you delete, and what should you look for? For the most part, you can delete anything you've created and no longer need: pictures you've saved to the hard drive; movies you've made; music you've downloaded; PDF files you've opened and saved; unzipped files; Excel, PowerPoint, FrontPage, and Access files; and documents you've written. You can also delete temporary files that Windows has saved all on its own.

Delete Files from the Root Directory (C:)

Your root directory is likely to be a place where you are storing files that you don't need. Let's quickly get rid of the unwanted files and then we'll move some files to better organize this directory. Open wide; let's take a look:

1. Right-click the Start button and choose Explore.

2. Expand My Computer and click Local Disk (C:).

3. If you see any files you no longer need, right-click and choose Delete. These should be personal files you've created, not folders. You do not want to delete the Windows folder, the Program Files folder, or the Documents And Settings folder! Keep an eye out for zip files, movie project files, picture files (.jpg, .bmp., .gif,. and .tif), documents, music, PDF files, PowerPoint and Excel files, or similar gunk you've created.

Once you've finished deleting what you no longer need from the root directory in the C: drive, you might still have some stuff there that you want to keep. Take a look at Figure 3-7. Even though we've deleted most of the stuff we don't want in the C: directory, there are still things we want to keep. The next task is to move them to a better location.

TIP: If you want to know more about what should be in the C: directory and what shouldn't, refer to the Gunkbuster's Notebook earlier.

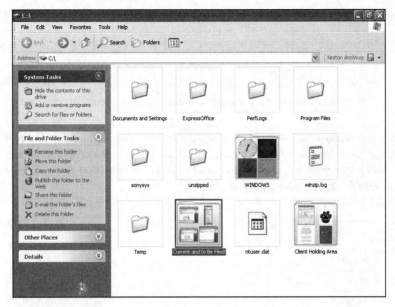

Figure 3-7
Here's a cleaned-up C: drive. It isn't clean enough though!

Better Organize Your Root Directory by Moving Files

You don't want to leave these remnants hanging around in your root directory. You want to move them to a more suitable holding area. Leave the folders that belong there where they are, like the Documents And Settings, PerfLogs, Programs Files, Unzipped, and other system folders. *If you don't know what it is—don't move it!* However, you will want to move the extraneous files like those stray music files, zip files, pictures, or folders you've created there by accident.

To move these files to a better location follow these steps:

1. Starting with something similar to Figure 3-7, select a file to move by hovering the mouse over it.

2. Click the View menu, point to Explorer Bar, and select Folders (this will place a check mark by it.) Locate, in the left pane, the My Documents folder. It will be located at the very top of the list on the left side. If you have a partitioned drive, where C: holds only the operating system and program files and you store your documents elsewhere, locate that folder in the left pane. It might be on the D: drive (or E: drive).

3. Expand the My Documents folder. You might see something like what is shown in Figure 3-8.

4. Drag the files and folders (that you created) from the C: drive to the proper folder in My Documents. (Remember, you might have configured My Documents on the D: drive.) When you're finished, the C: root directory should contain only folders that are necessary for the operating system and its programs to function. Don't move any folders created by other programs like Instant Messaging program, applications, or system or hidden files.

TIP: When you move a file like a picture or a song and some application needs it later, it might not be able to find it. You'll have to tell that program where the file has been moved. This might take a few minutes out of your day for the next few weeks or so, but take our word for it, you'll be glad you did!

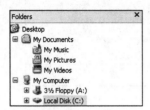

Figure 3-8
Locate the My Documents folder, and then drag those misplaced files to their proper places.

TIP: If you have a folder named Online Services in the Program Files folder, delete it. It contains files to help you get set up with AOL, MSN, and similar online services. Chances are, you're already online and you don't need to keep these files.

Delete Unused Files in Other Locations

Your root directory is an easy target to look at for removing unwanted files. But what about the rest of your hard drive? It is likely that you have unwanted files hanging out on your entire drive, hiding in places you haven't even thought to look. Fortunately, you can use the Search option to locate files on your main hard drive that you no longer need. For instance, if you know you have lots of JPEG files from your digital camera still stored on your computer but you haven't run across them yet while degunking, you can search for them using the Search command. If you have created art files in Photoshop, Arts & Letters, Corel, or a similar art program, you can locate those files by searching for their file extensions as well. For instance, Arts & Letters files all end in a .ged file name extension. Those files aren't stored in the usual My Pictures folder and might be hard to find. The same goes for Photoshop and Corel files. You can also manually locate and delete misplaced music or video files simply by searching for them. Let's give this a whirl:

1. Click Start, and click Search. (If you don't see the Search option on the Start menu, right-click the Taskbar, choose Properties, click the Start Menu tab, choose Start Menu, click Customize, click Advanced, and check Search. Okay your way out of the boxes.)

2. From the Search dialog box, perform independent searches for *.jpg and *.jpeg to locate missing digital camera files and pictures; *.psd to locate missing Photoshop files; *.gif, *.tif, *.bmp, and *.tiff to locate art files; *.midi, *.mp3, *.wav, *.avi, and *.wma to locate music files; *.doc for Word documents; and *.pdf to locate PDF files. Of course, there are hundreds of other file types to search for; this is only the beginning, but it will probably keep you busy for a while.

3. If you find files you don't need that you created, opened, or imported yourself (these don't include program files), you can delete them from the Search window by right-clicking and choosing Delete. There are several ways to delete files if you find you have a lot to delete. We'll talk about that in a minute.

4. You can also move the files by dragging and dropping. To do this from the Search window, click View, point to Explorer Bar, and check Folders; then drag and drop to the correct folder as detailed in the previous section. This might not be necessary though; the files might already be in the right location! To see where a file is stored, right-click it and choose Properties, or view the files using Details view.

If you run across a large group of files you want to delete, use the Search Results windows to view their details (click View, click Details). The files meeting the criteria you searched for will be listed in groups by their location by default, but you can change that if you desire. For instance, clicking once on the Name title sorts the files alphabetically; clicking once on the Size title sorts the file by their size. You can also right click on any title to remove it or to add a different title to the interface. We found literally hundreds of JPEG files on our computers.

Now, choose the items in the list you want to delete by selecting them separately, selecting them in nonsequential groups by holding down the Ctrl key, or selecting them in sequence by holding down the Shift key. Press Delete on the keyboard to delete the selected files.

Here is a list of other files types to look for:

*   ASA or ASP—Active Server documents
*   ASF—Windows Media Audio/Video files
*   CHK—Check Disk files

- COV and CPE—Fax cover page files
- FRM—WordPerfect 10 documents
- MPA, MPE, MPEG, MPG—Movie files
- PPT and PPS—PowerPoint files
- SCR—Screen saver files
- TXT—Text files
- XLS—Excel files

You can see all of the file types stored on your computer from Windows Explorer by clicking Tools and then Folder Options. Select the File Types tab. Remember, you're looking for files *you* created.

TIP: *There are lots of temporary files on your computer too, and although you can search for these files from the Search command window, we prefer to use a utility called Disk Cleanup. We'll talk about that shortly, and we'll also give you more insight into temporary files. However, if you are so inclined and want to remove your temporary files manually, search for *.tmp. You can safely delete files that are more than a week old.*

Clean Up the "Unzipped" Folder

If you use WinZip (a popular program for compressing files), the Unzipped folder is where your unzipped files are stored so that you can open them, read or look at them, and then save them if needed. When you download a file from the Internet or get it from another source, it will have an extension of .zip if the file is compressed. Once you uncompress this file and save the unzipped files to your hard drive in another folder, you've got two copies! You probably don't need much of what you've got saved in the Unzipped folder. Let's take a tour:

1. Right-click the Start button and click Explore.
2. Locate the Unzipped folder and click it. It's generally located near the bottom of the list of folders on the root drive.
3. Browse through what you see there, and delete any item you don't need.

In addition to simply looking in the Unzipped folder for unnecessary zip files, you should also use Search to locate ones you've created or ones that you saved in different places. Doing a search for *.zip on one of our test computers yields an additional 135 zip files!

Locating Duplicate Files

Locating duplicate files is a little more difficult than simply locating a JPEG or PDF file. Some duplicate files end in extensions such as .001 .002 and so on, and you can search for them using the Search utility. This usually isn't a very productive way to go, though. The best way to get rid of duplicate files on your system is to download, install, and/or purchase a disk cleaning software program. There are many on the market, including several free ones.

Enter the words *Windows XP Remove Duplicate Files* in a search engine in IE 6 and see what you get. Many utilities are free for 10 days or so, and that might be all the time you need to clean your system. Consider this if you can actually see duplicate files; you might not have a problem in that regard.

 In Figure 3-9, we're using a program called Check Identical Files, a duplicate file checking utility found on the Internet that is free for 10 days. It only took a few minutes to download and install, and it's easy to use. As you can see, it's found several instances of duplicate files, many of which are media files. Some files even have three copies!

Get Rid of Those Pesky Temp Files

If your computer is like ours, you likely have temporary (*.tmp) files hiding in every nook and cranny. If you've never taken the time to clean up your temp files, you're in for a big surprise! You can free up lots of hard drive space quickly and easily simply by deleting these unnecessary files.

There are lots of reasons temp files are created. When Windows locks up or crashes, or if you have to use Ctrl+Alt+Del to restart, some temporary files get left on your hard disk. Some installation routines also leave temporary files. Temp files can be files that the computer creates to use as backup files for office programs like Microsoft Word so that, if something happens and the program shuts down unexpectedly, a saved copy will be available. Programs create temporary files, too, to store frequently needed information in an easily retrievable folder. Temporary files are also created when you surf the Internet, and these files store information about the Web sites you visit. Most of the time, these files are created to save you time, but after a while, their buildup can cause a hard disk to bog down.

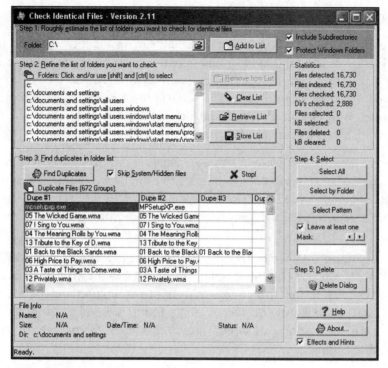

Figure 3-9
Here, we're using a program called Check Identical Files to locate and delete the identical files on my system.

It's best to clean up your temporary file folders occasionally, just to make sure you aren't causing the hard drive any unnecessary strain. There are several ways to do this, and using Disk Cleanup is the easiest.

Use Disk Cleanup

Disk Cleanup is a utility that ships with Windows XP and can be used to delete temporary Internet files, temporary (computer) files, offline Web pages, the files in the Recycle Bin, and more. Temporary files aren't needed, and if you've used offline Web pages, they're just taking up space too. Disk Cleanup is easy to use, but this first time you might want to lay off emptying the Recycle Bin, just to be safe.

To use Disk Cleanup:

1. Click Start, point to All Programs, point to Accessories, point to System Tools, and click Disk Cleanup.

2. Select the drive to clean up, and click OK.

3. In the Disk Cleanup dialog box, select the items to delete. I'd suggest unchecking the Recycle Bin and Compress Old Files, but the others you can leave checked as shown in Figure 3-10. Click OK, and then click Yes to tell XP that's what you really want to do.

Cleaning Up What Disk Cleanup Has Missed

You might have noticed that there weren't options in Disk Cleanup to remove cookies, browser caches, Internet Explorer history, recent documents, and similar items you might want to get rid of. In addition, if you use Search to locate the temporary files on your computer after running Disk Cleanup, you'll notice there are still some there. Here's how to clean up these additional temporary files:

1. Use the Search option and search your drive for *.tmp files.

2. Right-click Name in the Search window and verify that Date Modified is checked.

3. Click Date Modified in the Search window to sort the remaining temporary files by date.

4. Use the Shift key to select the files that are more than a week old.

5. Click Delete on the keyboard. (Not all files will be deleted.)

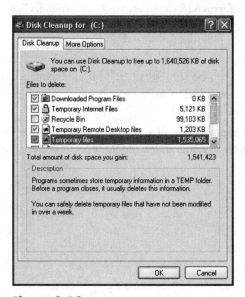

Figure 3-10
Use Disk Cleanup to delete unnecessary files from your computer.

Just for fun, delete these files too: *.dmp (dump files created when your computer crashes) and *.fts and *.gid (files that make searches faster; if you don't use Help a lot, delete these).

TIP: To clear the Recent Documents list, right-click the Windows Taskbar, click Properties, click the Start Menu tab, and click Customize. Depending on the theme chosen, click Clear or Clear List. Click OK.

Internet and E-Mail Files

You can manually clean up temporary Internet files, offline content, cookies, browser caches, Internet Explorer history, and more from inside the Internet Options dialog box:

1. Open Internet Explorer.

2. Click Tools, and click Internet Options.

3. From the General tab, click Delete Cookies to delete the cookies on your computer, and click Delete Files to delete temporary Internet files.

4. From the same tab, click Clear History to clear references to Internet sites you've visited.

5. To stop Internet Explorer from automatically using AutoComplete to finish entries for Web addresses, forms, or usernames and passwords, click the Content tab, click AutoComplete, and remove the checks for AutoComplete settings. You can also clear forms and clear passwords, as shown in Figure 3-11.

6. Click OK until you have exited the dialog box(es).

As for Outlook Express, for now, deleting the items in the Sent Items folder and the Deleted Items folder can be somewhat helpful, but there are a couple of chapters on Outlook Express later, so we'll save the nitty-gritty for then.

TIP: Norton SystemWorks provides tools to optimize the hard drive, remove unnecessary files, and clean up the computer in general. We highly recommend a program like this.

Figure 3-11
Clear Internet Explorer's cache.

Deleting User Files from Unused User Accounts

If you've ever created a user account for someone else so that they could access your computer, you'll have user account files for that person stored on the hard disk. If that person no longer accesses the computer and doesn't need the files he or she created, you can safely delete both the account and the files.

Here's how:

1. While logged on as an Administrator, open Control Panel and click User Accounts.
2. Take a look at the user accounts on the computer. You'll want to keep yours, of course, and hopefully the Guest account is disabled, but if you see additional accounts you don't need listed there, you can delete them. Click the account to delete, and from the resulting window, click Delete The Account.
3. In the next window, Do You Want To Keep <*username*>'s Files? (shown in Figure 3-12), click Delete Files.
4. In the next window, click Delete Account if desired.

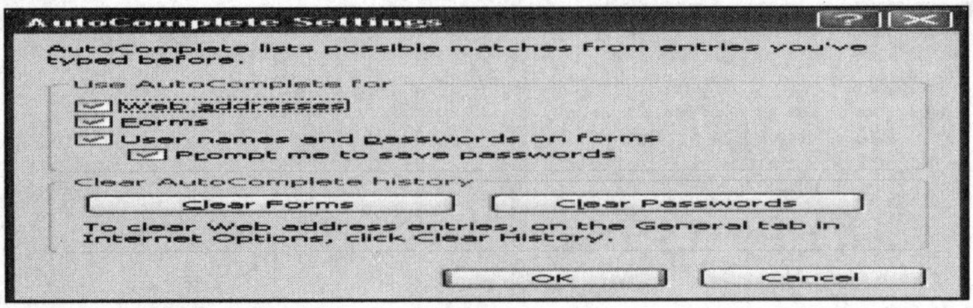

Figure 3-12
Delete a user's files.

Summing Up

To sum up, deleting files and folders *that you created* can be quite helpful in speeding up or improving the performance of your computer. If you took this first step seriously, chances are good your computer is now running better than it was before. Our gunked-up test machine is really screaming now, and we've only just begun!

Before you go to bed tonight, do a quick backup and run Disk Cleanup. In about a week, empty the Recycle Bin.

Uninstalling Programs You Don't Need and Tweaking Those You Do

Degunking Checklist:

√ Remove the programs you no longer use by utilizing the program's uninstall options.

√ Remove unwanted programs that don't have an uninstall option with the Control Panel.

√ Remove extraneous Windows components from Control Panel.

√ Search for programs you didn't know you had and remove them.

√ Remove programs for hardware you no longer own.

√ Fine-tune the programs you regularly use to improve their performance.

f you've deleted all of the unnecessary documents, temporary files, pictures, movies, and music from your computer, you've taken a gigantic step forward in reducing the amount of clutter on it. As you've learned, when you reduce clutter, you improve the performance of your system. The next step in the degunking process is to remove *programs* you don't use and their related files.

In addition to removing programs you don't use, though, you can remove programs that you can't use, like programs that you installed with your first Web cam, applications for a printer you no longer own, or programs for an older digital camera or scanner you no longer have.

Windows also automatically installs some components you might not need as well, like MSN Explorer or Games, and you could have chosen to install some things you no longer want, too. Windows Fax Services is one of them. For instance, if you recently purchased a dedicated fax machine and you don't use the fax application that comes with Windows XP, you can remove this Windows component.

CAUTION: *You should perform a comprehensive backup and create a System Restore point before starting this chapter.*

Remove Programs You Don't Use

Take a look at your All Programs list to see some of the programs you have installed on your computer. You can do this by clicking on the Start menu and selecting the Programs option. All of the programs installed on your computer won't be listed here, but many will. If anything strikes you as odd or if you don't know what a program is, open it up and take a gander. If it's a program you don't need or one that doesn't open, make a note of it. We'll uninstall it next. You should also make a list of programs that you are not sure if you use or not. You might encounter some programs that have names that are so cryptic or shortened that you might not be able to easily determine if the program is needed. Later, we'll show you how to play detective and uncover the mysteries of your installed programs.

GunkBuster's Notebook: Locating a Program's Uninstall Option

Programs that are installed on your computer are generally installed to the C: drive, and their files are usually located in the Program Files folder. If you accept the defaults while installing, chances are good most of your programs are installed there. When searching for an uninstallation program, check there first.

Sometimes though, you'll find programs and their uninstallation commands in the Windows folder. This is especially common when the program or application comes with a computer that already has XP installed and has bundled software. As an example, Corel's WordPerfect was found in one of our parent's Windows folder, and they didn't even know they had it! And right there, when no other uninstallation command could be found, not even in the Control Panel, was an uninstall icon!

Another place installed programs might be hanging out is in folders that were automatically created by the programs themselves. Generally, these folders are in regular places like the Program Files folder, but sometimes they're in more obscure places, like the Windows\System 32 folder.

If you've purchased a computer that had Windows preinstalled, look in the Windows folder for other telltale signs, like folders with names created from a variation of the manufacturer's name. There you're likely to find programs or shortcuts for subscribing to online services, help and support programs, and more.

NOTE: *Applications that you use regularly will move automatically to the left-hand column of the Start menu. You can also put shortcuts on the Desktop, access a program from the All Programs list, or run the program from its program icon in its program folder.*

TIP: *Before uninstalling any program, close all running programs.*

When choosing what to uninstall, don't uninstall any program if you aren't sure what it is used for. In addition, shy away from uninstalling Microsoft Updates, your computer manufacturer's help and support programs, or Hotfixes, as well as any programs that were upgraded from one version to another. In addition, if your computer came with XP preinstalled and included several programs with it, and all you got was a recovery disk, you shouldn't uninstall any of these programs unless you are positive you don't want them anymore. Many times, the only way to get these programs back (without the application's disks) is to format the drive and use the computer manufacturer's recovery disks.

Using a Program's Uninstall Command

Once you make a decision to remove a program, you should always first check to see if the program has an uninstall option. The uninstall option is the best way to go because it usually will take care of a number of important cleanup and "bookkeeping" tasks, such as updating the Windows Registry. This helps ensure that your system doesn't keep any junk around that's related to the program you're removing. The best way to see if a program you want to remove has an uninstall option is to check the All Programs list, as shown in Figure 4-1. The uninstall option is usually pretty complete and generally removes all instances of the program on the All Programs list and from the Programs folder. Figures 4-1 and 4-2 show the Uninstall choice and an uninstall in progress.

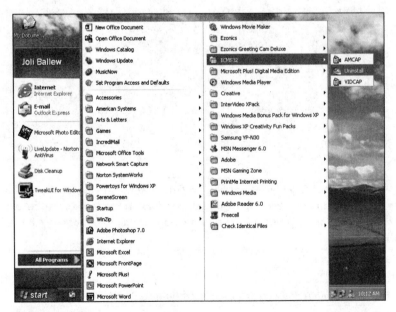

Figure 4-1
Use a program's own uninstall option to remove a program you no longer need.

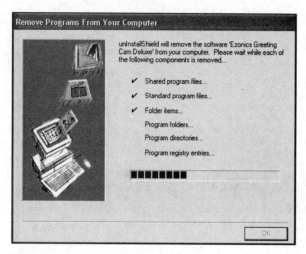

Figure 4-2
An uninstall in progress using a program's uninstall option.

TIP: If you receive a message that you are going to uninstall some shared files when uninstalling, be sure to choose the option not to delete them. These files don't take up much room, but uninstalling one that is needed by another program can cause problems.

If you see any programs on the All Programs menu that you want to remove that offer no uninstall choice, you'll need to remove them using the Control Panel and the Add Or Remove Programs option.

Using the Control Panel to Remove Programs

The Control Panel offers the Add Or Remove Programs option for uninstalling any program on your computer. If there's no uninstall option for a program, do this:

1. Open the Control Panel. If it isn't on the Desktop, open My Computer and look for it there. You can also access the Control Panel by clicking on the Start menu, selecting Settings, and then selecting the Control Panel option.

2. Double-click the Add Or Remove Programs option.

3. In the Add Or Remove Programs window, locate the program to uninstall.

4. Click Change/Remove, as shown in Figure 4-3.

5. Click OK if required, and wait while the program is uninstalled. Figure 4-4 shows an example of a Remove Shared File? dialog box. Selecting No To All is generally the best choice.

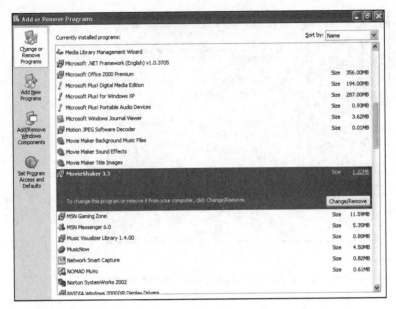

Figure 4-3
Use the Control Panel's Add Or Remove Programs to uninstall any application.

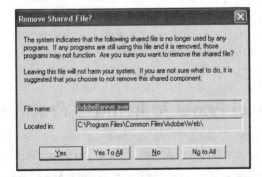

Figure 4-4
Choose No To All when prompted to remove shared files.

Extraneous Windows Components

You can also clean up your hard disk by removing or uninstalling Windows components you don't use. Earlier, we mentioned Windows Fax Services and Games, but there are others as well. Figure 4-5 shows some of the available Windows components.

To see what Windows components you have installed on your system and to uninstall the ones you don't need, follow these steps:

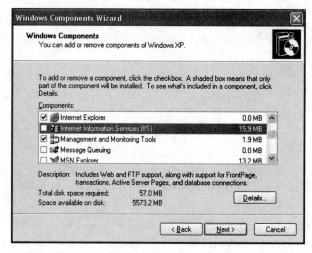

Figure 4-5

Windows components aren't always needed.

1. Open the Control Panel. If it isn't on the Desktop, open My Computer and look for it there.

2. Double-click Add Or Remove Programs.

3. Click Add/Remove Windows Components in the left pane of the Add Or Remove Programs window.

4. When the Windows Components Wizard opens, scroll down the list, clicking on the components you have installed one at a time, and read what they are used for in the description under the components list. If you have Internet Information Services installed but you aren't planning on creating your own personal Web server, you can uninstall it. You might also consider uninstalling MSN Explorer if you use IE6, Outlook Express if you use Incredimail or another e-mail client, Windows Messenger if you don't IM, and Games (under Accessories And Utilities) if you don't play. Select the item(s) to uninstall and click Next.

5. Wait while the Windows Components Wizard completes.

Cleaning Up the Start Menu

After uninstalling unnecessary programs, you might also need to remove references to them from the Start menu. This is pretty easy:

1. Click Start, point to All Programs, and from the list, locate the item to delete.

2. Right-click the item and choose Delete, as shown in Figure 4-6.

3. Click Yes to verify.

Figure 4-6
Remove uninstalled programs from the Start menu if it isn't done automatically.

Keep in mind that deleting an item from this menu does not delete the program. You should have already done that. This command simply removes the shortcut to the item on the Start menu if it still exists. If you have any other shortcuts you'd like to delete from the Start menu, even if they are for programs you still have installed, you can remove them in the same manner. But remember, removing them from the Start menu does not uninstall them.

Find Programs You Don't Even Know You Have

Some of the items in the Add Or Remove Programs window might have looked a bit unfamiliar. We found one named PicoPlayer, one named Open MGSecure Module 3.1, and one named Network Smart Capture. Of course, we didn't dare uninstall them, not knowing what they were, but we'd certainly like to find out. You might have run across a similar issue.

There are several ways to find out what a program does. You can search the Internet for the application's name, you can open the Program Files folder and launch the EXE file, or you can see if there's a matching item in the All Programs list. If you can start the program, you can decide if you'd like to keep it or not. As it turns out, the computer manufacturer installed all of the items we had questions about, and thus, we uninstalled them.

Check Out the Program Files Folder

You'll be surprised what lurks in the Program Files folder. There are programs that aren't listed on the All Programs menu, that aren't shown on the Desktop, and that aren't listed in Add Or Remove Programs. To find out what you've got hiding in there, follow these simple steps:

1. Right-click the Start button.
2. Click Explore, and browse to the Program Files folder.
3. Click the program folders to see what files are in each one.

If you find programs you don't want or need, there are really only three ways to get rid of them:

1. You can hope to find an uninstall option in the program folder.
2. You can visit the manufacturer's Web site for uninstallation instructions.
3. You can delete the entire folder by right-clicking and choosing Delete.

Use #3 as a last resort; deleting entire program folders can be hazardous to your computer's health!

About deleting program folders: Our test computer had a folder that contained several graphics-related program icons and EXE files. It was full of applications that weren't used, and there was no choice in the Control Panel to uninstall them. There was also no uninstall option that we could see in any of the Program File folders. The only way to get rid of this folder and its contents was to delete it entirely. After a successful reboot, the deletion was not hazardous to the computer's health. However, you won't always be that lucky, and this isn't meant to imply that the computer won't have problems at a later date. Delete program files with care (and keep a good backup)!

CAUTION: *Don't delete program file folders unless you are really, really sure you understand the consequences. For instance, don't delete the Photoshop 6 folder after upgrading to Photoshop 7! You might find later that you needed some of those files.*

GunkBuster's Notebook: Centralizing Storage of Install Suites

Windows provides ready-made folders for storing documents, music files, video files, and digital photo files. What it does *not* provide is a folder for "install suites," which are files that you download for installation as programs under Windows. When you download a utility from the Web somewhere (whether free or something you paid for) you're downloading a file. This may be a ZIP file (or some other type of compressed archive file, like a RAR file) or it may be an EXE (executable) file.

Whatever its format, this install suite file must be stored somewhere. Windows typically dumps it into your My Documents folder, and that's where it will remain unless you move it somewhere else. Some people move an install suite file from My Documents to the folder created when the utility is installed, somewhere under Program Files. Others move install suite files to the Program Files folder, above all the program-specific folders. Our advice is to create a separate folder for install suite files.

But first, why keep them at all? Once you've installed the utility, you don't need its install suite. That is, you don't need it...until you buy a new machine and need to install it on the new machine, or until your old machine crashes hard and must be reformatted and everything must be reinstalled. If you try a piece of software and don't like it (and then uninstall it), deleting its install suite is just good housekeeping. If you *do* like it, keeping the install suite file is essential.

Keeping install suites in one folder rather than scattering them "willy-nilly" across your hard drive is important for two reasons:

- If all install suites are together, you can spot duplicates and old versions that are no longer needed and delete them.
- If all install suites are together in one folder, you can back them up very easily by burning the folder to a CD. Backing up installed programs is pointless—you can't reinstall them just by copying them from a backup CD. That being the case, backing up install suites is essential.

What you name the folder is up to you, but something like "Install Suites" or "My Install Suites" works well.

One final note on install suites: Programs that you purchase by downloading from a Web site generally require an "unlock code" to make them fully functional. It's a good idea to create a document file that details all your unlock codes and the programs to which they apply. Store this document file in your install suites folder. An install suite without its unlock code is useless!

Remove Spyware

Spyware is another item you might not know you have on your computer. Spyware is a program that is installed on your computer either with or without your knowledge, and advertising companies use them to track what you do online, including what sites you visit. Sometimes they add new toolbars to your

Web browser, change your home page, or cause excessive pop-up ads to appear on your computer. Other times they can be more dangerous and do things like stealing your passwords, credit card numbers, or other forms of identification. Illegal Internet music download sites can be culprits, as can unscrupulous businesses such as pornography sites. Xupiter was on our computer once, and we had no idea how it got there. Besides being an invasion of your privacy, though, most of these programs are poorly written, causing your computer to act buggy or respond slowly.

If you think you might be infected because you've visited or downloaded software from a risky Web site, or if all of the sudden you are experiencing problems such as a change to your home page, you might want to have your system scanned. You can get a free scan from many Web sites, including **www.spywareinfo.com** and **www.spychecker.com**. Visit **www.spychecker.com/software/ freeware_antispy.html** for various choices. We tried X-Cleaner Free, a free spyware checker (and more) and found it to be quite easy to use as well as functional. The interface is shown in Figure 4-7.

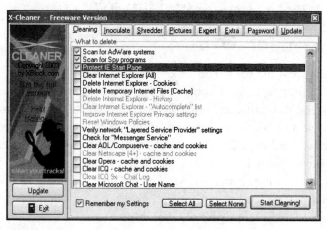

Figure 4-7
Download and use a spyware removal program to check for spyware on your computer.

We also tried SpyHunter, **http:www3.enigmasoftwaregroup.com**. It scanned the system for free, found no spyware (although it did find some cookies it felt were of "medium" danger as well as a couple of files), and displayed protection options. This interface is quite comprehensive and is shown in Figure 4-8.

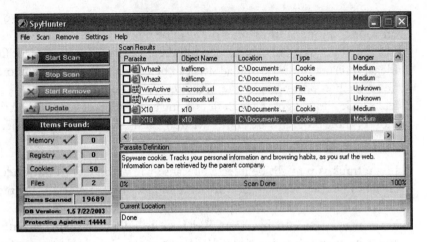

Figure 4-8
SpyHunter is quite comprehensive, but you have to buy it if you want it to use the removal tools.

Remove Programs for Hardware You No Longer Own

Take a look around the room and make a list of all of the hardware you currently have connected to your computer. Include printers, scanners, speakers, CD burners, and Web cams, and don't forget items like MP3 players and digital cameras that you connect intermittently. Next, take a look at the boxes that hold your dead hardware, like that pen/camera/Web cam/coffeemaker your mom got you for your birthday last year. Now, return to Add Or Remove Programs in the Control Panel, and see if it includes any items in your list of hardware that you no longer own or use. We'll bet you'll find a few printers, maybe a scanner, and probably an old Web cam.

Old printer software is the worst because printers generally come with programs for enhancing photos, cropping them, publishing or e-mailing them, and similar tasks. If you use a different program (such as Photoshop or Photoshop Elements), or any of the available Microsoft tools (like Publisher, Photo Editor, Paint), or any of the newer software available in Office 2003, you probably don't need this additional software at all. Figure 4-9 shows an example of some unnecessary software.

Keep uninstalling! Our test machine is running faster than ever, and we've only just begun!

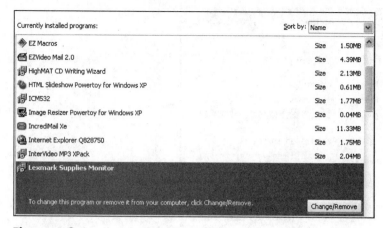

Figure 4-9
Remove programs for hardware you no longer own.

Tweaking Programs You Do Need

Now that you have only the programs you want installed on your computer, let's tweak those and the Windows components for ultimate performance. There are several options for increasing performance, including having the program open in a specific window size, having a program run in a different operating system environment (using Program Compatibility Mode), configuring System Restore to use minimal system resources, tweaking Performance options, and working with virtual memory settings.

Right-Click Your Program Icons

Right-clicking any program shortcut icon brings up a deluge of choices. Choose Properties to see the properties shown in Figure 4-10. Here, you can tell the program what to do when you click the shortcut icon. We like our programs to start in Maximized mode. You can also change the icon, set compatibility options, and more.

Program Compatibility Mode

If you find that an older program that worked fine on your Windows 98 machine doesn't run so well on your new Windows XP machine, you can tell Windows to run it in Program Compatibility Mode. When you choose this option, Windows XP changes the operating environment for the program and creates an area for the program to run in its native environment. While you can use the Program Compatibility Wizard, you can also configure it manually:

Figure 4-10
Set properties for applications.

1. Locate the program icon on the Desktop or the program name on the All Programs menu. The program has to be one that you've installed; you can't set compatibility options for Windows XP applications like Outlook Express, Internet Explorer, Paint, or similar programs.

2. Right-click and choose Properties.

3. Click the Compatibility tab, and check Run This Program In Compatibility Mode For:, and notice the options in the drop-down list become available. Choose a mode for the program from this drop-down list. See Figure 4-11.

TIP: For best results, don't run anti-virus software in Program Compatibility Mode.

If the program still seems buggy after configuring it to run in Program Compatibility Mode, check the manufacturer's Web site for updates or patches, check Windows Update for program fixes, or if the program is a game that uses DirectX technology, ensure that you are using the latest version of DirectX (see the next section).

Make Multimedia and Games Run Better

Multimedia and games use DirectX, a tool that enhances the multimedia capabilities of your computer. DirectX enables programs to determine the hardware capabilities of your computer and then sets program parameters to match,

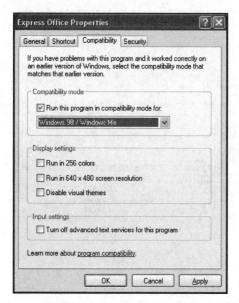

Figure 4-11
Program Compatibility Mode lets you run any program you've installed in another operating system environment.

thus making sure the program can access and use all of the high-performance options available. You can tweak DirectX using the DirectX Diagnostic Tool: Click Start, click Run, and type dxdiag. Then, click OK.

If you are familiar with DirectX terminology and tools, or if you just want to see if there are any problems, you can work through the tabs of the dialog box. Each offers various information and information on problems and features. You can also perform tests to see if the hardware and software are functioning properly, including tests on your display, sound devices, music devices, input devices, and more. As shown in Figure 4-12, We've tested the music devices on our system. You can see in the Notes section that all DirectMusic tests were successful.

If you do find problems or if DirectX sounds like a planet in a sci-fi movie to you, you'll be better off using the options under the More Help tab. There, you'll find various troubleshooters that will walk you through solving any problems you've found. You can also click Help from any tab to get more information.

Performance Options

Keeping in mind that entire books could be written on enhancing performance options, let's go over the basics of the basics. Locate My Computer, right-click, and choose Properties. Click the Advanced tab. Performance options are available by

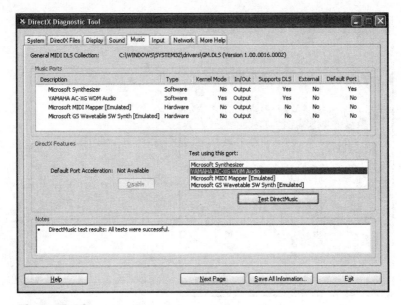

Figure 4-12

Testing a system using the DirectX Diagnostic Tool.

clicking the Settings button in the Performance section. Figure 4–13 shows both dialog boxes.

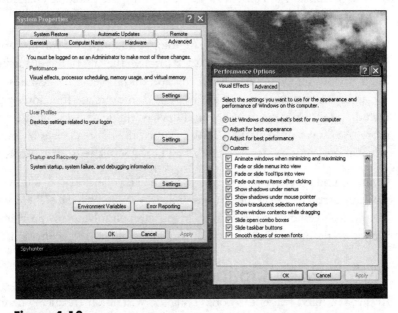

Figure 4-13

Performance options can be accessed from inside the System Properties dialog box.

Notice that in the Performance Options dialog box, we've chosen Let Windows Choose What's Best For My Computer. That's the default, but it can be changed. For instance, if you're interested in getting the best appearance from your computer, select Adjust For Best Appearance; if you want best performance, choose Adjust For Best Performance. You can also select Custom, and check or uncheck anything you desire.

The problem with adjusting for best performance is lack of appearance! No fading or sliding of menus, no smooth screen fonts, no visual styles on windows and buttons. Your best bet for enhancing performance is to choose Custom and uncheck as many boxes as you're comfortable with.

The Advanced tab offers some other performance tweaks:

- Processor Scheduling can be configured to use a greater share of process time for either Programs or for Background Services. By default, the computer uses a greater share of its resources on running programs, but if you'd rather have XP focus its attention on running background services, you can change the default. Generally, the default is fine.

- Memory Usage can be configured to use a greater share of memory to run either Programs or for System Cache. By default, the computer uses a greater share of available memory on running programs, but if you'd rather have XP focus its attention on system cache, you can change the default. Generally, the default is fine.

- Virtual Memory Settings can be configured for the paging file. The computer uses a specific area of the hard disk as if it were RAM, and XP sets a default paging file size. If you need to, you can click Change, and set this manually. Chapter 12 introduces virtual memory and gives suggestions for configuring this option.

TIP: *There are several sites on the Internet that offer performance-enhancing software. Check out www.5star-shareware.com for starters.*

System Restore

System Restore is a hard disk space hog. By default, System Restore is enabled on all drives when you first get Windows XP, unless you have less than 200 MB of free hard disk space. System Restore saves data on the hard drive so that if you have a computer problem, you can revert back to a saved state easily. It's an important feature, mind you, and we are not going to suggest you turn it off, but we are going to tell you how to tweak it, just in case you want to save a little (or possibly a lot of) hard drive space.

Let's check out your System Restore settings, and take a look at how much hard drive space is being used:

1. Click Start, point to All Programs, point to Accessories, point to System Tools, and click System Restore.

2. In the Welcome To System Restore dialog box, click System Restore Settings.

3. In the resulting System Properties dialog box (this should look familiar), notice that the available drives are listed and System Restore status is showing. In Figure 4-14, System Restore is monitoring both drives.

4. Select a drive, and click Settings. Figure 4-15 shows how your System Restore settings might be configured.

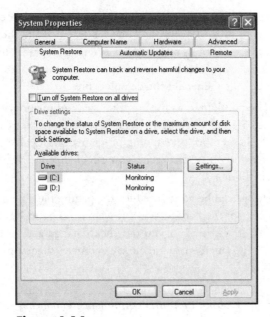

Figure 4-14

System Restore is monitoring both drives on this computer.

5. You can reduce the amount of disk space System Restore uses by moving the slider to the left. For the most part, 1 GB certainly suffices, and with 1 GB set aside for System Restore, you'll always have several restore points to choose. This will be a welcome relief if and when you need them. Reconfigure the slider if you'd like, and click OK.

6. Reconfigure any additional drives, and click OK. Close the System Restore dialog box.

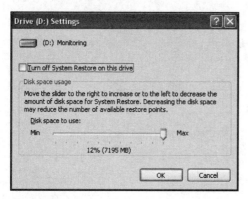

Figure 4-15
Notice that System Restore has 12% of the available disk space allocated for restore points. That's over 7 GB here!

Summing Up

By now, you should have deleted your unnecessary documents, pictures, music, and movies, as well as uninstalled unnecessary programs. Hopefully, your machine is running better than ever! Keep in mind that we've only just begun; there are plenty more things we can do to degunk your computer!

Before going to bed tonight, do a quick backup and run Disk Cleanup and Disk Defragmenter. Wait a while before deleting the items in the Recycle Bin too, just to make sure you won't need anything you deleted today.

Organizing Your Remaining Files and Folders

Degunking Checklist:

√   Organize the default folders by creating additional, embedded, folders and moving files into them.

√   Use the File and Folders tasks pane in Windows XP to rename, move, copy, or delete folders.

√   Create folders on partitions configured for data only.

√   Empty the Recycle Bin to free up space on your hard drive.

√   Use Disk Cleanup and Disk Defragmenter to finalize the cleansing process.

Now that you've deleted unnecessary files and applications, it's time to organize what you have remaining on your hard drive. Comparing this to our house cleaning analogy, this part of degunking is like cleaning out the garage: You need all of the stuff you have stored there, but you don't want to trip over it each time you need to use the car. You'll also need to be able to find the stuff easily when you need it!

In this chapter, you'll learn how to create folders and how to move files and folders. You'll also learn some techniques for getting organized (and staying that way). Once this bit of organizing is out of the way, we'll run Disk Cleanup one more time and hold our breath and empty the Recycle Bin. Last but not least, we'll defragment the hard drive. Once all this is done, your PC should be zipping along at breakneck speed.

Better Organize the Default Folders

The simplest way to organize your files is to create personal folders inside the default folders. As we discussed in Chapter 3, the default folders are My Documents, My Pictures, My Music, and My Videos. You can create subfolders inside of those and move data into them. These default folders make great storage areas and can be used to organize everything from your accounting files to your zoo pictures. Hopefully, you've moved some of your files there already.

Because the default folders are generally located on the C: drive, you might encounter a problem with using them—they can get really disorganized. (See the GunkBuster's Notebook tip later in this chapter where we'll show you how to change the default location of a default folder.) In this age of large hard drives (80 GB or more), many computers are partitioned into two drives: the C: drive, which holds the system files and programs, and the D: drive, which is supposed to store your personal data. This sounds good in theory, but unfortunately many people store personal stuff in the default folders, and one day they wake up and realize that their 16 GB C: drive is full, and their 64 GB D: drive is empty! What a mess.

It's likely that your system is set up in one of the following ways:
- You have a single partition and use the default folders. (Partitions are sections of a hard drive that are created to hold specific types of data, like system files or personal data.)
- You use a second partition or you have more than one hard drive and you create your own folders for storing personal data.
- You have been saving files haphazardly.

Fortunately, no matter what your particular set of circumstances, we can get it all straightened out here. The techniques we'll introduce will apply to everyone.

Where Should You Put Your Data?

Because computers come in all shapes and sizes, you have to look at your specific setup and decide where you want to store your files. Open My Computer and take a look at what you have. If you have a single hard drive that contains a single partition, C: for instance, you should store your files in the default folders on that drive. If this is the case, skip to the section "Personalize the Default Folders with Folders of Your Own" later in this chapter. If you have two or more hard disk drives or hard disk partitions, you'll need take a few extra steps. You can determine what your setup is by clicking on My Computer on your desktop. If your setup looks anything like the one shown in Figure 5-1, you'll know you have more than one hard drive or partition.

If you have a setup like this, you probably won't want to save to the default folders on the C: drive. Looking again at Figure 5-1, you can see that the Local Disk D: is a 58.5 GB hard disk and 52.5 GB are free. Now that's a good place to save data! (On this same computer, the C: drive is 16 GB, with about 7 GB free.)

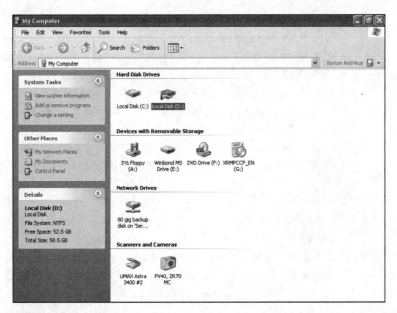

Figure 5-1

Here's a computer with two disk drives. The C: drive is for the system files and the D: drive is for the data.

GunkBuster's Notebook: Creating Default Folders for Multiple Partitioned Hard Drives

If you have multiple partitions or drives, you should create some new default folders on a drive or partition other than C: and move your personal data over there (if it isn't there already). You won't have the luxury of having the standard default folders such as My Documents, My Pictures, or My Music. Thus, you'll need to set up your own organizational system. Here are the steps to help you:

1. Open My Computer and open the drive where you want to place your data. On the computer shown in Figure 5-1, that would be the D: drive. Yours might have a different letter assigned.

2. Right-click an empty area of the folder window, point to New, and click Folder. Name the folder My Pictures.

3. Repeat step 2 and create three more folders: My Videos, My Music, and My Documents. You might also want to create My Webs if you create Web pages, My Current Projects to hold work in progress, or similar folders.

4. Close the window that shows the contents of the D: drive.

5. Open the My Documents folder on the C: drive, or open any other folder that contains data you'd like to move, as shown in Figure 5-2.

6. Select the items to move either by using the Edit menu and Select All or by selecting the files manually. In the folder shown in Figure 5-2, we will select all of the files. (The goal is to move your existing data—data you've created yourself—from the smaller drive to the larger one. When you're finished, the folders containing data on the C: drive should be just about empty.)

7. From the File And Folder Tasks pane, select Move The Selected Items.

8. In the Move Items dialog box, browse to the D: drive, locate the folder to move the data to, and click Move. The files will be moved automatically. The Move dialog box is shown later in Figure 5-5.

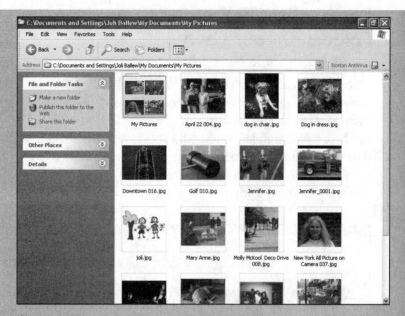

Figure 5-2
Locate the items you'd like to move from the C: drive to another drive.

CAUTION: Don't move program file folders, downloaded installation files, or any file that you did not create yourself. Doing so could cause system instability.

The next time you need to open a file, picture, project, or music, make sure you browse to the D: drive! You'll also want to tell applications like Windows Media Player that you've moved your files, if you have. To do this, for example, just open the player, click Tools, and click Search For Media Files. In the Search On drop-down list, choose the new drive.

Once you set up a new set of folders like this, you should take special care to ensure that your files are saved in the new location whenever you use applications like Word, Excel, and so on. Because the new default folders will have the same names as the ones that Windows XP set up for you (they are now just stored on a different drive or partition), you could easily save to the wrong drive or partition if you are not careful. You might want to regularly check the default folders on your C: drive (My Documents, My Music, and so on) and move the files found in these folders to their proper corresponding folders on the drive or partition you are using to actually store your personal data.

Personalize the Default Folders with Folders of Your Own

Once you've decided where to store your data, whether it's on the C: or some other drive, you can begin personalizing the folders by adding your own touches. For starters, open the My Documents folder and categorize the documents in there. Perhaps you might organize what's in the folder by projects you need to finish, projects completed, and projects yet to be started. You could also take a different approach and organize by the document type, like budgets, health, taxes, or letters. You can repeat this practice for each of the default folders. Figure 5-3 shows a fairly organized My Pictures folder.

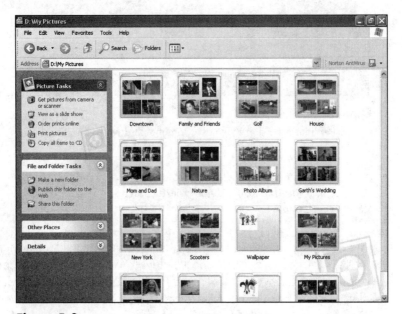

Figure 5-3

Organize your data in folders you create and name.

With ideas for folder names selected, create and organize your folders by following these steps:

1. Open the folder to organize. In the File And Folder Tasks pane, click Make A New Folder. If you can't see this pane, right click an empty area of the folder's window, point to New, and click Folder.

2. Name the folder and press Enter.

3. Click and drag items from the folder into the new one you just created.

4. Repeat these steps until all of the items are neatly organized in folders.

GunkBuster's Notebook: Change the Default Location of Your My Documents Folder

Windows XP places your My Documents folder in a default location:

C:\Documents And Settings\>user name> \My Documents.

Here *C* is the drive in which Windows is installed, and *<username>* is the currently logged-on user. (Remember that each user who uses your computer and has a logon name will have his or her own My Documents folder.) As you are moving your folders around, trying to better organize your hard drive, you might come up with a better location for your My Documents folder. The good news is that you can change the default location of this folder by following the simple steps presented here.

Here's another scenario to consider: If you have a computer that has two partitions, perhaps one for the operating system files (C:) and one for data (D:), you may have already moved the documents you've stored on the C: drive to the D: drive by using the Move command. While you can copy, paste, and/or move data from your old My Documents folder on the C: drive to the larger partition on the D: drive manually, changing the default location of the My Documents folder would be much easier. If you want to change the default location to the D: drive, for example, follow these steps:

1. Close all running programs.
2. Right-click the My Documents folder and select Properties.
3. Click the Target tab, and click Move.
4. In the Move dialog box, browse to the location where you want to move the file to. If the folder doesn't exist, browse to the location, and in the Select A Destination dialog box, click Make New Folder. Click OK.

Rename, Copy, and Delete Folders

You can rename, copy, and delete folders by right-clicking them. Renaming can also be done with the default folder names (for instance, if you would rather have the folder named Pics instead of My Pictures). Just select the task from the list after right-clicking.

Move Data into the New Folders

While it's easy to drag and drop a file from inside a single folder into a new folder created there, it's a little more difficult to drag and drop a file between folders that are completely separate. As mentioned in the GunkBuster's Notebook, "Creating Default Folders for Multiple Partitioned Hard Drives," Windows XP offers options to move folders and files in the Files And Folders Tasks pane. We'll go over it again in case you skipped that tip.

Assume you have some videos that you took with your digital camera on the memory card instead of the tape and you saved them in the My Pictures folder. After seeing that they are videos, you want to move them to the My Videos folder. You could open both folders, resize them so you can see each, and then drag and drop the files manually. The better method for doing this would be to use this simple command:

1. Select a file or folder to move. In this example, we'll be moving the Videos From Camera folder from My Pictures and putting it in My Videos.

2. In the File And Folder Tasks pane, click Move This Folder, or if appropriate, Move This File. See Figure 5-4.

Figure 5-4

Choose Move This Folder to move a file using the File And Folder Tasks pane.

3. In the Move Items dialog box, browse to the location to save the files and click Move. Figure 5-5 shows an example. The folder (or file) will be moved automatically.

Empty the Recycle Bin

In the first half of the chapter, we focused our efforts on organizing the data you have left on your hard drive. During this process, you might have found more junk to throw away. And, of course, we still have all of the data and programs that we threw away in Chapters 3 and 4. Now it's time to take that serious step of emptying the Recycle Bin.

Figure 5-5
You can access this dialog box by clicking Move This Folder in the File And Folder Tasks pane.

In case you are not aware, when you first delete files, folders, or programs, they are not actually physically removed from your hard drive. They are simply marked for deletion and placed in a location called the Recycle Bin. This sort of gives you a second chance in case you actually delete something that you later realize you might need. In order to physically remove data from your hard drive, you must go to the Recycle Bin and remove it. Once it's gone from there, it's gone for good. So, before you right-click, let's make sure of a few things first, including that the computer can be restarted without errors!

Restart the Computer

Before deleting the items from the Recycle Bin, restart the computer. If you get any errors, you'll need to seriously look into what's going on before you do any deleting. There are several types of errors you can get on boot-up, including the following. I've also offered a few solutions, so read the list carefully:

- Errors related to installed or uninstalled software: These errors can usually be repaired by reinstalling the application causing the error. You might also have to reinstall so you can successfully uninstall.

- Missing .dll files: .DLL files (files with the .dll extension) are Dynamic Link Library files and are shared files used by many programs installed on the computer. A shared DLL file could have been deleted when a program was uninstalled. Visit **http://support.Microsoft.com**, type in the error message, and follow the directions given for repairing the problem. You might also solve the problem by doing a repair installation using the XP CD, using a program like Norton's WinDoctor to replace the missing files automatically, or recovering the files from the Recycle Bin yourself.

- Stop errors: Stop errors occur when the missing file is a much needed one. Stop errors are generally caused by missing device drives or damaged system files. SYS files and DLL files can cause Stop errors. **Http://support.Microsoft.com** offers solutions to repairing hundreds of different Stop errors. Many solutions include recovering the damaged or missing file from the i386 folder of the XP CD.

- Missing Windows program files: "Windows could not start because of an error in the software" and "Load needed DLLs for Kernel" are caused by missing Windows program files. When a problem occurs as serious as this one, you'll need to "upgrade" to XP again and perform a reinstallation.

TIP: For unknown errors that can't be solved simply, read the Knowledge Base article #308041 on the Microsoft site. This article summarizes many different troubleshooting techniques.

In addition to repairing errors using the Knowledge Base articles, recovering from the Recycle Bin, performing an repair installation or upgrade, or copying the missing files from the i386 folder, you can also solve many problems with System Restore. Be sure to weigh all of your options before doing anything drastic, like formatting and reinstalling!

Make a Final Pass

Before deleting items from the Recycle Bin, make one final pass. Use Disk Cleanup to remove any unnecessary files that might have accumulated since the last time you ran it. Start each program that you have installed, and verify that they open and run correctly. If you find any errors, reinstall the program or recover the missing files from the Recycle Bin. Take a look at My Documents, My Pictures, My Videos, and My Music and make sure there isn't anything missing that you need. Additionally, verify that your anti-virus program is working and is up-to-date. You should always have current, up-to-date, running anti-virus programs and firewalls and have the programs set to automatically collect and install virus definitions automatically. Finally, do a backup of your most important files.

Ready? Empty!

If everything looks good (or after you've repaired any items mentioned in the list of errors earlier), right-click the Recycle Bin and click Empty Recycle Bin. In the Confirm Multiple File Delete dialog box, click Yes to delete. If you have Norton or some other anti-virus software, you might have a "protected" Recycle Bin too. If you'd like to delete the files there, follow the directions for your software. Generally, it's as simple as right-clicking the existing Recycle Bin and choosing the appropriate item. See Figure 5-6.

```
UnErase Wizard
Open
Explore
Empty Norton Protected Files
Empty Recycle Bin

Create Shortcut

Properties
```

Figure 5-6

If you have anti-virus software, you might have additional choices for emptying the Recycle Bin.

Use Disk Defragmenter

You can count on one thing: If you've deleted a lot of files, moved files from one partition to another, deleted programs and applications, and emptied the Recycle Bin, your hard drive will be a mess. When we say "a mess," we don't mean it's disorganized by our standards. We mean that the files on the actual hard drive are *fragmented,* or disorganized by Windows standards. There are files and parts of files stored everywhere, and they aren't stored contiguously. That causes problems and degrades the performance of your hard drive.

Here's basically how a hard drive works: A hard drive is a circular disk, kind of like an old LP record. As data is written to the hard disk, it is written sequentially using the first open space it finds. If you installed a program on that hard disk the day you purchased the computer, it would be located near the beginning. As time passes, files are saved after it and the disk begins to fill up. If you uninstall that same program a year later, you'll have a big gap on the hard disk where that program once was. The next time you install a program or save a file, Windows will begin writing that data to the first open space it sees, most likely this gap where you uninstalled the program and freed up some space. This means you could have part of a file stored at the very beginning of the hard drive, another part stored in the middle, and the rest of the file saved at the end. When you open that file, Windows has to search the entire hard drive to put the pieces together.

When Windows has to piece together a file in this manner, the computer slows down because it simply takes longer to find the data. The disk might have to spin several thousand more times than it should have to, which not only causes a slow response but also causes unnecessary wear and tear on your computer. After a computer is *defragmented,* the files are stored (more) contiguously and the computer's hard disk has to spend less time spinning around and looking for files. This makes for better performance and less stress on the computer. The problem is worse if *program files* are stored in a noncontiguous manner. See Figure 5-7 for a visual representation of a hard disk.

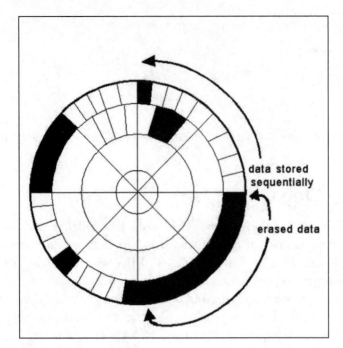

data stored
sequentially

erased data

Figure 5-7
This is how a hard drive looks and how data is stored.

Fortunately, Windows provides a utility called Disk Defragmenter that is designed to clean up the fragments in your hard dive. When you run this utility, Windows rearranges the files it knows should be placed together so that the disk will operate more efficiently. You'll see a huge difference after defragging your drive.

Are you ready to do some defragging? Make sure it's almost bedtime and you won't need your computer for a while and then follow these steps:

1. Close all open programs.

2. Turn off screensavers.

3. Turn off anti-virus software and disconnect from the Internet. (This is an important step.)

4. Click Start, point to All Programs, point to Accessories, point to System Tools, and click Disk Defragmenter.

5. Highlight a drive to defragment and either click Analyze to see whether or not the disk needs defragmenting or click Defragment to begin the process immediately. Figure 5-8 shows a disk being defragmented.

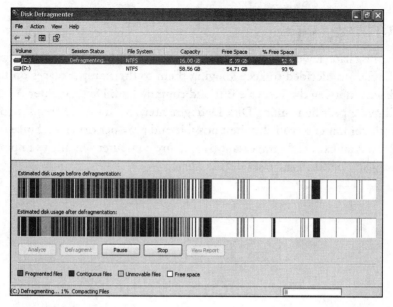

Figure 5-8

A defragmentation in progress.

Some final notes about defragmenting: You should analyze your hard disks once a week to see if another defragmenting session is in order. Just click Analyze and see what Windows suggests. This is important because how often you need to defragment depends on how active you are on your computer. If you turn the computer on once a week to e-mail your kids, you probably won't need to defrag for a long time, but if you use your computer a lot and install and uninstall lots of files and programs, you'll need to defrag a bit more often.

The length of time it takes for Disk Defragmenter to complete depends on the size of your hard disk and how defragmented it is. It's best just to let it run while you're asleep because it can take several hours on extremely gunked-up machines. Make sure to disable screensavers and anti-virus programs, too; sometimes they interfere with the process. And finally, if for some reason you can't get Disk Defragmenter to run correctly or to complete, try running it in Safe mode.

Disk Defragmenter is one utility you should make a point to use regularly. Once defragmented, a drive will perform better, and you can expect noticeable performance improvements. It's well worth the time it takes!

Summing Up

In this chapter, we completed the optimization of the hard drive by organizing the files we decided to keep, moving them to their proper places on the hard drive, emptying the Recycle Bin, and running Disk Defragmenter. All of these things, especially running Disk Defragmenter, are "must do" items if you want your computer to run at its best possible and peak performance. Since the hard drive is an extremely important part of any computer system, it's important to regularly perform the tasks detailed here.

Tweaking Your Desktop and Start Menu

Degunking Checklist:

√ Clean up and personalize the Taskbar so you can work faster and smarter.

√ Remove items from the System Tray that use valuable system resources.

√ Limit the programs that start when Windows starts.

√ Group running applications, use Quick Launch, and employ AutoHide.

√ Personalize the Start menu by adding or deleting programs, reordering the list, and more.

√ Personalize the Desktop with your favorite folders and shortcuts, and remove unused icons.

√ Use non-system-intensive screensavers and themes to enhance performance.

√ Personalize folder options.

In Chapters 3, 4, and 5, you learned how to remove and organize a lot of data and programs that reside in your folders. You might not realize it, but there are a number of cleanup and organizational tasks that you can perform on your Desktop to make Windows run much better. But degunking your Desktop doesn't just involve throwing stuff away and organizing the stuff you want to keep. It also involves making Windows run more efficiently and personalizing it so that it works *for you*, not the other way around! Personalizing XP might not seem like a big deal, but it is. You can tell XP how you want the Taskbar and Start menu to look, what should or shouldn't appear on the Desktop, and how you want to interact with it when you need information (setting Folder Options). By personalizing Windows XP, you can work faster and smarter and perform tasks more efficiently than if you didn't personalize it at all. You can put what you need where you need it, making it a snap to open a program, locate a file, or perform a task. This is the fun part of degunking!

Clean Up and Personalize the Taskbar

The Taskbar is that little blue bar across the bottom of your screen. You can use it to immediately find out what programs are running, what programs started automatically when you booted Windows, and what programs you have configured to launch quickly (see Figure 6-1). The Taskbar is full of information and, by its very nature, a busy place that tends to get more than a little cluttered.

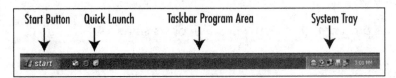

Figure 6-1
Having icons in the Taskbar makes opening a program as easy as a single click. However, too many icons in the System Tray can bog down the computer.

The Taskbar contains three main components: In the bottom-left corner, you'll find the trusty Start button. To the right of the Start button is the Quick Launch toolbar (assuming you have this feature selected), which contains a set of program icons that you can click to quickly launch the programs they represent. The area to the right of the Quick Launch toolbar is the area of the Taskbar that lists the programs currently running on your computer. Finally, the section to the far right is the System Tray. The System Tray shows the programs that started when Windows did, and each runs automatically and in the background.

The System Tray is where we'll focus our energies first; we bet you don't even know what you have in there! Every item in the System Tray is slowing down the boot process and bogging down your computer, and it's time to do a little cleaning.

TIP: Your System Tray will look different than this if you have AutoHide configured or if you don't use Quick Launch.

Look at Figure 6-1 again and you'll see that the Taskbar's Quick Launch area is configured to display the icons for the programs Outlook Express and Internet Explorer, and it also includes the Show Desktop icon. Notice also that icons for an anti-virus program and network connections, an Incredimail icon, the system clock, and even a little icon for Windows Media Player are all located in the System Tray. With these items on the Taskbar, they can be accessed easily. You might have similar icons.

In this section, you'll learn all the tips and tricks you need to know to clean up and personalize your Taskbar, including adding or removing icons, adding or removing toolbars, using AutoHide, locking the Taskbar, grouping applications, and configuring Quick Launch, just to name a few! There is a lot that you can do to clean up and personalize the Taskbar, but we'll start with the System Tray feature first because that is a likely place where you can do some serious degunking!

 If you want the icon for Windows Media Player to appear in the System Tray as shown in Figure 6-1, you'll need to get the Windows Media Player Tray Control. It's available in the Windows Media Bonus Pack for Windows XP here: **www.Microsoft.com/windows. windowsmedia/download.bonuspack.aspx**.

Managing the Taskbar's System Tray

We like to add to the System Tray in the Taskbar items that we deem important to work or play. However, it seems like we spend most of our time removing stuff from it. Programs, especially those downloaded from the Internet, like to place their icons there without our permission. If you don't monitor your System Tray regularly, it could become really cluttered. Very often, when you download a new program, it asks whether you want an icon placed in your System Tray. Many people don't think twice about clicking Yes to these requests.

You should also be very selective about what you place in the System Tray. When an icon is showing in the System Tray, the program it represents runs in the background and uses valuable system resources. You don't want a lot of icons there for that reason, because besides cluttering up the System Tray, their programs hog valuable RAM. It's best to have as few items as possible in the System Tray.

Some of the items you might want running in the System Tray include icons for programs you regularly use or want access to (such as an anti-virus program), or icons for applications that you use daily (such as music download software or Media Player). You can also configure your network connections so that when they are connected, an icon representing that connection shows in the System Tray. Using the connection's icon, you can disconnect, view properties, and make configuration changes quickly. Some items you probably don't want there are icons for programs you downloaded, tried out, and didn't like, such as RealPlayer, Napster, any instant messaging programs, and programs like wallpaper changers or jukeboxes. You should also remove the icon for any program you simply don't use that often. Remember, in this case, less is best, so don't gunk up your System Tray with unnecessary icons! Let's now look at how to both add or remove an item.

Add Program Icons to the System Tray

Some programs have a built-in feature that adds an icon to the System Tray. You can also instruct a program's icon to stay in the System Tray by checking an option from inside the desired program, as shown in Figure 6-2. This example shows a Norton Anti-Virus option, and it is checked so that the program's icon will be displayed in the tray. Different applications offer different ways to do this. I am just showing one example here to get you started. (Obviously, you would uncheck this option to remove the program.)

☑ Sh̲ow the Auto-Protect icon in the tray

Figure 6-2
Sometimes, applications have an option to be added or removed from the System Tray.

Locating a program's System Tray option can be difficult if not downright impossible. You can't just choose any program and instruct it to place a representative icon in the System Tray. The developer who created the program must put in this feature and, unfortunately, many don't. Fortunately, freeware and shareware utilities are available that can help you take control.

TIP: It's a good idea to have icons for your anti-virus and firewall applications in your System Tray. That way, you can always make sure that your Internet connection is secure.

One application for setting up the System Tray is the Tray Minimizer. You can get the evaluation version at **www.trayminimizer.com**. This application lets you minimize items to the System Tray instead of the larger Taskbar area. This unclutters the Taskbar and lets you locate and find things more quickly than if you had to sort through various grouped icons. Figure 6-3 and 6-4 show the Taskbar before and after using this utility.

Figure 6-3

A cluttered Taskbar.

Figure 6-4

Programs minimized to the System Tray using Tray Minimizer, one of many applications available from the Internet.

Remove Program Icons from the System Tray

As mentioned earlier and shown in Figure 6-2, some programs offer a choice so that you can remove their program icons from the System Tray. To find these options, right-click the program's icon and choose Properties, Preferences, or any other choice that will allow you to set the program's configuration. Look around, and you might find what you are looking for.

If you can't find an option to remove the icon and you see icons in the System Tray for items you don't need or use (like instant messaging, Napster, RealPlayer, jukebox or other music software, or programs you've downloaded but don't use), you can tell Windows you don't want those programs to automatically start and their icons appear in the System Tray when you start Windows. Here's how:

1. Click Start and then click Run. In the Run dialog box, type msconfig.exe. Click OK.

2. Click the Startup tab. Figure 6-5 shows an example. Here, an application we downloaded from the Internet is selected.

3. Uncheck items that you recognize and don't want to start automatically. In the screen shown in Figure 6-5, we can uncheck several, including Wallpaper Changer, VAIO Action Setup, Launchpad (we recognize ICM532 as a Web cam we don't use), WMPImporter (Music Now software), and Microsoft Office. If we want to use these programs, we'll start them manually! Don't uncheck anything you don't recognize though. If you are unsure about an

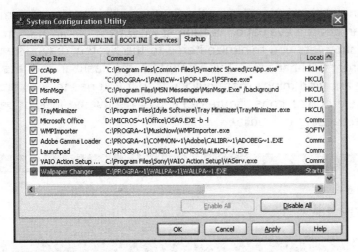

Figure 6-5

The Startup tab in the System Configuration Utility shows what starts when you start Windows. Much of this isn't needed.

item, jot down the path to the program and see if you can figure out what it is by browsing there and starting the program. If that doesn't work, you can look up the program in question on the Internet.

4. Click OK and restart your computer.

5. On reboot, read the information and click OK in the System Configuration Utility dialog box. You'll notice fewer icons in the System Tray.

Hide Inactive Icons in the System Tray

Now that you've decided what items you want in the System Tray, you can choose to hide them when the programs they represent are inactive, always show them, or never show them. With AutoHide, you can get rid of the icon, essentially hiding it, without getting rid of it completely. This is a great way to unclutter the Taskbar and System Tray without actually having to remove items from it that you'd really like to keep.

Here are the steps to follow:

1. Right-click an empty area of the Taskbar, and choose Properties.

2. From the Taskbar tab, verify that Hide Inactive Icons is selected, and click Customize.

3. Under Current Items, click to set the options. The options are Hide When Inactive, Always Show, or Always Hide. Hiding icons will leave them accessible but will hide them in the System Try under an arrow. Selecting Always Show will always show the item and never hide it. Click OK twice. Your

System Tray will now look like the one shown in Figure 6-6. You can access the hidden icons by clicking the arrow.

Figure 6-6

Hiding inactive icons can clean up the System Tray.

Here's a summary of programs you might want to keep running all the time, and thus keep in the System Tray and those you might not:

- If you use an instant messaging program, by all means, keep it in the System Tray; if not, remove it. Consider using the AutoHide feature here.

- If you use music software and a download site often, keep the software and connection to it in the System Tray. If you tried out the program, didn't like it, and don't use it, remove it.

- If you don't recognize a program in the System Tray, remove it.

- Leave items you access regularly like Power Management on a laptop, anti-virus software, the volume icon, firewall icon, or network connectivity status in the System Tray. Remove items that don't need to run all the time like QuickTime, e-bot, Napster, or video or music managers.

Add Quick Launch Icons

As you've seen, Quick Launch is an area of the Taskbar that is located just to the right of the Start menu and enables you to start applications quickly and with a single click. In addition to (or instead of) the default icons, though, you can add your own specific icons to start your favorite programs. This feature makes it easier to load frequently used programs; you don't have to go to the Start menu and search for the program you want each time. Turning on Quick Launch does not start the programs or cause them to run; it only creates a shortcut to them. It isn't like the System Tray, where valuable resources are sucked dry by programs that run in the background; Quick Launch only offers a place to access programs quickly.

So, turn on Quick Launch, add icons for your favorite programs, and then remove the shortcuts to those programs and other unnecessary icons from the Desktop if you desire. Doing so unclutters your Desktop while still offering quick and easy access to your most-used programs. Figure 6-7 shows an example of a customized Quick Launch toolbar.

Figure 6-7

Quick Launch holds shortcuts to programs and applications for easy access and startup.

You can use and/or customize Quick Launch by doing this:

1. Right-click an empty area of the Taskbar and click Properties.

2. From the Taskbar tab, check Show Quick Launch.

3. Click OK.

4. To add a program to the Quick Launch menu, locate the program from either the All Programs list or Windows Explorer.

5. Right-click and drag the program to the Quick Launch area.

6. Let go and choose Copy Here.

7. To remove a program from the Quick Launch area, right-click the icon. Then click Delete, and click Yes to verify.

Some people prefer to keep their Taskbar cleaner and just rely on placing their favorite programs in the Start menu, with Quick Launch hidden. This is a good technique if you usually have 3 or 4 programs running simultaneously with multiple documents open at one time and you want to see them all on your Taskbar.

Lock, AutoHide, and Group Options in the Taskbar

You can lock the Taskbar so that it cannot be moved or resized, or you can configure it to hide when inactive. You can also configure it to group files opened by the same program in the same area of the taskbar. If you choose to group files, when the Taskbar becomes crowded, the buttons for the same program are collapsed into a single button. Figure 6-8 shows an example.

Figure 6-8
Grouping files saves valuable Taskbar space.

To use AutoHide, to lock the Taskbar, or group items, right-click the Taskbar, choose the Taskbar tab, and select the appropriate boxes.

Customizing with TweakUI

While there are a few other things you can do with the Taskbar, we'll move on to some really cool tweaks. Are you tired of seeing those balloon tips pop up messages? Would you like to group files in a specific order? How about getting a warning in the Taskbar when you're low on disk space? You need TweakUI, a free and extremely powerful PowerToy.

Download and install TweakUI from **www.Microsoft.com/windowsxp/ pro/downloads/powertoys.asp** and use its simple interface to tweak the Taskbar to your heart's content.

Personalize the Start Menu

In order to work faster and smarter, you need to personalize the Start menu so the things you need are readily available and the things you don't need or no longer have installed aren't taking up unnecessary space. There's nothing worse than having to wade through a disorganized Start menu looking for some program you think should be there but isn't! As you can see from the screenshots in this book, we prefer the XP theme and default look. Figure 6-9 shows our Start menu. Yours could look much different than this. Notice that our most-used programs are showing on the left and My Computer has an arrow beside it. Pointing to this arrow or any other on the Start menu opens another menu with the item's contents.

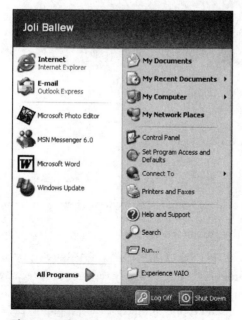

Figure 6-9
A customized Start menu.

You can customize your Start menu too; right-click the Taskbar, choose Properties, and click the Start Menu tab. Click the Customize button for your particular Start menu style. There, you'll find almost everything you need.

XP Start Menu

If you're tweaking your XP-themed Start menu, after opening the Start Menu tab as detailed in the preceding section, you'll see what is shown in Figure 6-10. (You can also right-click an empty area of the Start menu and select Properties.)

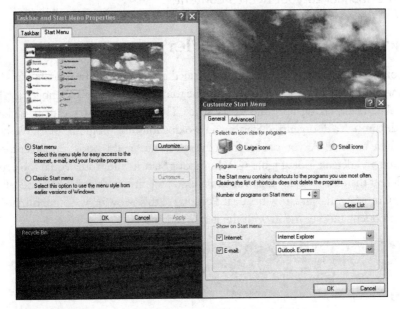

Figure 6-10
There are lots of Start menu options.

From the General tab you can do the following:

• Choose the icon size.

• Choose the number of programs on the Start menu or clear the list.

• Show or hide Internet and e-mail programs, and choose between them.

Here's what you can do from the Advanced tab:

• Choose to open submenus by pausing on them with the mouse.

• Highlight newly installed programs. (This is highly recommend, because newly installed programs might be installed under a non-descriptive name and be difficult to find. For instance, one of our favorite programs, EZ Macro, is listed in the Start Menu under the American Systems option.)

- Show, hide, and display as a link or a menu the Control Panel, My Computer, My Documents, My Music, My Pictures, Network Connections, and System Tools.
- Show or hide Favorites, Help And Support, My Network Places, Printers And Faxes, Run, Search, and Set Program Access And Defaults.
- Enable dragging and dropping from the Start menu.
- Enable Scroll Programs, which shows the programs list as a scrollable, single-pane list instead of horizontal pages.
- List or clear most recently opened documents.

Configure the items as you like them and OK your way out of the dialog boxes.

With the Start menu configured, you can perform several additional tweaks.

- Right-click any item in the left pane to pin it to the Start menu, remove it from the list, or rename it.
- Right-click any item in the right pane to rename it, view its properties, or see other information.
- Reorder the items in the All Programs list by right-clicking any program and clicking Sort By Name, rename or delete any items from the list, or see an item's properties.

Adding Items to the Start Menu

If you have the dragging and dropping option enabled, you can use drag and drop to add items to the Start menu or reorder them. (Although there are other ways, this is the easiest.) To add an item to the Start menu, follow these steps:

1. Locate the item using Windows Explorer, right-click, and drag the executable file to the Start menu.
2. Drop the file in the All Programs menu or the left pane of the Start menu.
3. Choose Copy Here when prompted. Figure 6-11 shows an example.

In addition to adding programs to the Start menu by dragging and dropping, you can also move programs around to reorder them. Just drag and drop!

Classic Menu

If you're using the Classic menu, you'll see different options when you customize the Start menu's properties. (Remember, right-click an empty area of the Taskbar, choose Properties, click the Start Menu tab, and then click Customize.)

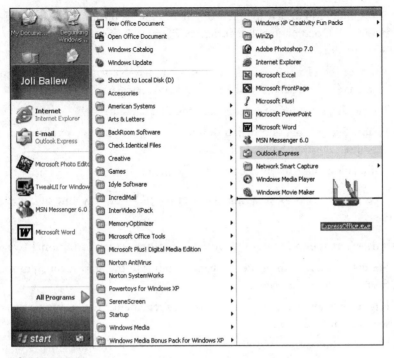

Figure 6-11
Drag and drop to add a program to the All Programs list.

Customizations are similar to those listed earlier for the XP Start menu:

*   Display Administrative Tools, Favorites, Log Off, and Run.
*   Expand the Control Panel, My Documents, My Pictures, Network Connections, and Printers.
*   Enable dragging and dropping, scrolling the Start menu, using Personalized menus, and selecting icon size.
*   Add or remove a program from the Start menu, or sort or clear items.

As with the XP Start menu, you can right-click any item on the Start menu and delete it, sort the items by name, use drag and drop to add programs or reorder them, and right-click see an item's properties.

TIP: TweakUI, mentioned earlier, offers one really nice option for tweaking the Start menu. You can select which items can or cannot appear on the Most Frequently Used Programs section of the Windows XP Start menu. This is not an option in Windows XP.

Clean Up and Personalize the Desktop

There's really only one more item we're going to clean up and then personalize with our own touches, and that's the Desktop. You can make the Desktop look however you want it to. It can have lots of icons or none at all; it can show My Computer, My Network Places, Internet Explorer, and/or the Recycle Bin; it can have shortcuts to programs you use a lot, folders you access daily, networks you connect to, and more. You can also choose screensavers, although for the purpose of degunking, we'll talk about non-system-intensive ones as well as non-system-intensive themes.

Get Your Desktop Organized

There is nothing worse as a productivity zapper than a really messy Desktop. Over the years, we've looked over the shoulders of friends and family only to discover a Desktop that looks really scary. Let's face it: Most of us simply drop applications and folders on our Desktop until we can't tell what the background screen is supposed to look like any more. Then, we search the screen whenever we are looking for a specific program to start up or folder to use. Not only that, but we'd venture to guess some of the links don't even work anymore. There must be a better way!

Our recommendation is that you develop a strategy for what you will allow to be displayed on your Desktop. You should be very picky—if you're right-brained, think of your desktop as really valuable real estate, like beachfront property—you don't want to junk it up with a bunch of broken beach chairs and fishing poles. If you're left-brained, imagine it's a filing cabinet and the icons on your Desktop are the tabs on your file folders. Either way, the idea is to clean it up, make it nice, and configure it so that you can find what you want, when you want it.

Your Desktop probably has icons on it for the Recycle Bin, maybe Internet Explorer or My Computer, and, most likely, My Documents. But you also probably have a lot of junk you don't need. To start with this process, take an inventory of all of the application icons that you currently have and divide this list into the following groups:

- Applications you can't live without (the ones you use quite regularly)
- Applications you never use any more or rarely use
- Applications you don't even recognize

If you still have too many applications in the first group, you'll need to go through it again and narrow it down to just your top applications. The applications listed in your second group can likely be taken off your Desktop entirely (we'll show you how this is done shortly). For the third group, you should take a little time and review all of the applications you have here and reduce the list down to just the applications you actually need.

Add or Remove Default Icons

You can remove many of the icons on your Desktop to make it look tidy and make your computer start up a little faster when you first boot up. Of course, you can add icons that are missing.

To add or remove default icons, follow these steps:

1. Right-click an empty area of the Desktop and choose Properties.
2. In the Properties dialog box, choose the Desktop tab.
3. Choose Customize Desktop to open the Desktop Items dialog box, which is shown in Figure 6-12.
4. In the Desktop Items dialog box, check or uncheck My Documents, My Computer, My Network Places, and Internet Explorer. (Notice you can also change the icons for these if you desire.)

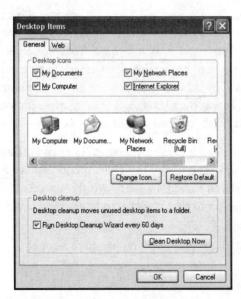

Figure 6-12
The Desktop Items dialog box enables the addition and deletion of many of the default icons.

5.   Click OK in the Desktop Items dialog box and again in the Display Proper-
     ties dialog box to apply the changes.

The Recycle Bin

You might have noticed that the Recycle Bin wasn't available for deletion
when you were customizing the Desktop. Removing the Recycle Bin requires
that you obtain a third-party application, and they are plentiful! If you've already obtained TweakUI from **www.Microsoft.com/windowsxp/pro/
downloads/powertoys.asp**, you already have the capability. Just open TweakUI,
click Desktop, and uncheck Recycle Bin. You'll want to remove the Recycle
Bin only if you're trying to create an "icon-less" Desktop. Generally, the Recycle Bin is a necessary icon for the Desktop and we recommend you keep it.

Create Folders and Program Shortcuts

Having items on the Desktop that you use often can also help you work faster
and smarter. You can add folders to the Desktop by either creating shortcuts to
existing folders or creating new ones. You can add program shortcuts just as
easily.

To create a shortcut to an existing folder that contains documents you access
often, simply follow these steps:

1.   Browse to the folder using Windows Explorer.
2.   Right-click, point to Send To, and click Desktop (Create Shortcut). A
     shortcut will be placed on the Desktop.

Do this to create a new folder on the Desktop:

1.   Right-click an empty area of the Desktop.
2.   Point to New, and click Folder.
3.   Name the folder, and then drag and drop files in there or add them there as
     they are created.

To create a shortcut to a program, locate it from the All Programs menu (refer
to the section "Personalize the Start Menu" earlier in this chapter to maintain
the Start menu) and drag it to the Desktop. If you can't find it on the All
Programs menu, look for it using Windows Explorer. A shortcut will automatically be created.

Removing Folders and Shortcuts

Removing shortcuts from the Desktop is as easy as right-clicking and choosing Delete. They just go away; no harm done. You can also right-click and delete folders like My Documents, My Network Places, My Computer, and Internet Explorer; they'll be removed but their contents won't be deleted and moved to the Recycle Bin. However, if you want to remove a folder that *you created* on the Desktop and the folder is *not a shortcut* to another folder, you have to be more careful. If you delete a folder you've created on the Desktop, its contents will be deleted as well. Figure 6-13 shows the warning box you'll see when you try to delete a folder that is not a shortcut to another folder.

Figure 6-13
If you delete a folder, you also delete its contents.

TIP: Folders that are shortcuts to others have a small arrow printed on them.

Therefore, if you have created a folder on the Desktop and have added data to it and you later decide that you don't want it on the Desktop anymore, your best bet is to drag and drop the file to another area. You can drag it to the My Documents folder, to somewhere in Windows Explorer, to a separate hard disk, or even to a network drive. Dragging and dropping moves the file from the Desktop without deleting its contents.

Run the Desktop Cleanup Wizard

Once the desktop is nice and neat and everything is organized just the way you want it, configure the Desktop Cleanup Wizard to run every 60 days so that you can avoid some of the major pitfalls in keeping your Desktop clean. The Desktop Cleanup Wizard scans the shortcuts on your desktop and determines if they've been used in the past 60 days or if they haven't. If they haven't, you'll be prompted to let Windows safely remove them.

To run the Desktop Cleanup Wizard and to configure it to run automatically every 60 days, follow these steps:

1. Right-click an empty area of the Desktop (by now that should be easy), and click Properties.
2. Click the Desktop tab and click Customize Desktop.
3. Verify that Run Desktop Cleanup Wizard Every 60 Days is checked.
4. To run the wizard now, click Clean Desktop Now.

Choose Non-System-Intensive Screensavers

If you've chosen a wacky screensaver, one that is complex, one that requires complex calculations, or one you've downloaded from a Web site that can't be trusted to create efficient program code, you might be seeing the effects of running a system-intensive or poorly designed screensaver. When a screensaver is used, the computer must offer up system resources to run it. If you're having problems with system performance, including slow response coming out of a screensaver, a screensaver that hangs or freezes up, or one that locks up the computer, you should switch to a non-system-intensive or a default Windows XP screensaver. Of course, the best option is to select None. This way, absolutely no system resources are used!

Even some of the Windows XP screensavers require a lot of system resources, though. Although one of our computers worked just fine when using the Windows XP Aquarium screensaver, when we upgraded, purchasing new fish and configuring seven of them to swim around on the office Desktop (that had 128 MB of RAM), it was just too much for it. It would hang up and sometimes even lock up the computer. These are common problems.

If you're having screensaver problems, select a screensaver that's not so complex, like the Windows XP screensaver or the Starfield screensaver:

1. Right-click an empty area of the Desktop, and then click Properties.
2. From the Screensaver tab, select a new screensaver.
3. Click OK.

About Themes

If you're concerned about performance, choose one of the default Windows XP themes, like Windows XP or Windows Classic. Other themes may use more resources with their fancy sounds and other amenities. However, if you're in it for the simple pleasure of having a nice background, screensaver, mouse pointer, colors, and interface, and if you have plenty of resources, by all means, browse for and choose a theme!

Here's how to explore additional themes and install them:

1. Right-click an empty area of the Desktop and click Properties.

2. From the Themes tab, use the drop-down list to see the available themes. If you've purchased and installed Microsoft Plus! or other software, you might have some already. If you only have the default themes, click More Themes Online, and click OK.

3. Browse through the information.

TIP: *We'll suggest you stay away from themes unless you have a screaming computer with resources that you don't need. Even our best computer gets sluggish when we apply one!*

Explore Folder Options

The Folder Options icon in the Control Panel offers many ways to enhance your computer's performance, enhance productivity, and enhance how you view windows and folders in Windows XP. To view the available folder options, open the Control Panel and open Folder Options, or right-click the Start menu, choose Explore, click Tools, and click Folder Options. You can also open this dialog box from inside the Control Panel, using the Folder Options icon. The Folder Options dialog box will appear, as shown in Figure 6-14. You can enhance the performance of your computer by making some changes here:

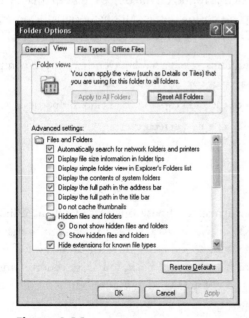

Figure 6-14

There are plenty of ways to enhance performance using Folder Options.

- If you have a specific file type that you'd always like to open in a specific program, you can configure file associations using the File Types tab. For example, if you want all of your JPEG files to open in Photoshop instead of Paint or the Windows Picture And Fax Viewer, you can make that change easily. Just click the File Types tab, locate the file type, click Change, and pick a program from the list. See Figure 6-15.

Figure 6-15
Open a specific file type with a specific program.

- If you are running Windows XP on a laptop, if you spend most of your time computing in a non-networked environment, or if you only access one or two specific folders on a network, you can disable the Automatic Search For Network Printers And Folders. While this feature doesn't take up too many system resources, it does continuously scan for changes to shared resources on a network. If you don't need this, disable it from the View menu. It's the first option.

- Windows creates and caches folder thumbnails in a cache file so that it can reuse them instead of creating new thumbnails each time you open the folder. You'll want this to be enabled, so verify in the View tab that Do Not Cache Thumbnails is not checked.

- If you are tired of Windows showing you pop-up descriptions for folder and desktop items, from the View tab, deselect Show Pop-Up Descriptions For Folder And Desktop Items.

- To change the default double-clicking with the mouse to single-clicking for opening files, from the General tab, make the desired changes.

- Offline files are files that you copy from a shared folder on a network so that you can work on them while not connected. Upon reconnection, the files are synchronized. Offline files take up a lot of hard disk space, and if you aren't going to need them, don't enable them from the Offline Files tab. Check that tab to verify that this is unchecked.

- From the View tab, verify that Launch Folder Windows In A Separate Process is not checked. Checking this will cause each program to open in a separate memory space and will slow down your computer's performance.

You should look through the items available to see if there's anything else you'd like to change. We choose to turn off Simple File Sharing, Show Control Panel In My Computer, and Show Hidden Files And Folders. You might decide after researching these options that you feel the same.

TIP: Click the question mark in the top-right corner of the Folder Options dialog box and then click anywhere in the box to get more information about a particular option.

Summing Up

Cleaning up and tweaking the Start menu, Desktop, and Taskbar might seem like simple cosmetic enhancements at first, but they aren't. Making programs readily accessible, having what you need on the Start menu, and using Quick Launch helps *you* work faster, and the result of that is that *Windows* works faster. Cleaning up the System Tray, limiting what programs start automatically when Windows starts, and using non-system-intensive screensavers and themes dramatically increases performance as well. Finally, configuring folder options can also increase performance in a variety of ways, including disabling functions that aren't necessary.

Preventing Spam Gunk

Degunking Checklist:

√ Develop a strategy of having three different e-mail accounts—primary, backup, and disposable—to minimize spam.

√ Choose a primary e-mail address that is *not* vulnerable to dictionary attacks.

√ Choose your e-mail client carefully—some clients are "gunk magnets."

√ Don't post your primary e-mail address on the Web or allow others to do so.

√ Obfuscate (obscure) your primary e-mail address when posting to Usenet newsgroups.

√ *Never* try to "unsubscribe" from spammer mailings. (It's really "subscribing" to *more* spam.)

√ Use a disposable e-mail address for communicating with online vendors and discussion boards.

√ Choose, use, and update a separate spam filtering product to reduce spam.

√ Learn about mail proxies and POPFile.

E-mail is the glue that holds your personal and business computing together. But careless use of e-mail will attract gunk. Unfortunately, only a little carelessness will attract an almost *unimaginable* amount of gunk, in the form of spam. Spam is one of those phenomena where prevention is the very best cure. In this chapter, we'll show you how to degunk your PC by preventing spam from entering your inbox in the first place.

You probably are aware that spam is unwanted commercial e-mail, unless you've been living in a refrigerator box for the past several years. It is generally sent from companies that you have never had dealings with and want no part of. Much spam is fraudulent—get-rich quick schemes, phony penis- and breast-enlargement pills, controlled drugs without a prescription, and so on. Most people agree that when they want to buy online, they will go looking for products. They do *not* want products to come looking for them in the form of spam.

As you'll learn in this chapter, you can do many things to minimize spam. Most of the suggestions are preventive, and only a modest amount of vigilance and housekeeping is required on an ongoing basis. Of course, if you let spam get out of control, you'll have a massive mess to clean up. In Chapter 8, e-mail housecleaning will be covered in more detail, where you'll learn how to clean up and organize your legitimate mail as well as deal with spam that gets through your defenses. (Alas, some always will.)

Choose the Best E-Mail Addresses

Spam prevention begins with your e-mail address. Smart and serious e-mail users have more than one address to minimize their encounters with spam. There are three general categories of e-mail address that we recommend you set up:

- Primary e-mail address
- Backup e-mail address
- Disposable e-mail addresses

Your primary e-mail address is the one on your business card. You give it to your friends and business associates. It's the address that you want the world to use. It's also the one where you'll be fighting most of your spam battles. Your backup e-mail address should be a second e-mail account obtained from a separate e-mail hosting company that is not tied to your primary address. If the company hosting your primary address is down for some reason, you can then use your backup e-mail address until your primary address comes back online.

Your disposable e-mail addresses are those that you use knowing that you can cancel them at any point and lose nothing. Disposable e-mail addresses are often obtained from free Webmail sites. You generally shouldn't share them with friends and business associates. You use them for online commerce and other circumstances where you don't trust a person or (more likely) a company or Web site not to misuse the address. If anyone misuses a disposable address, you simply cancel the address and obtain a new, different one for further use.

Set Up Your Primary E-Mail Address

Your primary e-mail address should be accessible from anywhere. Here are some guidelines you should follow for setting up your primary address:

- Your primary address should not be the e-mail address that you obtain when signing up for a broadband Internet connection at home. Many broadband providers do not allow you access to your e-mail account when you connect to the Internet at a wireless Wi-Fi hotspot or from a dial-up connection.

- If you connect via a dial-up network like AOL, that address is suitable as a primary address. AOL and other similar networks like MSN have many dial-up "points of presence" around the country, and you can get in from any of them.

- The best primary e-mail address to have is one associated with a Web hosting account. Most Web hosting firms offer some number of e-mail addresses (5 to 10) with a hosting account for your personal or business Web site. Multiple e-mail accounts are good, in case you have to abandon a primary account for spam reasons (more on this later). You'll find that there are virtues to setting up a primary address in this manner:

- You can access the account from anywhere you can connect to the Net. This is *extremely* important if you travel a lot.

- The e-mail address will be associated with the name of your domain, so it's easier for people to remember. It will also look "official" and professional. As an example, if your name is Andy Stanton and you own the domain **stantonservices.com**, your e-mail could be **astanton@stantonservices.com** and your web site could be **www.stantonservices.com**.

Set Up Your Backup and Disposable E-Mail Addresses

The address you obtain from your broadband provider makes a good backup address, as does an address from one of the free Webmail sites. Disposable addresses are also best obtained from a Webmail site. Here are a few guidelines to follow:

- Make your backup e-mail account either your broadband ISP e-mail address or an account with one of the national e-mail providers like AOL. In a pinch, an address from a free Webmail account will do.

• Obtain one or more disposable e-mail accounts from one of the free Webmail services. (More on using disposable e-mail addresses shortly.)

Avoid Spammer Dictionary Attacks

Many people who register their own personal or business names create an associated e-mail address by using their first name and the domain name. A consultant like our mythical Andy Stanton might register the domain stantonservices.com and create an e-mail account **andy@stantonservices.com**. You'd have to forgive poor Andy for not suspecting how much spam gunk such an address would attract. The problem lies with something called a *dictionary attack*.

Spammers pay nothing per message to send out spam. With broadband access, they can send literally millions of messages per day, making possible a peculiar way to gather e-mail addresses as spam targets. Spammers (using custom mailer utilities intended for spamming) choose a domain, like stantonservices.com, and start cranking out e-mail to addresses in a sequence that might look like this:

Abe@stantonservices.com

Abby@stantonservices.com

Al@stantonservices.com

Alan@stantonservices.com

Albert@stantonservices.com

Andrew@stantonservices.com

Andy@stantonservices.com

Ann@stantonservices.com

Anna@stantonservices.com

These names come from a dictionary of names and common words compiled by spammers from online dictionaries and e-mail addresses that they find on the Web. They use automatic mailer software, which generates small test messages. Many of these test messages have no body text at all. The mailer software keeps track of bounces—messages that come back because an e-mail address does not exist—and purges the address of any bounced message from the list of addresses mailed to. If a generated address receives a message that doesn't bounce, that address is considered "live," and spam will soon begin to be sent to it—*even if the address has never actually been used!*

This is legal, and costs nothing per address. Every day, spammers send literally billions of such test messages looking for new addresses. Avoiding dictionary attacks is simple, if not foolproof, by following these guidelines:

- *Choose your e-mail address carefully by choosing a name or word that is not in any dictionary.* For example, don't use **andy@stantonservices.com**; instead, use something not easily guessed by a program. This could be your first initial and last name, like **astanton@stantonservices.com**, or something you make up yourself, like **rugster@stantonservices.com**, where "rugster" is a word you make up from whole cloth.

- Don't use ordinary words that are in the dictionary (even peculiar ones like "hellion" or "symbiont") or words and names from popular culture, like "Gandalf" or "muggle."

- *String words together, or make up new ones.* A well-known artist hit upon a magnificent e-mail address, which is **slavetohercat@stantonservices.com**. (The domain has been changed to protect her privacy.) She will never be hit in a dictionary attack, that's for sure.

- *Don't use random strings of letters, like* **jkwts@stantonservices.com**. This looks like a "from" address generated by spammer utilities, and there are now filters that look for random-looking "from" addresses and treat them as spam.

- *Don't use a middle initial.* It used to be effective to add a middle initial after a common first name, in an address like **AndyR@stantonservices.com**. In recent years, spammers have been cycling through first names and middle initials as well. If you have an unusual first name, it might be effective, but nothing beats a totally made-up word or phrase!

Choose Your E-Mail Client Carefully

You might be surprised to learn that the e-mail client you use makes a tremendous difference in how much gunk your e-mail system collects. This applies to both spam (the subject of this chapter) and e-mail gunk of other kinds, which will be explored in Chapter 8. There are hundreds of e-mail clients out there, many of them free but a few of them costing much money. In this section, we'll discuss what to look for in a gunk-resistant e-mail client.

Be Careful with Outlook

Because of certain features in both Microsoft Outlook and Outlook Express, clever spammers have developed unique techniques for gunking up these clients with spam. Both these clients fail several crucial gunk tests, none of which is essential to their operation. (This subject will be explored again in Chapter 8, with respect to things other than spam.) The problem with both Outlooks concerning spam is fairly simple: Both are vulnerable to "spam beacons" executed with HTML images. (Some people call them "Web bugs" or "image beacons.") This is another scurvy spammer trick, one even cleverer than the dictionary attack mechanism described earlier.

You can protect yourself better with Outlook or Outlook Express by using a third-party spam filtering package that integrates tightly with them. Neither package provides sufficient spam filtering capabilities, and Outlook Express stores what spam filtering word lists it supports in the Registry, which contributes massively to Registry gunk (more on that in Chapter 8).

One late note: At this writing, word has it that the next version of Outlook has the capability to disable the downloading of "external content", that is, images and documents that come from remote servers. This feature should defeat spam beacons, but there are several reasons not to use it, which will be covered in Chapter 8. If you're considering adopting Outlook or Outlook Express, we recommend turning to Chapter 8 now and reading the appropriate sections.

Watch Out for Spam Beacons

Understanding spam beacons requires understanding how spammers work. Spammers gather e-mail addresses however they can, via dictionary attacks and Web spiders or simply by buying existing lists of addresses. They send out messages indiscriminately to millions of addresses. They sometimes remove addresses that bounce messages. However, whenever they can verify that an address is good, they copy that address to a special list of verified addresses that they can then sell at a premium price to other spammers.

You do *not* want to verify your address to a spammer. Needless to say, replying to a spam message is one way to verify that your address is good. (You don't actually *buy* things offered in spam messages, do you?) A spam beacon can verify your address to the spammer if you simply open the message—or even preview it in the Outlook preview pane!

Here's how spam beacons work: Nearly all spam these days is formatted as HTML, which allows the embedding of images in text. A spam beacon consists of an image embedded in an HTML e-mail message. This image (which can be part of the message's art or advertising pitch, or even a single white pixel lurking in a corner of the message as a tiny "invisible" image) has a name that is uniquely coded to your e-mail address. The image's name doesn't have to *contain* your e-mail address, but it may contain a long string of numbers or characters that is linked, in the spammer's database, to your e-mail address.

When you open or preview a spam message, any images in the message's HTML are requested and downloaded from the spammer's image server. The server's log records which images are downloaded, and then the spammer database program builds a list of e-mail addresses from which the beacon image was downloaded. *Shazam!* The spammer knows the message arrived at your inbox intact and was opened for display.

The key to avoiding spam beacons is to avoid downloading images embedded in HTML-formatted messages. One way to do this is never to open a spam message. Some messages, however, are carefully crafted so that you can't easily tell whether it's spam or not. Deceptive message subject headers like "In response to your recent message" may prompt you to open yet another stupid pitch for penis pills. After awhile, most of us can smell spam a mile away, but those of us who get lot of mail from people we've never met (contact people at businesses are a good example) get messages that must actually be opened. It's also easy to open spam messages by accident, and it only takes one spam beacon hit to get your e-mail address on yet another list of "preferred" addresses.

The central spam problem with both Outlook and Outlook Express is that there is no good way with either program to inspect the text of a message without also downloading the message's images. Both Outlooks use Internet Explorer to display the message body. There is a way to disable image downloads in Explorer, but if you do, you can't use Internet Explorer to surf the Web and see images on Web pages. Worse, if you receive a message containing images that you do want to see (and there are lots of legitimate e-mail newsletters that contain images), there is no way to selectively turn image downloading off for individual messages.

Because the preview pane is simply an IE window, previewing a message in the preview pane is no different from opening it in a separate window. The images come down from the spammer's server, and the spammer has your number.

Use Alternative E-Mail Clients

When you go shopping for gunk-resistant e-mail clients, your top priority should be to look for features that circumvent spam beacons. There are two ways that e-mail clients finesse spam beacons:

- Simple clients don't render HTML tags and simply display whatever text is in the message. Because images are downloaded by the HTML <IMG> tag, this defeats spam beacons completely—but it also prevents you from seeing images in mail that you request or otherwise want to read. The client PCPine is free and perhaps the best example in this class, though it is *not* for beginners.

- More sophisticated clients provide features for you to turn image downloads on and off *on a per-message basis*. They have a button allowing you to toggle image downloading on and off. Typically, you turn image downloading off and only turn it on if you receive a message containing images that you want to see. Highlight that message, and toggle images on. *Don't forget to toggle images off again before you move the message highlight bar to another message!*

The following e-mail clients from the second category include ways to defeat spam beacons. There are certainly others, and you should look closely before installing any client!

- Poco Mail 2.6 and later allows you to "sanitize" a message by preventing image downloading on a per-message basis or alternatively (with V3.0) stripping out HTML tags entirely before display. (Earlier versions lack this feature.) The cost is $35. Visit **www.pocomail.com**.

- Pegasus mail V4.1 calls spam beacons "Web bugs" but it's the same villain. Pegasus allows you to prevent image downloading, though not in as flexible a manner as you can with Poco. Pegasus is an excellent program and has the advantage of being free. Visit **www.pmail.com**.

- Eudora V6 allows you to disable downloading of images from e-mail messages. The product is generally good, but at $50 it is significantly more expensive than PocoMail without being significantly more capable. Visit **www.eudora.com**.

Use Your E-Mail Address Carefully

If you're not careful about what you do with your primary e-mail address, nothing else matters. Once spammers lay hands on your primary e-mail address, they will send you spam forever. Verifying to spammers that your e-mail address is "live" and working (as explained below) definitely makes things worse, but as best we in the industry can tell, addresses never "time-out," and experiments have shown that spam will be sent for years to an address picked up by spammers only once.

The following sections explain what *not* to do with your e-mail address, and why. None of this is any guarantee against ever getting spam in your inbox. Use an address long enough and spam happens. In general, you can't tell how a spammer gets your address, so trying to figure it out after it happens is pointless.

Never "Unsubscribe" from a Spammer Mailing List

Ever find it funny that a spam message rarely gives any crisp information concerning who and where the spammer is, but almost always includes a link to "unsubscribe?" That's because unsubscribing from a spammer's mailing list is *always* a hoax and a lie. The whole purpose of that unsubscribe link is to verify that your e-mail address is "live" and functional and that whoever it belongs to pays enough attention to their e-mail to attempt to get off of a spammer's list. That tags you not only as a live address but as a good prospect, one that the spammer can sell to other spammers for a good deal of money.

Never Post (or Let Others Post) Your E-Mail Address on the Web

Getting new addresses to spam is one of a spammer's highest priorities, and they go to great technological lengths to snag them. In the late 1990s, spammers took a hint from Web search engines and created "Web crawlers" or "spiders" that simply pulled down Web page after Web page, 24/7, and searched for that telltale @ symbol. If your e-mail address (which contains one of those @ symbols) happened to be in one of those Web pages, you were hosed, er, spammed.

The lesson is plain: Do *not* post your e-mail address in "naked" form on your Web page. The spamspiders are still out there, crawling day and night. Furthermore, make it clear to your friends and other contacts that they cannot post your e-mail address on the Web. This is a problem for people who are publicly known for some reason, and people who serve on nonprofit boards and other things for which Web contacts are useful.

TIP: If you create a Web page for or serve as an officer or other significant figure in an organization with a Web page, use a disposable address for your entry in the "contacts" section of that Web page.

The only unbreakable (so far, at least) workaround for the spamspiders is to render your e-mail address in a graphic image and post the graphic image on the Web. The spamspiders are searching for text, so if there is no text associated with the image, there's nothing for them to grab. The downside to this is that people cannot simply click on the image and bring up an e-mail edit window, but that's the price you have to pay.

Many people have written and used clever JavaScript functions that "obfuscate" (obscure) an e-mail address in the JavaScript source code, which then assembles it "on the fly" into a cleartext (readable) e-mail address when someone clicks on the link. This may reduce the number of spamspider hits, but it has two disadvantages:

- No such system is unbreakable, and there are spammers who brag about their efforts to break JavaScript obfuscation code. Web spiders have been written that parse and execute JavaScript code copied from Web pages, and if the code can turn an obfuscated address into cleartext, the spider can too. Because systems like this are an affront to spammers' intelligence, they are willing to spend enormous efforts to break them—and once broken, they're broken forever.

- The number is uncertain, but somewhere between 10-15 percent of all Web browsers disable JavaScript completely, and people using those browsers will not be able to click on your JavaScript obfuscated address link anyway.

Obfuscate Your E-Mail Address on Newsgroups and Discussion Boards

Just as there are spamspiders that crawl the Web searching for e-mail addresses to spam, there are spiders that download and scan Usenet newsgroups and Web discussion board postings for e-mail addresses. Postings to newsgroups and discussion boards often require the entry of an e-mail address of some kind. Some people who post anonymously simply make up a phony address, but if you want people to be able to reach you apart from the newsgroup or discussion board, obfuscating an address is necessary.

The idea is to create an address that is "broken" in a way that a spider cannot fix but that any reasonably intelligent human being can. For example, here are a couple of obfuscated forms of Andy Stanton's e-mail address, **rugster@stantonservices.com**:

rugster@stantonNOSPAMservices.com

rugster@stantonPULLTHISservices.com

As given, these addresses will bounce, unless you delete the "NOSPAM" or "PULLTHIS" text.

This system worked well for many years, but spammers (to whom such mechanisms are a terrible affront) have created ever more sophisticated spiders. These days, spiders are regularly searching for blocks of uppercase letters within an address that is otherwise completely in lowercase, and stripping out anything in uppercase.

The current solution (current for how long, we're not sure) is to mix cases in an obfuscation, like this:

rugster@stantonPuLLThISservices.com

It takes a little more thought to remove the obfuscation, but most people (especially those used to the conventions of newsgroups and discussion boards) will catch on quickly.

By the way, it's now unwise to use the word "spam" in an obfuscation, whether in upper- or lowercase. Some have tried to spell it backwards, but "MAPS" has other meanings and can be confusing to newcomers.

One final note about discussion groups: Many people have reported that signing up for a Yahoo! Groups account opened the gates to huge quantities of spam, even though Yahoo insists it does not sell lists of e-mail addresses to spammers. This has happened to many people in our immediate acquaintance, so we strongly recommend *against* creating a Yahoo! Groups account.

Use Disposable E-Mail Addresses for E-Commerce

The largest and best-known e-commerce retailers like Amazon.com can probably be trusted not to sell your e-mail address to spammers. (They have too much to lose if it ever came out, for way too small a financial gain.) Unfortunately, midsize and especially smaller retailers are another matter. When creating an account with online retailers, always use a disposable e-mail address. These are e-mail addresses obtained from one of the many free e-mail services that are everywhere on the Web. They cost nothing, and when an address inevitably becomes a spam magnet, it can be discarded and another one obtained.

Nearly all e-mail clients of any consequence can support multiple e-mail accounts, with one e-mail address per account. Here are the steps to follow:

1. Set up a separate account for each address you use.

2. When you click the check mail button, the client will read them all and deposit all the mail from any of the several accounts in your inbox.

3. Consider creating a filter that will deposit all the mail sent to a disposable address (say, one devoted to use with a single e-commerce retailer) into a specific mail folder. Creating filters can be an advanced topic, and it's always very specific to a particular mail client. Whatever mail client you use, read your documentation and give it a try. Filtering can be very useful, even though it takes some practice to get it right.

If you limit the use of a disposable address to a single vendor, you'll be able to tell quickly if that vendor is selling your address to spammers, especially if you direct all mail sent to that address to a single folder. If the vendor does sell your address, write an angry letter to the people in charge there, indicating that you'll never buy anything from them again. It's the only way we'll ever break them of that habit!

Services That Manage Disposable E-Mail Addresses

There are online sites that offer paid services for creating and managing disposable e-mail addresses:

www.emailias.com/

www.spamex.com/

www.spamgourmet.com/

All these sites work pretty much the same way by allowing you to create what amounts to a self-destructing e-mail alias for your primary e-mail address. These aliases can then be sent to e-commerce retailers, and after a predetermined amount of time, or a predetermined number of messages sent back to the address, the address self-destructs.

These services are not hideously expensive ($9 to $20 per year, typically), but some of them allow you to make the mistake of replying to a message with your real e-mail address in the From field, which completely negates any benefit to using the services. Because there are so many free e-mail services out there, we don't recommend the use of online disposable e-mail services. Just get an account with BoxFrog or one of the multitude of others and use the address until spam kills it. It's as simple as that.

Use a Separate Spam Filtering Utility

As hard as you may try to avoid being spam bait, there's really no getting around it: Sooner or later they'll find you and the spam will begin arriving. The only way to deal with spam once it actually happens is to use some sort of spam filtering technology. Spam filtering is done when a program of some kind (whether your e-mail client or a separate spam filtering utility) inspects an incoming e-mail message and decides whether it's legitimate or spam. How it makes this decision is crucial, but how that decision is made may also be highly technical and difficult to describe.

In this section, we'll explain how spam filtering works and suggest how to use it to divide your spam from your "ham" (your legitimate e-mail.)

A Short Spam Filtering Glossary

The best way to start is to define a few terms from the jargon associated with spam filtering. Most spam filtering products use more than one means of making the spam/ham decision, and you'll have to understand what they are to make them work.

Bayesian filtering. This is a fascinating technology that allows a spam filter to "learn" how to spot spam by using statistical analysis of message length and the distribution of words present in a message. Basically, you pass a certain number (at least 100) messages through a Bayesian filter and somehow indicate to the filter (generally by clicking a button) whether each message is spam or legitimate e-mail. The filter analyzes what words tend to be in spam versus real e-mail and then uses that analysis to "guess" whether a message is spam or not. If you're persistent about training a Bayesian filter, the filter gets better with each message it analyzes, and after a week or so its "guesses" will be accurate to better than 90 percent, and probably closer to 95 percent. Later in this section, we'll explain how to use POPFile, a completely free Bayesian spam filter that works very well.

Blacklist. A blacklist is a list of e-mail addresses or Internet domains from which all mail is to be considered spam and discarded. No further analysis is done. If a message's sender or the sender's domain is on the blacklist, it's spam. Some e-mail clients call this a *blocked senders list* or *banned senders list.*

False negative. When a spam message is mistakenly identified as a legitimate message, this is a false negative. A false negative will show up in your inbox with all your legitimate e-mail and you will have to delete it manually. It is very difficult to eliminate false negatives entirely, and if you try, you may increase the rate of false positives (see the next entry), which are *much* worse.

False positive. When a legitimate e-mail message is tagged as spam (and, worse, discarded with the rest of the trash), it's called a false positive. These are the bane of spam filters, and your main job will be to tweak your spam filter technology so that your false positive rate goes to zero. Doing so may increase your false negatives, but those are easier to deal with.

Magnet. This is a term used primarily by POPFile, but other filtering technologies are beginning to adopt it. A magnet is a user-defined term or address that "pulls" a message toward a spam classification or a non-spam classification. In

POPFile, for example, if you create a magnet based on seeing your boss's e-mail address in the From field, that magnet will "pull" all messages from your boss into your inbox as real e-mail. On the flip side, you can define a magnet based on the word "Viagra" that will "pull" any messages with "Viagra" in the subject line to the trash folder, or wherever else you banish spam to. More on this later, in the description of POPFile.

Mail proxy. Nearly all e-mail clients allow some sort of spam filtering. However, many of the best spam filtering products are not e-mail clients at all but *mail proxies,* or programs that insert themselves between your e-mail client and the POP server from which your e-mail is delivered. All your e-mail passes through the mail proxy, which then filters for spam and either deletes it or marks it so that your e-mail client can delete it after you inspect it. POPFile, Norton Anti-Spam, and McAfee SpamKiller are all mail proxies.

Whitelist. Many e-mail clients allow you to create a whitelist, which is a list of e-mail addresses or Internet domains from which you will always accept e-mail as legitimate. Your whitelist would thus contain the e-mail addresses of people and organizations that you trust—such as your spouse, friends, children, and coworkers—or newsletters or e-mail lists that you subscribe to. (A whitelist is the reverse of a blacklist.) Many spam filtering products allow you to import your Windows address book as a ready-made whitelist, under the reasonable assumption that your address book does *not* contain the addresses of spammers!

Filtering Within Your E-Mail Client Is Not Enough

Virtually all e-mail clients have some ability to filter e-mail based on words found in the various message header fields or the message body. Some e-mail clients make this filtering easier to use than others. Perhaps the best in terms of filtering is PocoMail, especially in adding senders or whole domains to the blacklist. In PocoMail, you can right-click a message in the summary window and, from the context menu, choose to ban either the sender (for example, **kgrtn@spammer.com**) or the whole domain (spammer.com).

If you get only a little spam, PocoMail or something like it may be all you need. However, simple sender or key word filters like those found in e-mail clients are becoming less and less effective as spammers become ever more clever at providing fewer "hooks" for a keyword filter to grab. Most modern spam has become exceedingly vague, using short, common words as much as possible. The worst spam (offering porn and drugs) is almost always sent using forged headers, which is something few e-mail clients can detect on their own.

Combating spam effectively, especially if you get more than 20 spam messages per day, really requires a separate spam filtering utility. There are many, and although most are commercial products, several free products exist. If you're shopping for a commercial product, be sure that the following is true:

- *It supports your e-mail client and/or your e-mail service.* Some spam filtering products do not support MAPI mail systems, for example, or will work only with a short list of popular e-mail clients, typically Outlook, Outlook Express, and Eudora. Most spam filtering utilities do *not* work with Webmail accounts.

- *You understand the costs and installation limitations.* Some products require an annual subscription fee. Many now require "activation," meaning that the software "phones home" for permission to run and cannot be installed on more than one computer in your home.

How Mail Proxies Work

Nearly all standalone spam filtering utilities are mail proxies. Unless you have some experience in the server world, the term "mail proxy" is probably new to you. In the simplest possible terms, a mail proxy is a software utility that you insert between your mail client and your mail server to process your e-mail before it is delivered to your inbox.

Mail proxies can be used for various purposes, but nearly all are used to filter spam. This filtering can be done in several ways, and many filtering utilities use several different methods to separate spam from legitimate e-mail, including whitelists, blacklists, keyword and key phrase filters, and Bayesian statistical analysis. Typically, a mail proxy will look at a message in the light of its various filtering technologies and then decide whether it's spam or legitimate. The mail proxy will then mark the message somehow, often by inserting a short tag at the beginning of the subject line, and then send it down to the e-mail client.

The e-mail client still has a part in the filtering task: It looks at the markers added by the mail proxy and routes anything marked as spam to its trash folder and any marked as legitimate e-mail to its inbox.

This process is shown in Figure 7-1. The mail server is somewhere off on the Internet, typically owned and operated by your Internet service provider (ISP). The mail proxy and e-mail client are both programs that run on your PC, which is represented by the shaded box. When your e-mail client sends out its request for new mail, this request (which usually goes directly to the server) passes through the mail proxy. The mail proxy passes on the request for new e-mail to the server, which delivers new e-mail to the proxy. The proxy inspects and marks the new e-mail and then passes it on down to the e-mail client.

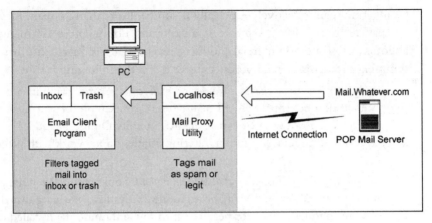

Figure 7-1
E-mail downloaded through a mail proxy.

In a sense, the mail proxy has two different "faces." From the perspective of the e-mail client, the proxy looks like an e-mail server. The proxy accepts requests for new mail and sends mail back to the client. From the perspective of the e-mail server, the proxy looks like an e-mail client. The proxy sends the server a username and password and accepts the mail that the server sends back. This allows both the client and the server to operate pretty much as they always did, when they only spoke to one another, without the mail proxy in between.

A mail proxy must be configured with your e-mail account information because it acts as an e-mail client "by proxy" when communicating with your e-mail server. How this is done varies by product, so follow the installer wizard or other documentation for the product that you choose. In the next section, we'll explain how to configure POPFile, one of the best spam filter products that you'll find anywhere.

POPFile: Excellent…and Free!

One of the most popular spam filtering utilities is also one of the most effective, as well as among the cheapest: Free! For these reasons, we'll explain POPFile in detail in this section. POPFile is a trainable Bayesian filter built into a mail proxy, and in our tests, it has managed to eliminate as much as 99 percent of incoming spam. You have to be diligent about training it and keeping it trained over time, but if you do, the results are nothing short of magical.

POPFile is free and open source, and it may be downloaded from this URL: **http://popfile.sourceforge.net/**

POPFile and Its Buckets

POPFile is downloaded as a zip file containing a single setup.exe file. Once you download and unzip it, run setup.exe. It installs just as any Windows application installs, using a wizard that asks you questions until it knows enough to complete and configure the installed program. You can safely accept all the install wizard's default values until you get to the Buckets screen.

Most of the way through the POPFile install, you'll be shown a dialog box that asks you to choose the buckets that you'll need when using POPFile. A bucket is simply POPFile's name for a category into which e-mail may be classified. By default, POPFile creates four buckets on install: Inbox, Spam, Personal, and Work. Unless you intend to do more with POPFile than simply separate spam from ham, you only need the Inbox and Spam buckets. To eliminate the other two, check Remove for them before clicking Continue, as shown in Figure 7-2.

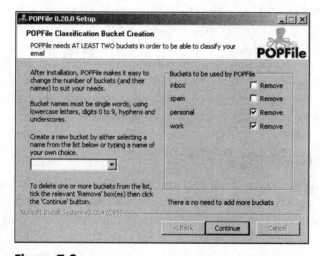

Figure 7-2
Removing unnecessary POPFile buckets.

With the Inbox and Spam buckets defined, POPFile's install can go to completion, after which it will begin working. A yellow octopus icon will appear in the System Tray.

Configuring Your E-Mail Client to Use POPFile

The only real subtlety in configuring POPFile for simple spam filtering actually lies in setting up the mail server addresses in your e-mail client. POPFile itself requires almost no configuration at all. It doesn't need to know your mail server's address. It gets that from your e-mail client.

What you need to do is find the place in your e-mail client where addresses for mail servers are displayed and edited and change them in the following fashion:

1. Change the address of the POP e-mail server that delivers your e-mail to 127.0.0.1. That is the IP address on which POPFile "listens" for commands and from which it delivers mail. From the perspective of your e-mail client, POPFile is your POP mail server.

2. This is the tricky one: Change the value in the username field to the real name of your POP mail server followed by a colon and the username you use to log into that server. For example, if the name of Andy Stanton's POP server is **mail.stantonservices.com** and his username is **astanton**, the value he would need to enter here is **mail.stantonservices.com:astanton**. (Bold is used for clarity only.)

What happens here is that when Andy Stanton clicks the button directing his e-mail client to check mail, his e-mail client will send the string **mail.stantonservices.com:astanton** to POPFile at the IP address 127.0.0.1. POPFile separates the mail server name and the username and uses those two separate strings to log into the remote POP server. Once the connection has been established, the e-mail client sends its password to POPFile, and POPFile simply passes it along to the remote POP server. After that, the conversation between the mail client and the mail server continues normally until the connection opens for the downloading of new mail from the POP server.

Using and Training POPFile

POPFile is unobtrusive and runs silently in the background. You'll know it's working if you see a little yellow octopus icon in your Windows System Tray. (It's not a very good icon, and at very high screen resolutions, it may look like a nondescript yellow splotch.) You don't have to tell POPFile to download mail. You tell your e-mail client to download mail and the client requests mail from POPFile. POPFile then requests mail from your remote POP mail server and examines the mail as it passes through on the way to your e-mail client. Unless you configure it otherwise, it will add a little prefix to the subject header of each message: [spam] or [inbox]. This allows your e-mail client to filter messages to either the trash (for spam) or to your inbox.

The real work in using POPFile lies in training it. After you bring e-mail down to your e-mail client, you must double-click the octopus icon in the System Tray to bring up POPFile's management window, which will appear in your default Web browser. Click on the History link in the upper-left corner and you'll see a screen like the one shown in Figure 7-3.

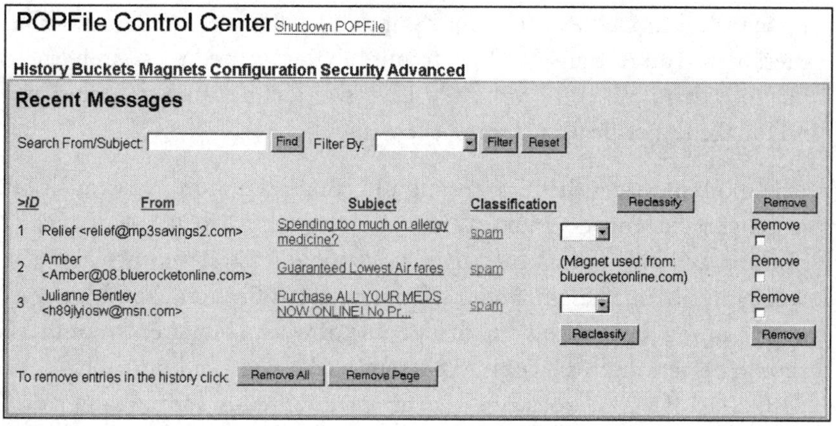

Figure 7-3
The POPFile History screen.

The History screen contains one line for each message that has passed through POPFile. A message will remain in the History screen until you delete it. You can delete messages from the underlying History database one message at a time, an entire screen of messages at a time, or all messages (however many there might be) at once.

Note that each message has a classification; in Figure 7-3, all three messages shown are classified as spam. If all messages are classified correctly, nothing further need be done and you can delete the messages from the History screen. If any messages are misclassified, you can train POPFile to do better by changing the classification shown. This is done by selecting a new classification from the drop-down list to the right of the classification link. This pull-down list will contain all buckets defined within POPFile and in most cases will consist of only Spam and Inbox. Change the classification of any messages that you consider misclassified, and then click the Reclassify button. POPFile will change the classification of those messages and redisplay the History screen with the new classifications displayed.

TIP: If you forget to click the Reclassify button after changing a message's classification, the training will not "take." Also, once you delete a message line from the History screen, you can no longer go back and reclassify it. Make sure you're certain of message classifications before you delete messages from History!

POPFile does its best to come to a reliable decision on which bucket a message belongs in. However, when the decision proves difficult to make according to its statistical model, POPFile may punt and call a message "unclassified." It is then up to you to train POPFile to put the unclassified message in the correct bucket. Each time you do this, POPFile's model becomes a little sharper and will make future decisions more accurately.

The more messages that pass through POPFile, the more "certain" it becomes of its classification decisions. When you first install POPFile, it will "know" nothing and will call all messages "unclassified." Over the first few days, you will probably be changing a lot of message classifications. You'll be reasonably busy training for probably the first couple of weeks, but after a month POPFile should be accurate well over 90 percent of the time, and probably higher than that. (One of the consolations of getting a hundred or more spams a day is that POPFile will learn *very* quickly to distinguish between spam and ham.) Achieving accuracy well over the 90 percent depends on savvy use of POPFile's magnets, as explained in the following section.

Creating POPFile Magnets

POPFile lets you create any reasonable number of magnets, and if carefully used, magnets will allow you to reduce your false positive rate to almost zero. (One of our associates recently announced that POPFile had been trained to be 99.46 percent accurate for his mail, which is frankly astonishing. He said it was due to having about 40 very carefully chosen magnets.) Taken together, POPFile's list of magnets is both your blacklist and your whitelist. Each magnet is defined separately and can pull toward any existing bucket.

Creating a magnet is done from the Magnets screen, shown in Figure 7-4. There is some helpful explanation right on the Magnets screen, but the process is really very simple: You specify the type of magnet, which in POPFile's context indicates to which e-mail message field to look in. You can choose the From field, the To field, and the Subject field. The value is the word, phrase, e-mail address, or domain to look for in that field. A partial match is still a match; in other words, the e-mail address **tjkqv@spammer.com** will match **spammer.com**. Finally, you specify the bucket into which a matching message will always go. POPFile can be used to classify legitimate e-mail into any number of buckets, but most users simply specify two buckets: Spam and the legitimate mail bucket, called Inbox.

When you have all three fields filled out, simply click the Create button to create the magnet.

Defining magnets is like automatic training for POPFile: Each time a message is "pulled" to a bucket by a magnet, POPFile learns from that message without

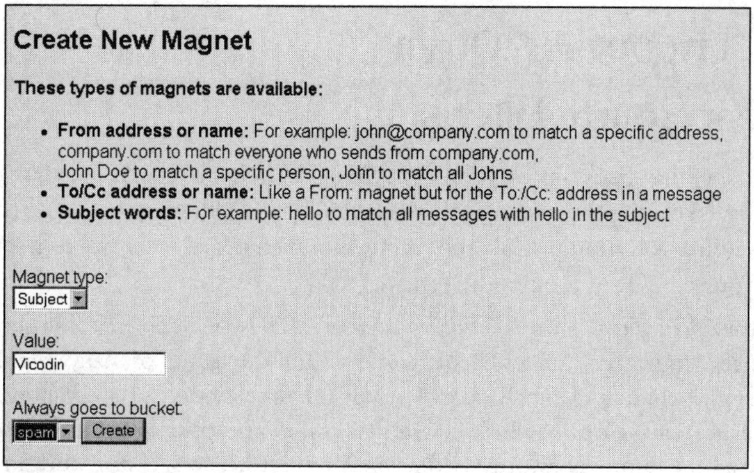

Create New Magnet

These types of magnets are available:

- **From address or name:** For example: john@company.com to match a specific address,
  company.com to match everyone who sends from company.com,
  John Doe to match a specific person, John to match all Johns
- **To/Cc address or name:** Like a From: magnet but for the To:/Cc: address in a message
- **Subject words:** For example: hello to match all messages with hello in the subject

Magnet type:
Subject ▼

Value:
Vicodin

Always goes to bucket:
spam ▼   Create

Figure 7-4
Creating a POPFile magnet.

your having to manually specify anything. So even though creating magnets takes a little time up front, over the long haul it saves you a great deal of time that would otherwise be spent manually training POPFile.

Now, what magnets should you create? Here are some guidelines:

- Create inbox magnets, one for each of the people who send you legitimate e-mail most often. That is, create a magnet for your spouse, one each for your boss and close coworkers, one for each of your children and close relatives with whom you communicate via e-mail, and one for each of your friends whom you hear from regularly.

- Create an inbox magnet for each e-commerce company with whom you do business. E-mail from online retailers is easily mistaken for spam—after all, a lot of spam is from online retailers whom you've never heard of. If you buy books from Amazon.com, create a magnet for Amazon.com. If you use eBay, create a magnet for eBay, and so on.

- Create an inbox magnet for each e-mail newsletter or list server that you subscribe to. Spammers often call their messages newsletters, so it's easy to mistake a real newsletter for a fake one.

- Create a spam magnet for any obvious spam senders or spam keywords that seem to predominate in your spam pile. Keywords like "penis," "Vicodin," and so on make great spam magnets because they rarely turn up in subject lines of real e-mail, unless you work in the medical field.

- On an ongoing basis, create an appropriate magnet for senders or subjects that POPFile tends to misclassify. POPFile can seem mysterious at times, so when you discern any pattern in what it's getting wrong, try to figure out a magnet to pull similar messages in the proper direction.

Avoid Triggering Other People's Spam Filters

While keeping spam out of your own inbox is probably much on your mind these days, keeping the messages that you send out of other people's spam filters is something you should also be thinking about. Here are a few tips to help you keep your mail from looking like spam:

- *Avoid putting certain words in the subject header.* These include "free," "insurance," "mortgage," "penis," "enlargement," and the names of many popular drugs, including Viagra, Xanaxx, Vicodin, Hydrocodone, Lortabs, Valium, Levitra, and so on. Watch the spam that comes into your own inbox and avoid the distinctive words used in their subject headers. If you work in a field that uses certain spam-favored terms like "mortgage," "refinance," or "meds," try to keep them out of your subject line if possible.

- *Avoid using certain words in the body of your message.* The big offender here is "unsubscribe," which many people filter out as a sure-fire spam telltale. Don't write things that sound like a sales pitch if you can avoid it. Phrases like "limited time," "great deals," and so on will trigger a lot of spam filters, as will any verbiage that comes from the gutter or can be mistaken for gutter talk by a spam filter. (The sad poster child here is "summa cum laude.")

- *Avoid including images in your e-mail.* Many people have become so desperate to filter spam (much of which uses images) that they filter on the HTML <IMG> tag and consign any message containing an <IMG> tag to the trash folder. If you need to send an image to someone, it might make more sense to direct them to a file on your FTP site (if you have one). You could also tell them in a separate e-mail that you're sending an image so that they can watch their spam folder.

- *Send your e-mail as plain text rather than HTML.* Spam is virtually always sent as text formatted with HTML because many spammer tricks depend on HTML tags and comments. If you send plain text rather than HTML, many Bayesian filters will be more inclined to consider your note as legitimate.

- *Make sure your PC's system clock is correct.* This is an odd one, but for reasons unclear (and spammers *always* have reasons!), much spam is sent with incorrect dates and times in the "time sent" field. We have heard reports of spam being sent that is two or three years old—and more than a few that are from several years in the future! (It is as easy to forge sent dates as anything else in e-mail headers.) Some major e-mail systems have begun to tag such misdated mail as spam. So if your PC thinks it's running in the year 2000, your e-mail will be sent with a 2000 date on it—and other people's mail servers may call it spam.

Summing Up

This chapter is about preventing spam from getting into your inbox. Spam is by far your worst e-mail problem. If you get enough e-mail, the sheer quantity can be a source of gunk all by itself, especially as the years roll by.

Cleaning Up E-Mail Gunk

Degunking Checklist:

√ Learn how to keep your current e-mail from going "under the fold" in your inbox.

√ Create a system of folders for classifying e-mail you want to keep.

√ Isolate time-delimited e-mails in folders that can be deleted or archived to CD after they're no longer current.

√ Don't retain e-mails with large binary attachments. Save the attachments elsewhere and delete them from your inbox.

√ Inspect your attachments folder (if you have one) and delete binary files that have been saved elsewhere.

√ Check your outbox and drafts folders to make sure gunk isn't accumulating there.

√ Check to see if copies of your mailbase from previous e-mail clients are still on your hard drive.

√ Consider using a "file shredder" utility so that sensitive personal or financial data cannot be recovered after deletion.

Most households have something (usually in the kitchen) affectionately called a "junk drawer." It's the drawer where stuff gathers that doesn't fall into any of the other major stuff categories. If it's not pots, pans, silverware, or kitchen gadgets, well…throw it in the junk drawer.

The junk drawer is the place originally intended to hold just a few things: scissors, a ruler, and maybe a little box of rubber bands. Over the years, however, people end up tossing in wine corks with clever designs, 17 promotional beer openers gathered at home-and-garden shows, coupons, poker chips that Mom found under the refrigerator, Dad's spare sunglasses, old toothbrushes used to scrub grout, loose screws that fell out of something, and on and on and on. Eventually you have to dig hard just to find the scissors—assuming they're still in there somewhere.

Without realizing it, most people have allowed their e-mail inboxes to become e-mail junk drawers. Messages accumulate for many reasons, but they *do* accumulate, and before you know it you have hundreds—even thousands!—of messages sitting around. The oldest are forgotten, and it doesn't take long for any single message to pass "under the fold" (that is, scroll off the bottom of the display) and quickly slip your mind, perhaps for good.

The public has had access to the Internet for more than 10 years now. E-mail is no longer a new technology, and people who have used it heavily over the years can gather a great deal of e-mail that isn't spam. This "wanted" e-mail becomes gunk when it is simply forgotten or can no longer be located within the mass of other messages. In this chapter, we'll talk about how to keep your e-mail from congealing into endless megabytes of gunk. We're not dealing with spam here; for that, see Chapter 7. This is about the organization and housekeeping of your *mailbase*; that is, the body of "real" messages that actually matter to you.

Keep, Hold, or Pitch?

As with spam, the best way to eliminate "real" e-mail gunk is to prevent it from piling up in the first place. This requires that you think hard about each message as it comes in. In general, any e-mail message falls into one of three categories:

- Mail with lasting value, which should be retained indefinitely.
- Mail associated with a current project or otherwise limited by a calendar date that needs to be held for a period of time and then either archived or deleted.
- Mail that can be dealt with right now and then deleted immediately.

These three categories of mail require action that you could characterize as "keep," "hold," or "pitch." Each time you look at a message entering your inbox, those three words should be kept in mind.

The 100-Message Rule

Most people who depend on e-mail try to adhere to a 100-message rule for their inboxes. Keep an eye on the number of messages your inbox contains, and when it tops 100, budget some time *right now* to get it down to about 50—or fewer. When you have more than 100 messages in your inbox, chances are that the oldest will be forgotten and just sit there gathering dust, making searches more difficult and time consuming.

If you're *really* disciplined, try to adhere to a one-screen rule. In other words, keep no more messages in your inbox than will display on a single screen. If you're busy and communicate a lot over e-mail, this will be extremely hard. Don't feel like a failure if you can't manage it. It's an ideal to strive for, not a requirement!

Is Autosorting a Good Idea?

Most e-mail clients have built-in general-purpose filtering machinery. With a little cleverness, you can create a filter to move incoming mail out of your inbox automatically, assuming you have someplace else to put it. (We'll cover creating a folder hierarchy for your e-mail in the next major section.) Most people think of e-mail filters in connection with spam, but in truth, filters have other uses.

For example, many people belong to e-mail mailing lists (often informally called *listservs*), which are party-line forums conducted over e-mail and associated with a given topic. For example, a listserv might be devoted to people who fly radio-controlled model airplanes as a hobby. Many of these lists have a lot of members who generate a great deal of e-mail, and these messages can gunk up your inbox very quickly. A filter can be created to look for some characteristic element in e-mail coming from that listserv and automatically move messages that satisfy the filter criteria to a folder created specifically for that list traffic.

Many mailing lists add a tag to the beginning of the subject line of messages sent out from the listserv. For example, the tag [RC-Airmodels] might be added to the subject line of mail sent from a radio-controlled model listserv. You can set up a filter to look for "[RC-Airmodels]" and move all messages bearing that tag to a folder you create for them.

This may sound useful, but it's a two-edged sword. Out of sight, out of mind, it's true—but "out of sight, forever in your mailbase" can be just as true. If you don't diligently classify mail from listservs as it comes in, you run the risk of having *huge* quantities of mail piling up in a folder somewhere. Some of that may be worth keeping, but if you use autosorting to put off the necessary decision making until later, you may be faced with having to read and judge hundreds of messages in one sitting, which would make anyone cross-eyed and after awhile may drive you to simply nuke everything in a fury of frustration.

It's Psychology, not Technology!

Deciding what messages to keep and what to pitch is really a matter of psychology rather than technology. You have to make those decisions sometime, and although technology can make some of those decisions easier, it can't make all of them for you. It's very easy to convince yourself that almost any message needs to be saved forever. Who knows whether it'll become useful in the future? Well, nobody—and that's what judgment is all about.

If you're really nervous about nuking messages, you can always consider the extra work of archiving them onto a CD so that they're not irretrievably lost. Almost certainly better is to develop the discipline of just letting them go. Time is precious these days—almost no one goes back and reads old e-mail "just for fun." Unless it has an objectively identifiable value for the future—financial or legal records, family history discussions, unique technical advice, or content that you can refer back to and use, things like that—steel yourself to just let it go.

Create a One-Screen Folder Hierarchy

The single biggest secret to keeping your mailbase manageable lies in creating a suitable hierarchy for folders in which to store your messages. Most e-mail clients come to you with just a few folders: Inbox, Outbox, Trash, and Drafts. These four folders are the ones through which your daily mail passes. They are *not* for storing mail over the long haul! For those "keep" and "hold" messages, you need to create folders.

Nearly all e-mail clients allow you to create folders or mailboxes, which may be displayed in a window to the left of the message panes themselves. Most clients allow a folder *hierarchy*—that is, folders that contain subfolders—and this makes organizing a very large mailbase much easier. It's not uncommon to find computer professionals with *tens of thousands* of messages in their mailbases, and for people like that, a good many folders may be required to make sense of it all and allow individual messages to be found quickly when needed.

Keep Your Folder List to One Screen

The key to creating a folder hierarchy is not to have so many folders in the left margin that you forget you have them. The way to do that is to limit your folders to a single screen's worth. The rule of thumb is this: If you have to scroll a list of folders up and down, you have too many. If you feel you absolutely need more folders than will fit in a single screen, nest related folders together under a parent folder.

Deciding what folders to create (like deciding when to nuke a message) is more psychology than technology. Think hard about how you use e-mail, not so much in terms of who it comes from but rather what the messages are *about*. When at some point in the future you want to refer back to a message, you may recall who sent it, but primarily what you'll be looking for is the message's topic. Folders should thus be about topics and not people. Here are some examples of mail for which you could create folders:

- Mail relating to your job
- Mail relating to your church or civic groups (such as Lions, Chamber of Commerce, neighborhood association, PTA)
- Mail relating to your hobbies and interests (such as programming, model railroading, kite flying, ham radio)
- Mail relating to projects or research you're undertaking (such as research on a medical condition or for an article you're writing)

Just to give you an example, let's postulate a set of mail folders for our mythical Everyman, Andy Stanton, a computer consultant living down the street from the Andersons in Springfield:

In	
Out	These four come standard with most e-mail clients
Sent	
Drafts	

Boy Scouts	Mail about Andy Jr.'s Boy Scouts activities
Chamber of Commerce	Mail relating to Andy's C of C activities
Church	Mail about events and other things at St. James
Consulting Practice	A folder containing other folders; more on this a little later.
Genealogy	Mail from relatives gathering family history data
Humor	For those funny messages Andy's brother sends out
Kitchen Remodel Project	Mail relating to Andy's remodel job on the kitchen
RC Airmodels	A hobby listserv Andy subscribes to

This folder hierarchy is pretty straightforward, and it serves Andy well. It's a very nice folder list because it can be displayed on one single screen.

Keep Time-Delimited Mail in Separate Folders

Note in the list Andy's "Kitchen Remodel Project" folder. It contains mail from the suppliers and contractor who are rebuilding the kitchen in Andy's house. The project is pretty intense, but it is definitely time delimited. After the project is done, the mail in the folder is no longer especially useful, and it certainly won't be referred to on a daily basis, as it was during the project's execution. Once his kitchen is completed, Andy can delete this folder or (more likely) archive the folder's messages to a CD and put it in a drawer somewhere. The folder itself can then be deleted from his folder hierarchy.

How you separately archive one folder among many depends completely on your e-mail client. With some clients (primarily the Outlooks), it's not easy; with others, it may be as simple as exporting a folder to a separate file. If your e-mail client gives you the option of exporting individual messages as separate EML files, this may be ideal because you can read the archived messages separately using a simple text editor like Windows Notepad if you ever need to refer back to them. If you archive a whole folder as a single file, you may have to reimport the folder into your e-mail client to read the archived messages again. Note that if you change e-mail clients after archiving a whole folder, your new client may not be able to read an archived folder exported from a different client. This is yet another reason to archive messages as individual EML message files and not whole folders.

Gunkbusters' Notebook: Managing Your Sent Items Folder

Every time you send a message to someone, a copy of it is saved in your Sent Items folder—and if you don't delete or move messages out of Sent Items, they remain there forever. People who have used e-mail for a number of years are often surprised to find that thousands of messages have accumulated in their Sent Items folder. Some management is called for.

Sent Items is useful as "short term memory" of messages that you've sent. Sometimes you recall that someone asked you to send a message to them for some reason, and you can't recall if you actually did or not. If you are unsure, look for messages to that person in Sent Items. This feature becomes less useful as time passes—e-mail conversations grow cold over a few months' time, and at some point messages in Sent Items might as well be trashed. This is *especially* true if they have attachments, as will be discussed a little later in this chapter.

A good rule of thumb is to remove messages from Sent Items after 90 days' time or less. "Removing" may mean deleting, but it may sometimes happen that a message that you sent someone is worth retaining as part of a larger conversation. For example, if you have a folder on Genealogy, you probably use it to store messages from relatives researching your family history with you on a collaborative basis. Information sent to them by you should probably be kept for future reference, and possible future sharing with other people whom you have not yet contacted. In cases like that, simply move the pertinent messages from Sent Items to Genealogy.

The important thing is simply to look in on Sent Items on a regular basis, or after any period of especially intense e-mail interchanges, especially if you've been sending messages with large attachments. Monthly is a good suggestion. Stick to it!

Use Nested Folders Carefully

Andy is a computer consultant, and he has a separate folder for all mail relating to his consulting practice. His consulting practice generates far more e-mail than all of his other interests and activities combined. Is one folder enough to manage it all?

No, it isn't. However, the single folder "Consulting Practice" doesn't tell the whole story. It contains a number of other folders that relate to his consulting practice:

Accounting	Mail from and to Andy's accountant
Clufre Realty	One of Andy's clients
Continuing Ed	Mail relating to night courses Andy takes
Dell Tech Support	Technical info about Andy's main PC
Gas Transport Inc.	One of Andy's clients
Harvest Moo Dairy	One of Andy's clients
Insurance	Mail relating to Andy's business insurance
Network Tech Support	Technical info about Andy's network
Sergeant Ron's Army Surplus	One of Andy's clients
Tax Matters	Mail concerning all tax issues

Andy actually has more folders within "Consulting Practice" than on his main screen. That's fine because Andy uses these folders on a daily basis and none of them is ever out of sight for very long. However, in general it's not a good idea to put folders within folders unless you refer to the subfolders often. It's much too easy to forget a rarely used folder hiding under another rarely used folder in your hierarchy.

Even if you do create folders within folders, limit yourself to two folders deep. Go three deep or more and eventually you *will* forget about one or more of those deeply buried folders!

Don't Accumulate Attachments

E-mail attachments are separate files that "ride along" on an e-mail message. Attachments can be any sort of file, but often they are files that contain content other than text, like images or sound files. This means that they are often very large—sometimes megabytes in size—and if you accumulate enough of them, they can become a huge source of e-mail gunk.

An associate of ours tells the story of a clueless employee at his firm who was sent a humorous animation of an alien singing a disco song and decided to send it to every single person in the company. The animation was 4 megabytes in size, and when multiplied by the hundred-odd people in the company, it completely filled the company's already-strapped mail server. (This was some years ago, before 100 gigabyte hard drives were commonplace.)

How e-mail clients handle attachments varies. Attachments begin as separate files, but when mailed, they are encoded within the message, and then when received, they are again broken out into separate files. Most clients allow you to click a Save As link or button to store the attachment somewhere else on your hard drive. What you must remember is that even after you save an attachment somewhere, *it most likely still exists in your mailbase* until you delete the message it came with.

Worse yet, some older clients save attachments as separate files into a folder somewhere and the attachments remain in that folder even after you delete the message that carried the attachment. What you must do is look in your e-mail client's documentation to see where and how it stores attachments. There may be a separate folder (perhaps called Attach) where attachments live. Go to that folder and see what it contains—and be prepared to be surprised. You may be looking at 100 megabytes or more of files you don't need and may already have stored elsewhere.

If you have a folder with a lot of messages in it and you are looking for those messages containing attachments, see if your e-mail client has a column (most do) for an attachment icon (this is typically a paper clip). If so, make sure that column is displayed. You can also sort messages in a folder by size: The larger messages will almost certainly be carrying attachments.

Here are some guidelines for dealing with attachments:

- Do not use your mailbase as a storehouse for attached files. When a message arrives with an attachment, *immediately* save the attachment to a separate location on your hard drive if it is to be retained. Otherwise, delete both the message and the attachment. If you want to retain the message but *not* the attachment, attempt to delete the attachment separately. (Some clients may not allow separate deletion of attachments and messages.)

- Don't open an attachment unless you know what it is. If a message arrives with an attachment and you are not *absolutely* sure of what it is or who it came from, *don't open it to see what it is!* This is how viruses propagate. Be particularly wary of files with the extensions.exe, .com, .scr, and .pif. Remember that under Windows, opening an executable file runs it! This is idiotic, but it's a fact of life. "Opening" *should* mean "looking at" rather than "running," but we must deal with Windows as it is.

- Enable the full display of file extensions in Windows Explorer. Most Windows installations default to hiding the file extension, which is a *very* bad idea. Why? A Windows filename can legally have more than one period character in it. A virus can send a copy of itself with the name ParisHilton.jpg.exe. If your Windows installation is hiding file extensions, the filename of the virus will appear as ParisHilton.jpg. Double-click it in an attempt to view the "picture" and the virus has you by the hindquarters. To disable hiding of file extensions, bring up Windows Explorer and select Tools and then Folder Options. Click the View tab and uncheck the item marked "Hide file extensions for known file types." Then click OK.

- Delete small files containing background graphics and other decorative items. Many e-mail clients send HTML backgrounds and decorative graphics as attachments, so you may see a multitude of very small files with obscure names in your attachments folder. If you don't recognize an attachment's name, you probably don't need it and can safely delete it.

- Watch out for attachments in your Sent folder! If you send messages with attachments to other people, most e-mail clients will save a copy of that message *and the attachments* in your Sent folder. If those attachments are large (say, an image or sound file), you may have a hundred or more megabytes of gunk cluttering up your mailbase in your Sent folder. This is almost certainly needless duplicate storage because you had to have a copy of each attachment file stored elsewhere to attach it to a message to begin with. The solution? Sort your Sent folder by message size and nuke every message containing an attachment.

GunkBusters Notebook: Spring Cleaning Your E-mail

If you send and receive any significant quantity of e-mail—and especially if you have a complicated folder hierarchy to store it in—you should budget one day a year for "spring cleaning" to make sure gunk isn't quietly accumulating in the far corners of your e-mail machinery. As with all e-mail management, it's less technology than psychology. The hardest part is simply deciding to do it, and then following through.

Here's a simple checklist for your annual e-mail spring cleaning:

1. Schedule a full day for it. This might sound like a lot of time but if you let your mailbase get away from you and gunk up, you will spend a lot more time than that over the coming year, straightening things out and looking for lost messages in the morass.

2. Before you do anything else, count the number of messages in your mailbase. No e-mail client that we know of will give you a single figure totaling your stored messages, but many (PocoMail first among them) will tell you how many messages are in each folder. Just take a pocket calculator, go down your list of folders, and add them up. Prepare to be surprised! (And if you're a good record keeper, try to keep a record of the size of your mailbase over time. If it's significantly bigger each time you check, you've got some serious degunking to do!)

3. Begin with your Sent Items folder. It keeps a copy of every single message you send, and few of those are worth keeping. Keep nothing in Sent Items that's more than 90 days old. Older messages should either be deleted or (if they're important enough to keep) moved to a folder where related messages (say, for tax matters, discussions on genealogy, and so on) are kept.

4. Next, go through your inbox and either delete or classify anything beyond your 100 most recent arrivals. Pay particular attention to that murky area below the fold, where messages have been lying fallow for a month or more. Force yourself to deal with anything unpleasant or difficult that's been awaiting action. If you're convinced you can't bring it down under 100 messages, you're fooling yourself. See if you need to add a folder or two for new interests or topics that have generated e-mail that doesn't quite fit anywhere else. But whatever you have to do, get it down to 100 messages or fewer!

5. Delete or Archive. Pour yourself a cup of strong coffee, start at the top of your folder list, and see what you no longer need to keep in each folder. No longer interested in radio controlled models, sold your plane, and haven't flown since last April? Archive or delete the whole folder. Sometimes a message that looked like a keeper last year doesn't look quite as essential this year. Let it go. Sometimes messages that you thought were forever were really time-limited. Be ruthless. It's the only way to stay ahead of your mailbase.

6. Keep Records. This is pure psychology, but it works: When you're done, count up the messages left in your mailbase to see how many you've eliminated. Keep a record somewhere (a short text file in your mailbase folder will do) indicating how large your mailbase is this time. It helps make it all seem worthwhile to know that you're actually staying ahead of things. You don't necessarily have to *shrink* your mailbase (unless it had gotten out of control to begin with) but you sure don't want it to grow like a fungus!

Miscellaneous E-Mail Housecleaning Pointers

Beyond what we've previously mentioned in this chapter, there are some odds and ends to think about in terms of e-mail gunk. These are minor compared to sifting and organizing your mail and managing attachments, but every little bit of degunking counts.

Watch Out for Abandoned Drafts

Most e-mail clients have a folder for messages that you begin writing but can't finish in one session. This is generally called the Drafts folder, but some clients may call it the Outbox. (The term "outbox" is more commonly used for mail that is completed and waiting to be sent.) Some e-mail clients will automatically save a message that you're writing to the Drafts folder after you've worked on it for more than a certain amount of time—and if you forget to send it, it will remain in the Drafts folder until you explicitly send or delete it.

You may well have several incomplete and abandoned messages in your Drafts folder. Open Drafts and take a look at what's in there. There may be nothing at all—or it may contain a lot of *really* moldy leftovers! Delete all messages in this folder that are not active projects.

Delete Duplicate Copies of Your Mailbase

All the major e-mail clients have the capability to import an existing mailbase from the other major e-mail clients. (If you're moving to or from a more obscure e-mail client, you may have trouble bringing your mailbase over.) However, after it has been copied over to your new e-mail client, there is still a copy of your entire mailbase stored with the old e-mail client, and that copy of the mailbase will remain on your hard drive, *even if you uninstall the old e-mail client.* If your mailbase is substantial, that can mean a *lot* of wasted disk space.

Of course, keeping the copy of your old mailbase on hard disk for a couple of weeks while you become familiar with the new e-mail client is not a bad idea (in case you decide you really don't like the new client). But at some point you should delete the copy of the old mailbase. Deleting it is easy using Windows Explorer—the mailbase is nothing more than one or more files in a directory. Delete the directory containing the mailbase files and the mailbase is gone. Sometimes, however, the tricky part is just *finding* the mailbase on today's cavernous hard drives. Table 8.1 summarizes how find the mailbases for some of the major e-mail clients.

Keep in mind that all modern e-mail clients allow you to specify where the mailbase is stored. If you don't specify a location, it will use a default path, which is listed in Table 8.1. If you (or someone who configured your PC) changed the default so that your mailbase is stored elsewhere, you may have to find it by searching for distinctive filenames or extensions.

Table 8.1   How to Find Mailbases for Common E-Mail Clients

Client Name	Path to check	Search for
AOL Mail	Program Files\America Online\idb	main.idx, main.ind
Eudora	Program Files\Qualcomm\Eudora\	in.mbx
Pegasus Mail	PMAIL\MAIL	*.pmm or *.cnm
PocoMail	Program Files\PocoMail\Mail	in.mbx
Outlook	(see below)	*.pst files
Outlook Express	(see below)	inbox.dbx

Outlook and Outlook Express can be configured many different ways, and there is no single path to check for either program. Outlook Express mailbases may be found by searching for "inbox.dbx" (the name of the inbox) and Outlook mailbases may be found by searching for files with a .pst extension.

There is a very big warning to be heeded when you want to delete a mailbase for "big" Outlook. Outlook's PST files may contain your copy of the Windows Address Book! Delete a PST file and you may delete your entire address book. This is unfortunate, because PST files are often very large and they do not compress very easily, even after you delete some or all of the e-mail messages they contain.

The rule is this: If you use Outlook, your Windows Address Book will almost certainly be stored in a PST file. If you do not use Outlook, your Windows Address Book will be stored in a WAB file. Keep in mind that if you change from Outlook to some other e-mail client, your Windows Address Book will remain in the PST file you used while you used Outlook as your e-mail client. Unfortunately, exporting mailbase and address book information out of Outlook to another e-mail client is extremely difficult.

Outlook Express E-Mail Gunk in the Windows Registry

Outlook Express has a habit of storing inappropriate things in the Windows Registry. The prime example is Outlook Express' blocked senders list, which is the list of addresses or domains whose mail should go directly to the Deleted Items folder. This list is stored in the Registry, and if you end up blocking hundreds of senders or domains (as most people who use e-mail a lot inevitably do), you will be gunking up the Windows Registry big time.

If you use Outlook Express, blocked senders will be stored in the Registry. If you stop using Outlook Express and even uninstall it, the blocked senders entries will remain in the Registry until they are manually removed.

The only really safe way to remove these blocked sender entries from the Registry is to do it from within Outlook Express. You remove them using the same dialog box that you used to add them, and it's easy except for one thing: You cannot select more than one blocked sender at a time, and therefore you must remove them one at a time, selecting and deleting each one individually. If you have hundreds of blocked senders, this is a nuisance that may take some time.

Here's how it's done:

1. From within Outlook Express, select Tools, then Message Rules, and then Blocked Senders.
2. In the Blocked Senders dialog box that appears, you'll see that each blocked sender entry is a separate line.
3. Highlight the first entry and click the Remove button.
4. Repeat step 3 on subsequent entries until they are all gone.

If Outlook Express no longer functions correctly, or if it cannot see the list of blocked senders stored in the Registry, you have no choice but to edit the Registry directly to remove the entries. This is not tremendously difficult, but it's something that you do *not* want to get wrong! Damage the wrong items in the Registry and your Windows installation won't work correctly—and perhaps not at all. You should not attempt it without a solid understanding of what the Registry is and how it works.

It can be useful to examine the Registry to see if any blocked sender entries are stored there. We'll be explaining how you work with the Registry and use tools such as REGEDT32 in more detail in Chapter 9. For now, we'll show you how to how to quickly use REGEDT32 to locate blocked sender entries. Here are the steps to follow:

1. Run REGEDT32.exe.
2. Expand My Computer and highlight HKEY_CURRENT_USER.
3. Choose Find from the Edit menu and search for the string "Block Senders."
4. Expand Block Senders, and expand Mail beneath it.
5. Expand Criteria under Mail. You'll see a long list of Registry entries with hexadecimal numeric names like 001, 002, and so on. Each one represents a blocked sender. If you click on one of the entries, you will see it expanded in the right pane and the address or domain of the blocked sender will be visible.

REGEDT32 can also remove individual entries from the Registry, but unless you know *precisely* what you're doing, it's not a good idea to try.

Use a File Shredder for Messages with Personal or Financial Data

Most people send and receive e-mail messages containing personal or financial information that should not be available to all and sundry. If in the course of degunking your mailbase you delete messages containing such sensitive information, understand that a clever enough person can recover that information, *even after it's deleted.* This is particularly important if you intend to sell or even junk your PC. Stories have circulated about people who deleted everything on their PC hard drives and put the machines out on the curb only to discover that identity thieves later recovered virtually everything that had previously existed on the hard drives.

The answer to this problem is to use what is called a "shredder" utility periodically. One of the best such utilities is Eraser, which is completely free and works very well. You can find Eraser at **www.heidi.ie/eraser/**.

Eraser has three general functions:

*   It erases files from the Windows Recycle Bin so that they cannot be recovered.
*   It erases individual files and folders so that they cannot be recovered.
*   It erases any data from the pool of unused space on your hard drive.

This last function is the important one when deleting messages from your mailbase. When you delete a message within your e-mail client, the disk space that that message originally occupied is returned to the hard drive's pool of free space. *The data is still present in that space*; the only difference is that the space may now be used for writing other files and other e-mail messages. Precisely when a given block of free disk space is reused cannot be predicted, and your sensitive data may be lying around naked in the hard drive's free space pool for weeks or months before being used again.

When you give it the command, Eraser goes out and overwrites all the free space on your hard drive with random data patterns. Thus, anything previously stored in that free space is gone forever and beyond recovery.

When you install Eraser, it adds a small icon to the Windows System Tray. Double-clicking on this icon brings up the window shown in Figure 8-1.

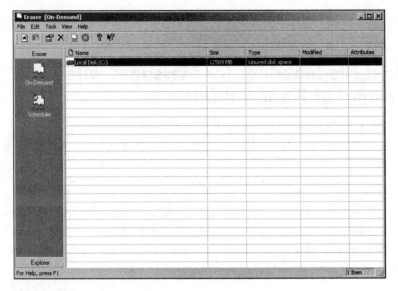

Figure 8-1
Eraser's main window.

If there is no line in the task window like that shown in Figure 8-1, you will have to create one. Select File and then New Task. The dialog box shown in Figure 8-2 will appear. Select your main hard drive (or whatever drive your mailbase is stored on) from the drop-down list under the Unused Space On Drive radio button. Click OK and the task will be created.

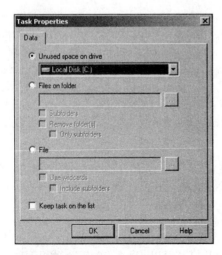

Figure 8-2
Eraser's Create Task dialog.

You then run the task by highlighting the "Unused disk space" task and selecting Task and Run.

It's a good idea to run Eraser on the unused space on your hard drive regularly; once a week is probably often enough. Certainly if you intend to sell your computer or give it to someone who should not see your personal data, delete everything that you don't want others to see and then run Eraser on the unused disk space.

Summing Up

The e-mail that you *want* to receive is no better than spam if it turns into gunk on your PC. Unlike spam, however, your own e-mail responds better to psychological than technological measures. You need to be ready to deal with e-mail *as it arrives*—and you can become an ace at deciding when to keep a message, hold it for a limited time, or deal with it (read it or reply) right now. As important as organizing e-mail into folders might be, no skill is more crucial than simply keeping the overall size of your mailbase down.

Ultimately, e-mail management is a lot like housecleaning: Devote a little daily effort to keeping things under control, and then once a year be prepared to turn the place inside out and make it shine. Keep in mind that the more diligently you perform those daily chores, the less of an ordeal that annual "spring cleaning" will turn out to be!

Cleaning and Tweaking the Registry

Degunking Checklist:

√ Learn what the Registry is, why it isn't scary, and why it is important for degunking your PC.

√ Learn how to use REGEDT32 to view the Registry.

√ Use the System Restore feature to back up and restore the Registry.

√ Back up sections of the Registry using REGEDT32.

√ Use the Registry Clean Pro utility to automatically scan and clean the Registry.

√ Use REGEDT32 to make tweaks to the Registry that can help you with your degunking chores.

Oh no, here comes the Registry! Just hearing the name of this creature might send shivers down your spine. But the Registry is like the man behind the curtain in the *Wizard of Oz*. Once you finally meet this character, you'll find that it isn't that scary. Of course, the Registry plays a very critical role in Windows. It also is a critical component that needs to be cleaned periodically to keep your computer running in top form. The Registry can easily get gunked up because Windows applications often store data in it but don't always clean up after themselves properly. As you learn about how to clean and degunk the Registry in this chapter, you should always keep in mind that safety is our top priority when making changes to it.

The Registry is one of those Windows features that everyone is constantly warning you about. Many Windows users (and even power users) are afraid of it because they don't fully understand what it does and how it works. But in order to really degunk your PC, there are things you must know about the Registry, including how it is used by Windows, how program information is stored in the Registry, how you can clean it both automatically and manually, and how you can tweak it to improve the performance of your PC.

As you'll learn in this chapter, there are two categories of activities you can perform on the Registry that are critical to helping you degunk your PC:

• Cleaning the Registry and repairing Registry keys

• Tweaking and optimizing the Registry

To help you understand how the Registry works, we'll also show you how to manually view and edit data that is stored in there.

CAUTION! *Before you make any changes to the Registry, you should make a backup copy of it. If you edit the Registry and make a major mistake, you risk destroying your system. If you don't have a backup, your only recourse would be to reinstall Windows. Don't be foolish and learn this lesson the hard way! Take a moment now to skip ahead in this chapter to the section that shows you how to back up the Registry.*

Inside the Registry

Windows used to have simple configuration files (called INI files) that stored important configuration information the operating system needed to perform critical tasks, such as starting up and loading programs, keeping track of program preferences, and storing and loading system settings for the Desktop. If you have been using Windows for a while, you probably remember these pesky INI files.

When Windows NT was born, these configuration files disappeared and were replaced by the mighty Registry. The Registry is essentially a big relational database that stores information such as operating system configuration data, application settings, hardware settings, networking settings, and much more. This information is stored in a hierarchical format, much like your Desktop file folder system.

As an example, let's say that you are using Microsoft Word to edit a file. During your editing session, you resize your main document window. When you quit Word, the settings will be saved in the Registry so that next time you use Word, it will operate just as you last left it. And you thought Windows did stuff like this by magic!

Because so much information is stored in the Registry, the Registry can easily get gunked up over time. Many of the applications you use on a regular basis will write to the Registry, and Windows itself is always storing information. Most applications write to the Registry properly, but some don't. This can leave you with a Registry that has incomplete data and extraneous data, which in turn makes your computer run slower.

What makes the Registry so critical and complex is that it touches just about everything that Windows does. To manage all of the tasks that take place with the Registry, Windows fortunately provides built-in tools that help to keep the Registry working properly. But as with any component of Windows, gunk will seep into the Registry, and it can cause a lot of problems, such as slow performance and system crashes.

To operate as efficiently as it can, the Registry data is stored in a binary format. This means that you can't simply read or change the data in the Registry without using a special tool. In this chapter, we'll use the powerful REGEDT32 program to show you how to manually view and change data in the Registry. Then, we'll use a third-party tool to clean the Registry.

A Quick Note about Windows Versions

As mentioned earlier, the Registry has been around for a while, and it has evolved just as Windows has grown up and improved. Because of this, you'll find that different tools and procedures are required to work with the various versions of Windows (NT, 98, ME, 2000, and XP). Since the primary focus of this book is on degunking computers running Windows XP, we'll focus on the tools and procedures required to view, clean, and tweak the Windows XP Registry. As we go along, however, we will point out some of the tools and procedures that will work with other versions of Windows. The following list includes some of the main issues for working with the different Registry versions:

- REGCLEAN.EXE, the popular Registry cleaning tool developed by Microsoft, does not work with Windows XP. It was designed for earlier versions of Windows and is no longer supported by Microsoft.

- Techniques for backing up and restoring the Registry differ significantly from version to version of Windows. For example, Windows 98 and ME provide a system tool called Registry Checker that you can use to back up the Registry; this tool is not available with Windows XP.

- While searching the Web for tips and utilities to clean, repair, and restore the Registry, be sure to match up the information and software you find with your version of Windows. Often, information on the Web may refer to older versions of Windows. If you are running XP, be sure to obtain the very latest information and utilities.

REGEDT32 Is Your Gateway to the Registry

Windows XP actually includes two Registry editing tools, REGEDIT and REGEDT32. We'll be using REGEDT32 in this book because it is a safer tool to use for viewing and making changes to the Registry. REGEDT32 is safer because it does not apply the changes that you make to the Registry immediately. To apply the changes that you make, you must first close REDEDT32. This gives you a sort of insurance policy. By comparison, REGEDIT applies your changes as soon as you make them.

Here's a tour of REGEDT32:

1. Choose Run from the Start menu and type in REGEDT32.EXE.

2. The window shown in Figure 9-1 should appear. The information that is first displayed might look unfamiliar to you. Each entry listed is called a top-level *key* or *hive*. (You can think of a hive as a broad category.) Notice that there are five hives listed. Each hive stores all of the values that represent individual system settings.

3. Double-click the hive or folder labeled HKEY_USERS. Then double-click the folder labeled .DEFAULT that appears. This should create the screen shown in Figure 9-2.

4. If you then double-click one of the subfolders that appear, such as Console or Environment, you will see a window pane that displays specific keys along with their settings. For example, Figure 9-3 shows the view displayed when the Console folder is selected. Notice that the window displays keys with labels like FaceName, FontFamily, and FontSize.

Each stored Registry entry is essentially a setting with an assigned value. The value tells Windows how to treat a specific setting. For example, the value assigned to the FontSize setting would tell Windows which font size to use as the default setting for the console display.

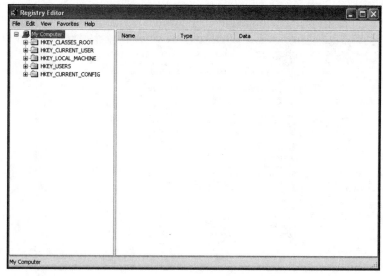

Figure 9-1

Viewing your top-level Registry data with the REGEDT32 tool.

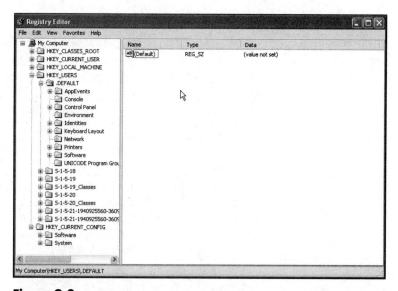

Figure 9-2

Viewing the default user setup data.

The trick to dealing with the Registry is to realize that all of the data is stored (keys and values) in a hierarchical manner. At the top level of the Registry hierarchy are the hives, or folders, listed in Table 9-1.

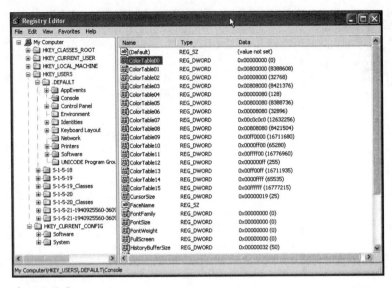

Figure 9-3

Viewing Registry keys and values.

Table 9-1   Top-Level Windows Registry Keys

Hive	Description
HKEY_CLASSES_ROOT	This hive stores information about all file extensions, descriptions, icons, associations, shortcuts, automation, class IDs, and more.
HKEY_CURRENT_USER	This hive serves as a link to the currently logged-in user's key stored in KKEY_USERS.
HKEY_LOCAL_MACHINE	This hive stores all software, hardware, network, security, and Windows system information. This is the area where most of the Registry keys and values are located.
HKEY_USERS	This hive stores all of the information about all users and their individual settings. The setting values include environment variables, color schemes, fonts, icons, Desktop configuration, Start menu items, network, and more. Each time a new user logs on, a new key is created based on a default key.
HKEY_CURRENT_CONFIG	This hive is actually a link that points to the currently selected hardware profile stored in HKEY_LOCAL_MACHINE.

Back Up and Restore the Registry

Take a moment to follow these instructions and make a backup copy of your Registry. Put your backup in a safe place, and always make sure you create a new backup before you start to make any editing changes to the Registry.

The tricky part about backing up and restoring the Registry is twofold:

- Because Windows is always using the Registry and part of it is always open, it is difficult to back up the entire Registry.

- Each version of Windows provides a different process and tools for backing up and restoring the Registry.

In this section, we'll focus on backing up and restoring the Registry for Windows XP.

Fortunately, Windows XP (and all versions of Windows) automatically creates a backup copy of the Registry each time Windows is started. But for smart and cautious degunkers like us, this isn't good enough. You should also keep an additional backup in a safe place—you never want to take chances when it comes to the Registry! There are essentially three different techniques you can use to back up the Registry:

- Use the Windows XP Backup utility, as covered in Chapter 15. This utility provides an easy solution to back up your entire system. The only caveat is that you need to be running Windows XP Professional to have access to this backup program.

- Use Windows XP's System Restore feature to create a restore point, which will back up all of the system data, including the Registry. The benefit of this approach is that you can easily restore your full system back to a previous state that you specify. The System Restore feature is described in more detail in Chapter 16, but we'll show you how to use it to back up and restore the Registry here.

- Back up and restore selected parts of the Registry using the REGEDT32 utility. Technically, this utility provides a feature to back up the entire Registry; however, we recommend you only use this utility to back up selected Registry keys. We make this recommendation because the Registry is always accessed by Windows, and although you can save the entire Registry manually to one large file using REGEDT32, you will not be able to fully restore it. The Registry has special security settings on certain keys that prevent you from restoring it manually.

CAUTION! One common misconception about the Windows XP Registry is that you can back up the entire Registry by simply making a copy of the Registry files. Although this technique could be used for Windows 98, Windows XP accesses many sections of the Registry directly. This means that Registry files could be open at all times, and you won't be able to back them up fully because they are in use.

Use System Restore to Back Up and Restore the Full Registry

Using System Restore to back up and restore the full Registry is the preferred option because it will safely back up the full Registry. We suggest that you run System Restore manually and follow the steps provided next before you make changes to the Registry. You should also do this before you make major hardware and software changes to your system.

Follow these steps to use System Restore:

1. Click Start and point to Programs, then Accessories, then System Tools and then click System Restore. This will produce the screen shown in Figure 9-4.

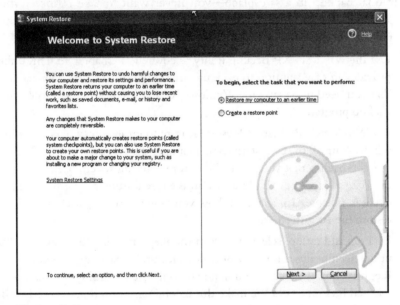

Figure 9-4
Using the System Restore feature to set a restore point.

2. Select the Create A Restore Point option and click Next.

3. Type in a name for the restore point you are creating and then click the Create button. Use a descriptive name such as "Backup before changing Registry."

4. The restore point will be created using the current date and time. The nice thing with this feature is that all of your system settings (including the entire Registry) will be saved.

To later restore your system using a restore point that you've created, do this:

1. Click Start and point to Programs, then Accessories, then System Tools and then click System Restore. This will produce the same screen shown in Figure 9-4.

2. Select the Restore My Computer To An Earlier Time option. Then click Next.

3. Select the restore point that you have previously saved from the list presented (see Figure 9-5) and click Next.

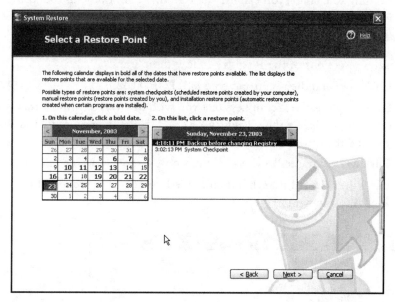

Figure 9-5
Selecting a previously saved restore point.

4. When the final screen is presented, click Next to start the process. Before you do this, be sure that all of your open programs have been closed and all of your data files have been saved. The System Restore feature will then shut down Windows and do its magic. After the restoration is complete, Windows will restart and return the settings that were in effect at the time you created the restore point. Keep in mind that System Restore may take a few minutes to restore your system.

When using the System Restore feature to create a restore point and then later restore your system, keep in mind that not only is the Registry data replaced but all of your system-level information is restored as well. The restore process allows you to restore your computer without losing recently added items, such as documents, Internet Favorites, e-mail messages, or your

Internet History files. For more information on the benefits of the System Restore feature and to learn additional techniques for how to use it, read Chapter 16.

Use REGEDT32 to Back Up and Restore Selected Parts of the Registry

If you need to back up a section of the Registry, such as a set of keys that you are planning to change, you can use the REGEDT32 tool. This tool provides a handy export and import capability so that you can back up parts of the Registry that you first select.

To back up sections of the Registry, follow these steps:

1. Click Start and then Run and type in REGEDT32.EXE.

2. Locate the top-level set of keys that you wish to save. Remember that you can navigate through the Registry keys as if they were a set of folders. When you find the top-level key you want, click on it to highlight it.

3. Click My Computer to select it, and choose Export from the File menu.

4. Select the Selected Branch button in the Export Range section of the window, as shown in Figure 9-6.

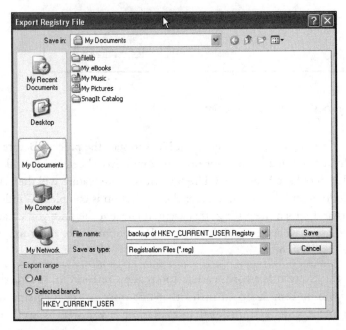

Figure 9-6
Exporting a section of the Registry using REGEDT32.

5. Type in the name for the file and browse to a place to save it. In our example, we are saving the set of keys and their associated values that are assigned to the HKEY_CURRENT_USER section or hive.

6. Click Save to create the backup file.

To later restore the section of the Registry that you saved, follow these steps:

7. Click Start and then Run and then type in REGEDT32.EXE.

8. Locate the top-level set of keys that you wish to restore. When you find the top-level key you want, click on it to highlight it.

9. Click My Computer to select it, and choose import from the File menu.

10. Select the file that you created to store your backup data and click the Open button.

Clean the Registry

Because the Registry is like the central control system of your computer, whenever you install, uninstall, or reinstall software, changes will be made to the Registry keys. Usually the programs you install and uninstall will do a good job of setting themselves up and cleaning up after themselves; however, not all programs work with the Registry properly. Some applications simply don't remove all traces of themselves when you uninstall them. In addition, you might have programs that you simply deleted from your computer without running the proper uninstall procedures. (Now you know why you should not just delete a program by placing it in the trash. You actually need to run its associated uninstall program.)

Over time, the Registry can get gunked up, and this can cause problems such as these for your computer:

- You computer may boot very slowly.
- Your programs may not launch properly.
- Your computer could crash unexpectedly.
- Your programs might have problems performing some operations, such as saving files to the proper directories, launching properly with the correct settings, and so on.

The more you do on your computer (if you install and remove lots of programs, for example), the more cluttered and bloated the Registry can become. In fact, if you followed the instructions in Chapter 4 and removed the extra programs that you don't need, it's likely that you've contributed to the clutter in the Registry. But help is on the way! By using a few carefully chosen products, we can clean up your Registry so it won't bog down your computer.

Use Registry Cleaning Software

Cleaning the Registry manually can an enormous task. As you learned earlier in this chapter, there are hundreds of keys to work with and potentially clean up. You could really damage the Registry if you are not really careful (or if you don't know what you are doing). A better way to clean the Registry is to use a third-party Windows Registry cleaning tool. There are many to choose from, which is both good news and bad news. Table 9-2 lists some of the commercial tools that are available.

Table 9-2   Tools that can be used to clean the Registry

Tool	Estimated Cost	Description
Norton SystemWorks	$70	Full-featured set of utilities that include a tool for cleaning the Registry.
Registry Clean Pro	$29.95	A safe utility that specializes in fixing errors and optimizing the performance of the Registry.
Registry Mechanic	$19.99	A program that allows you to safely clean and repair Windows Registry problems with a few simple mouse clicks.
Registry First Aid	$21.00	This tool is covered in Chapter 13.

In this chapter, we'll be using the Registry Clean Pro utility because it is easy to use, it provides a safe way to clean the Registry, and the company provides a free trial version that you can use for 30 days. Registry Clean Pro is safe because it never deletes a Registry key if this action could harm your computer. It also automatically creates a backup file before it removes any entries from the Registry. To clean the Registry, this utility scans all of your hard drives for the files and folders you have. It then scans the Registry to match up the files you have on your hard drives with the entries stored in the Registry. Its goal is to search out the Registry entries that are no longer valid and delete them. It can also produce a descriptive report that shows you the invalid Registry entries that Registry Clean Pro locates.

Here's how to clean the Registry with Registry Clean Pro:

1. Download and install the trial version of Registry Clean Pro from the company's Web site (**www.registry-clean.com**). You can also purchase the full version of the utility for $29.95 from the Web site. The trial version of the software does a good job; however, there are a few sections of the Registry that it doesn't clean out, including the file extensions and COM/ActiveX sections.

2. Run the program, and the startup screen shown in Figure 9-7 appears.

3. Select the Clean the Registry option and click Next.

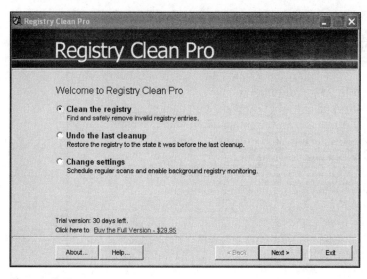

Figure 9-7
The startup screen for Registry Clean Pro.

4. Select the Full Scan option and click Next. Registry Clean Pro will warn you to close all open applications that you have running. This is crucial because some programs may try to access the Registry during the scanning process.

5. Once you have closed all open applications, click Next to start the scan. Registry Clean Pro will then take a few minutes to scan your hard drives and the Registry. It will create a list of the invalid entries that it finds.

6. After Registry Clean Pro completes its scan, it will display a screen listing the total number of invalid entries that it locates. At this point, you can instruct the program to clean the Registry automatically or display the list of errors found. We suggest you first review the list of errors before you start the actual cleaning process.

7. Select the Display The List Of Errors option and click Next.

8. Registry Clean Pro will then display a screen showing the errors found. You can sort this view by description by selecting the Description option in the Show As drop-down box. Figure 9-8 shows an example of the descriptive list. We recommend that you scan through the list of errors and make sure you don't see any you want to keep in the Registry. If you desire, you can unselect an entry.

9. After you have scanned the set of errors, click the Next button to return to the main scanning screen. Select the Clean The Registry option and click Next. Registry Clean Pro will then remove the invalid entries that it found.

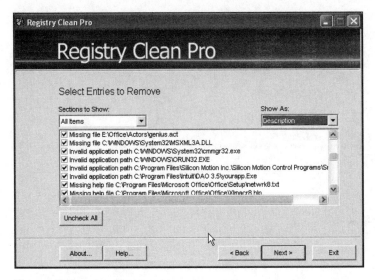

Figure 9-8
Viewing the errors found in a descriptive format from a Registry scan.

TIP: If you perform a Registry clean operation with Registry Clean Pro and you later decide you want to undo the cleaning operation, select the Undo The Last Cleanup option from the main screen and click Next. The Registry will then be fully restored to the state it was in before the last cleanup.

The following sections of the Registry will be cleaned by Registry Clean Pro:

- Startup
- Shared DLLs
- Fonts
- Application info
- Shared files
- Help files
- Most recently used list
- File extensions
- COM/ActiveX

Use Microsoft's RegClean to Clean the Registry in Windows 95/98/NT or Windows 2000

A few years back, Microsoft created a utility called RegClean.exe to help Windows 95/98/NT and Windows 2000 users clean the Registry. Unfortunately, this tool does not work with Windows XP. As you might have guessed, RegClean is an older program and Microsoft no longer distributes it. It is, however, a free program and does a good job of performing a basic clean operation of Windows 95, 98, NT, and Windows 2000 registries.

Tweak the Registry

Now that you've learned the basics of how to use the Registry and how to clean it with an automated tool, let's look at some changes you can make to it manually to improve the performance of your PC. The tweaks we'll make can also help you with some of your degunking chores. As we discussed earlier, it is very important that you back up the Registry before you make any changes to it. This is especially important if you make manual changes. The tweaks that we are introducing here are very simple ones and should not harm your Registry; however, you should always exercise caution.

TIP: We also recommend that you make only one change to the Registry at a time. After you make the change, you should restart Windows and make sure that the change you made produces the effect you want. When it comes to tweaking the Registry, don't try to be too ambitious. Simple and slow is the best policy.

There are many different types of tweaks that you can perform to enhance the workings of your PC. For example, you can improve the appearance of your Desktop and display, make changes to the Start menu and Taskbar, improve how critical applications such as Windows Explorer operate, and much more. For this chapter, we'll focus on some simple tweaks that can help you with your degunking chores. If you want to learn more about how to safely tweak and optimize the Registry, a good site to explore is **www.winguides.com/registry.**

GunkBuster's Notebook: Editing Values in the Registry

As you start to change values in the Registry to perform different system tweaks, you'll quickly encounter the different types of data that are stored there. To make a Registry change, you'll need to understand the basics of data types. A data type essentially specifies the data format of the value stored for a setting. The following list includes some of the more common data types that are stored in the Registry:

- **REG_SZ** This data type is used to store text strings such as "Yes," "No," "filename," and so on.

- **REG_DWORD** This data type stores numerical data in hexadecimal or decimal format.

- **REG_BINARY** This data type stores binary data (0 or 1 values).

- **REG_EXPAND_SZ** This data type stores variables in string data format. The variables are replaced by applications.

- **REG_MULTI_SZ** This data type is used for lists or multiple values.

When you work with the Registry, you can easily determine the data type for a value that you want to view or change. Once you select a Registry key to view, as shown in Figure 9-9, you'll see three attributes displayed for each value in the viewing pane: Name, Type, and Data. The Name attribute provides the name of the value or setting that you can view and change. The Type attribute specifies the data type for the value. If you examine Figure 9-9, you'll notice that most of the data types for the values listed are REG_DWORD, which indicates they store a numeric value. Finally, the Data attribute shows the actual data value that is assigned to the setting.

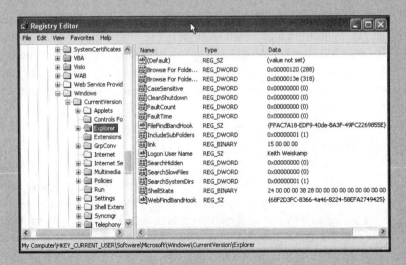

Figure 9-9

Viewing data types for Registry values.

To edit the data value for a setting, double-click the name of the setting. Figure 9-10 shows an example of the Edit Value dialog box that appears. In this example, we are editing the FaultTime setting. The value for this setting is entered in the Value Data field. Notice that it currently has a value of 0. Because this setting has a data type of double, you must enter a numeric value.

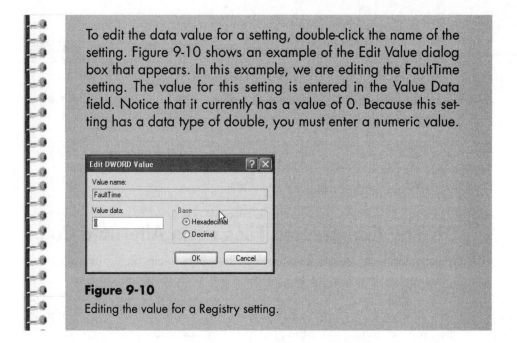

Figure 9-10
Editing the value for a Registry setting.

Turn My Documents Into a Cascading Folder

If you've been following our advice earlier in this book to better organize your My Documents folder by creating subfolders within it, you probably have a number of folders stored within My Documents. Using the Registry, you can easily turn My Documents into a cascading folder, which will then allow you to easily access the subfolders. The best part is that you won't have to first open the My Documents folder to get to your subfolders. This might encourage you to keep your personal data better organized because you'll easily be able to get at the folders stored inside My Documents.

Here's how to make My Documents a cascading folder:

1. Choose Run from the Start menu and type in REGEDT32.EXE.
2. Locate and open the key HKEY_CURRENT_USER\Software\Microsoft\ Windows\CurrentVersion\Explorer\Advanced.
3. Within this key or folder, you will find values, or settings, that control different settings for Explorer. Locate the one named CascadeMyDocuments. (If this value is not available, you will need to create one, which we'll explain in step 5.)
4. If the CascadeMyDocuments value is present, double-click it. Change the value to Yes.

5. If the CascadeMyDocuments value is not present, right-click inside the window view pane where the values are listed and select New | String Value. A new string value will be created with a default name. You can then rename it CascadeMyDocuments and assign it the value Yes as shown in step 4.

6. Quit the Registry editor and restart Windows in order for this change to take effect.

TIP: You can also set up your My Pictures folder as a cascading folder on the Desktop by following the preceding instructions, but this time, you add the string value "CascadeMyPictures" and assign it the value Yes.

Display Compressed Files in an Alternate Color

If you receive numerous compressed files, such as zip files, you might have difficulty cleaning them up from your folders because they might blend in with all the other files. Once you uncompress a compressed file, you likely won't need to keep the compressed file around. By eliminating unused compressed files, you can really reduce the gunk on your machine.

Fortunately, you can use the Registry to tweak Windows Explorer so that compressed files and folders will be displayed in an alternate color. This tweak involves a two-step process. First you must "turn on" the alternate color feature, and then you need to assign a new color (if you don't want to use the default color of blue):

1. Choose Run from the Start menu and type in REGEDT32.EXE.

2. Locate and open the key HKEY_CURRENT_USER\Software\Microsoft_Windows\CurrentVersion\Explorer.

3. Locate the value named ShowCompColor. This value is a DWORD value. (If this value is not available, you will need to create it.)

4. Set the value to 1 to enable the use of alternate colors. (The value 0 is used to apply default colors.) When this setting is turned on, the default color used will be blue.

5. If you want to use a color other than blue, create a new binary value named AltColor and set it to equal the hexadecimal RGB color value you want to use.

6. Quit the Registry editor and restart Windows in order for this change to take effect.

By highlighting unused compressed files, it will be easier to see the files you've uncompressed. If you regularly delete uncompressed files (after you've saved the components under their separate file names), you won't have a lot of gunk accumulating in this folder.

Display Hidden Files with Explorer

As you are using Windows Explorer to locate files to delete as part of the degunking process, you may need to view the hidden files. You can easily use the Registry to tweak Windows Explorer so that it always displays hidden files by default. Here are the steps to follow:

1. Choose Run from the Start menu and type in REGEDT32.EXE.

2. Locate and open the key HKEY_CURRENT_USER\Software\Microsoft_ Windows\CurrentVersion\Explorer/Advanced.

3. Locate the value named Hidden. This value is a DWORD value.

4. Set the value to 1 to enable the viewing of hidden files. (The value 2 is used to disable the viewing of hidden files.)

5. Quit the Registry editor and restart Windows in order for this change to take effect.

You can also view the hidden system-level operating system files with Windows Explorer by setting a different value in the Registry:

1. Locate and open the key HKEY_CURRENT_USER\Software\Microsoft_ Windows\CurrentVersion\Explorer/Advanced.

2. Set the value SuperHidden to 1 to show all hidden system files. (A value of 0 will hide system files.)

Once all of your personal files and folders (as well as system files) have been unhidden, you'll be able to see everything that is stored in your various folders. Hidden files can add more gunk to your hard drive because you won't know they are there and they will likely never be removed. Out-of-sight is not always the best policy when it comes to degunking.

Remove All Icons from Your Desktop

You can remove all icons from the Desktop if you desire. This is a good way to really clean off your Desktop. It involves another Registry tweak, so make sure you back up the system before you begin.

To clear the Desktop of icons, follow these steps:

1. Choose Run from the Start menu and type in REGEDT32.EXE.

2. Locate and open the key named HKEY_CURRENT_USER\Software_ Microsoft\Windows\CurrentVersion\Policies\Explorer.

3. Locate the NoDesktop value and double-click it. (If this value is not present, you will need to create it.)

4. Change the value to 1.

5. Quit the Registry editor and restart Windows in order for this change to take effect.

Summing Up

Cleaning your Registry can be an important part of the degunking process. And the best part is that you can use a safe third-party utility, such as Registry Clean Pro, to clean your Registry on a regular basis. But as you would before you make any changes to the Registry, make sure that you back it up first. With a clean Registry, Windows will function much more efficiently and you'll find that Windows and your various applications will load quicker. After you clean the Registry, you also might find that certain problems that you have been encountering with your computer go away. In addition to cleaning the Registry, you can perform a variety of Registry tweaks to help you improve the performance of your computer and the degunking process.

Optimizing Your Hard Drive and Startup System

Degunking Checklist:

√ Convert your file system to NTFS for better performance and security.

√ Resize hard drive partitions using third-party utilities to make more room for your applications.

√ Accelerate the boot process by cleaning up the Startup folder, tweaking the BIOS, and logging on automatically.

√ Use third-party utilities to enhance the boot-up process.

√ Use system utilities like Dr. Watson, Network Diagnostics, and others to find problems and optimize performance.

√ Get rid of unsigned files and drivers to speed up the boot process and your drive in general.

√ Configure System Properties to enhance system performance.

Your hard drive must be optimized for you to get the most out of your computer. We've done a little of that by deleting unnecessary files and programs, running Disk Cleanup, and running Disk Defragmenter. However, there are other things you can do to enhance your hard drive's performance. We call this "advanced degunking," and it includes using NTFS, configuring the startup options, using system diagnostic tools, and tweaking System Properties for enhancing system performance.

Use NTFS

Whether you are using Windows XP Home or Professional, NTFS (NT File System) is the recommended file system. If you aren't familiar with file systems, you have the option of choosing between three: NTFS, FAT (short for file allocation table), and FAT32. NTFS is the most powerful of the three because it offers enhanced security features, including file encryption, and disk quotas. It also works better with large disks than other file system configurations. With NTFS, you can maintain control of the files and folders on your system and protect them from being viewed by other users on your computer. With FAT32, all users have access to all files on the hard drive regardless of their account type. If you share a computer, NTFS is certainly necessary.

It's easy to find out what file system you use and convert if necessary. Once you convert to NTFS, though, you can't covert back without reformatting the drive, so make sure you won't need to. The only reasons to keep a FAT or FAT32 file system is if you dual-boot with an earlier operating system like Windows 98 or Windows NT 4.0. Most earlier versions of Windows cannot access an NTFS partition. If you aren't dual-booting, you're good to go with NTFS.

Converting to NTFS

You can find out if you have drives formatted with NTFS by using the Control Panel. Open Administrative Tools (click Performance And Maintenance if you're using the default theme), open Computer Management, and click Disk Management. The Disk Management console is shown in Figure 10-1.

Converting to NTFS is done from a command prompt:

1. Click Start, point to All Programs, point to Accessories, and click Command Prompt.

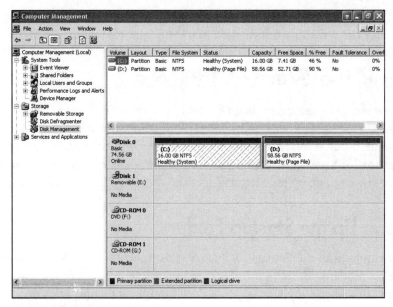

Figure 10-1

What file system does your computer use? If your screen shows that NTFS is enabled and the status is "Healthy (System)," then you don't need to do anything else.

2. Type convert *drive_letter*. /fs:ntfs. Press Enter. For example, to convert the C: drive, type the following:

    convert C: /fs:ntfs.

    If the drive is already formatted as NTFS, your screen will say "Drive C: is already NTFS."

3. Reboot as prompted.

Resize Your Partitions

You might have noticed in Figure 10-1 that there are two partitions created on a single hard drive. C: contains the system files, and D: contains data. The C: partition is usually quite small compared to the D: partition. If you've installed lots of applications, games, service packs, updates, and other necessary items on this partition, you might be running a little low on disk space here.

If you want to enlarge the space given to the C: partition, you'll have to purchase a third-party utility like Partition Magic. Partition Magic and programs like it can be purchased online or at your local computer store. Once the program is installed, you'll have the option to drag using graphical partition windows to increase or decrease the size of the partitions. Having the freedom to resize partitions on the fly is quite powerful. By increasing the space for the system partition, you can increase performance.

Degunk the Startup Process

Does it seem like the time it takes for your Windows XP machine to boot up is longer than it used to be? It probably is. By the time your office suite, anti-virus program, music software, drivers, Internet connection firewall, and all of your programs load, you've booted a lot of software! You can speed up the boot process by cleaning up the Startup folder and deciding what starts automatically.

Clean Up the Startup Folder

The programs in the Startup folder start automatically when Windows starts. The more items you have in there, the longer the boot up process will take. Figure 10-2 shows my Startup folder. You'll notice it's empty. We don't like to sit around and wait when our computers boot!

By default, many programs place themselves in the Startup folder and thus start automatically at boot up. The sad thing is that you probably don't even need these programs. You can remove them from the boot-up process by using the

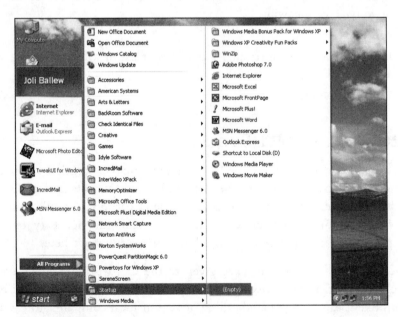

Figure 10-2
An empty Startup folder accelerates the boot up process.

Start Menu Properties dialog boxes or simply by right-clicking, which we'll do next. However, many programs that aren't listed in the Startup folder start automatically. We discussed those programs in Chapter 4, and used msconfig.exe at the Run line to open the System Configuration Utility to tell XP not to start them. Refer to Chapter 6 if you skipped that part.

For items you see in the Startup folder and no longer want to start automatically, remove them by following these steps:

1. Click Start, point to All Programs, point to Startup, and take a look at the entries.

2. To delete an entry, right-click and choose Delete. This will not delete the program; it will only remove the shortcut from the Startup folder.

TIP: To add entries to the Startup folder, simply drag and drop them there. If you drag and drop an EXE file, the program will start automatically. You can test it by moving Notepad there; on boot up, Notepad will open automatically.

You should notice a change already in how fast the computer boots once the Startup folder is cleaned up. Next, we'll clean up the boot process even more.

Clean Up the Boot Process

There are lots of other ways to clean up the boot process to make it faster. Some, like enabling Quick Boot in your BIOS, have their downsides, and I'm not going to mention them here. There are specific tests your computer really needs to run, and I'm all for letting the boot-up process take two or three more seconds rather than disable important system checks. Our goal is to degunk our machines as much as possible, but we also want to do this safely. There are a few things you can do that might not hurt, like skipping the floppy drive search (a second or two), disabling boot delays, logging on automatically, and disabling unnecessary services.

Tell the BIOS to Skip the Floppy Drive Search

Chances are good that your computer spends a few seconds looking to the floppy disk drive for operating system files when it boots. This might not be necessary if you have a fairly new computer and can boot to a CD (if booting to the hard drive fails). To change this default setting, you'll have to enter the BIOS.

While entering the BIOS might seem like a simple task (just press the right key combination or the correct function key at the right time during boot up), it isn't always that easy. Some computer manufacturers would rather you not be messing around in there and don't make it that easy to find. We remember one computer we had required that we wait until the blinking dash appeared in the top-right corner of the splash screen, and then we had to hold down the F3 key (while touching a nose with a left index finger). If you did that at the wrong time, no BIOS!

If you don't know your key combination and it isn't listed at boot up, try pressing F1, F2, F3, or similar keys at the splash screen. If that doesn't work, you might have to visit the Web site of your computer maker and search through their knowledge base. Once you can access your BIOS, walk through the pages using the arrow keys and change or disable the floppy drive search option at boot up.

TIP: Before getting too involved in changing advanced features of your BIOS, back it up. There are several third-party utilities available for this purpose, including Bios1.35.1 from www.bioscentral.com.

Don't Configure a Boot Delay

If you have a boot delay configured and you don't have a dual-boot system, you're just wasting time! Do this to find out if you have a boot delay:

1. Open the Control Panel (click Performance And Maintenance if you're using the default theme), and then open System.
2. Click the Advanced tab.
3. Under Startup And Recovery, click Settings.
4. Change the Time To Display List Of Operating Systems field to 0 seconds. Click OK twice to close out the dialog boxes.

Log On Automatically

If you are the only user of your computer, and if the computer is in a safe environment, you can configure Windows XP to log you on automatically, without using the Welcome screen and without using the standard Log On To Windows dialog box. Be warned, though, each time the computer boots up, your account will open automatically!

Here's how to configure automatic logon:

1. Click Start, and click Run.
2. Type control userpasswords2, and click OK.
3. Verify that the box called Users Must Enter A User Name And Password To Use This Computer is checked, and then select the account that you want to configure as the primary logon. See Figure 10-3.

Figure 10-3
Enable Automatic Logon.

4. Next, remove the check from Users Must Enter A User Name And Password To Use This Computer and click OK. Confirm your password and click OK.

One of our computers is configured for automatic logon, but only one person uses it, and there are few guests. However, when guests do arrive, auto logon is disabled and the Guest account is enabled, just to be safe.

Use the System Configuration Utility to Speed Up the Boot Process

In Chapter 6, we used the System Configuration Utility to disable unwanted programs that start automatically and store themselves in the System Tray. (Typing msconfig.exe at the Run prompt opens the System Configuration Utility.) By disabling unwanted programs, you can make the boot process a bit faster. There are other options that can be configured using this utility to enhance your computer's performance.

Generally, the System Configuration Utility is used as a diagnostic tool to uncover and repair boot problems. It allows you to check and uncheck items like drivers, services, startup programs, and to see which other items are the culprit for the particular problem you are having. In our case, though, we simply want to enhance the boot process, so we'll concentrate on that for now. The following list includes some of the useful degunking/souped-up tasks you can perform:

- Remove unwanted boot paths: When your system boots, Windows will search specified directories (boot paths) to look for files that it might need. Over time, various boot paths might get set up that you no longer need. These unnecessary boot paths can be acquired when Windows is reinstalled or if a reinstallation fails, or if you copy or delete partitions. The fewer places that Windows needs to search when it boots, the better.

- Remove programs that aren't required at boot up: These are located under the Startup tab. We talked about this in Chapter 6.

- Remove services you no longer need: Services are located under the Services tab; there will be more on what services you can uncheck later in this section.

To perform one or more of these tasks, open the System Configuration Utility by typing msconfig.exe in the Run dialog box. Then verify, check, delete, and uncheck the following items as they pertain to your system and needs:

- From the Boot.ini tab, click Check All Boot Paths. If you see a boot path that is no longer needed, you'll be prompted to remove it from the Boot.ini file.

- From the General tab, Selective Startup should already be selected and Load Startup Items should be filled in with a square. If the General tab does not look like the one shown in Figure 10-4, select Selective Startup, click the Startup tab, and uncheck programs you know are not needed at boot up. Refer to Chapter 6 for more help on this.

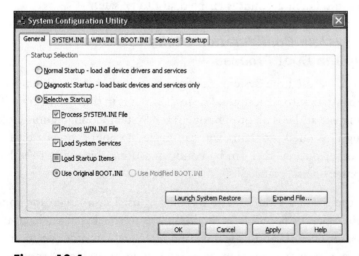

Figure 10-4
Use Selective Startup to tell Windows how to boot.

- Click the Services tab and sort the services by clicking Essential. Make sure that Hide All Microsoft Services is not checked. If a service is essential, you'll see the word "Yes" in the Essential column. You'll notice right off that many of the services *aren't* essential, including Fast User Switching Compatibility, Help And Support, Messenger, Smart Card, Task Scheduler, and items that came preinstalled on your computer, like a Media Music Server or programs you installed yourself. If you decide that you never use Help And Support, Task Scheduler, and smart cards to log on, you can uncheck these items. Don't uncheck anything that you don't recognize or can't find information about in the Help files though. For instance, don't uncheck DNS Client, DHCP Client, or Internet Connection Firewall or your Internet adventures will be greatly affected.

- From the Services tab, you can view the services in one of two ways. To view all services, leave Hide All Microsoft Services unchecked; to view only third-party services check Hide All Microsoft Services. Many of these services are certainly not needed. Leave checked anything that has your anti-virus program's name listed in it, and don't uncheck anything you don't recognize, but certainly uncheck things you don't need. I unchecked several here, including VAIO Media Music Server (Application), VAIO Media Music Server (HTTP), and VAIO Media Music Server (UpnP). We know we don't need any of these things. Uncheck what you deem unnecessary (nothing essential) and reboot.

***TIP:** Keep in mind that you can always go back and recheck anything you've disabled.*

GunkBuster's Notebook: Finding Performance Utilities on the Internet

You can find a lot of software utilities on the Internet that are either free or really inexpensive and can be used to improve the performance of your system. To see just how many there are, type *Freeware Shareware Windows XP Performance* into your favorite search engine. My most recent search yielded almost 45,000 hits!

There are applications that claim to speed up the boot process, clean the Registry, "heal" the Registry, maintain peak performance automatically, optimize Windows, tune up Windows, edit partitions, and more. Be careful when you select, download, install, and/or purchase this software! Some of the code might not have been written by the most experienced programmers, some might contain spyware or adware, some might enable pop-ups or annoy you with a registration dialog for the rest of your life, or, worse, they might even crash your computer.

Before downloading and installing anything, visit various sites and compare notes. You'll be able to find reviews on the latest freeware and shareware in a number of places, including reputable sites like **www.winfiles.com**, **www.pcworld.com** and **http://download.com**. Read the reviews first!

View Errors with Dr. Watson

If you are having unknown problems with your computer and you think you might be having some internal issues, you can check Dr. Watson's log for details. If you see a lot of errors in there, you might consider calling Microsoft tech support, doing a repair installation, or disabling incompatible software or drivers. Dr. Watson is a well-hidden feature of Windows XP, but it can be easily opened from the Run line. If you don't have any errors listed, you can be pretty sure that Windows XP is running well and has no internal errors.

Running Dr. Watson (Drwtsn32.exe)

Click Start, click Run, and type Drwtsn32.exe in the Run dialog box. Then click OK to start the program. You'll see a screen like the one shown in Figure 10-5. Notice that I'm having problems with Outlook Express; it shuts down on me from time to time, usually when I'm trying to do too many things at once, like sending an e-mail from a floppy disk, or composing an e-mail while receiving e-mail simultaneously. This is probably just too much for my poor little 128 MB computer to handle!

You can view error logs by clicking the application error and clicking View. This information can be helpful when trying to solve a particular problem with a qualified tech support person. In fact, if you call tech support and say that Dr. Watson has determined that you're having problems with Outlook Express, you'll be one step ahead of the game!

Get Rid of Unsigned Files and Drivers

Signed device drivers and files have been tested by Microsoft and are deemed safe and compatible. Those that are not signed might not be safe and might not be compatible. Unsigned device drivers and files associated with incompatible software is another area that can cause a computer to have a slow boot process, have a slow reaction time, or generally have unexpected performance errors

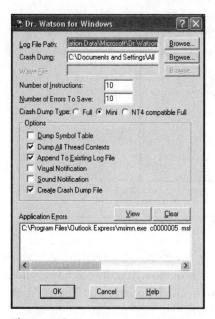

Figure 10-5
Dr. Watson is a hidden diagnostic tool.

(like blue screens). This incompatibility can cause major problems, including unexpected shutdowns of applications, hardware that sometimes works and sometimes doesn't, hard-to-diagnose problems with the shutdown process, including the inability of the computer to shut down at all, and even blue screens and memory dumps.

You can see what files (including drivers) are installed on your system that are not signed using the File Signature Verification utility, and you can do a little preventive maintenance by telling Windows you don't want to ever install unsigned drivers once these are uninstalled or updated.

Using File Signature Verification

Here are the steps to follow to scan for files and programs that do not have valid digital signatures:

1. At the Run line, type Sigverif.exe and click OK. You'll see the File Signature Verification dialog box shown in Figure 10-6.

2. Click Advanced and notice that the box called Notify Me If Any System Files Are Not Signed is checked. You'll run the utility twice, once with this checked and once with Look For Other Files That Are Not Digitally Signed checked.

3. Click OK and then click the Start button to have Windows look for files that do not have valid digital signatures.

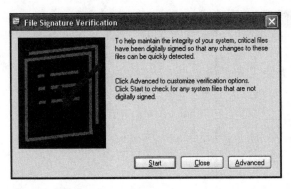

Figure 10-6
Use the File Signature Verification utility to search for unsigned files.

Once the scan is complete, you'll see a report similar to the one shown in Figure 10-7. Sort by file type to view programs that do not have valid signatures. These programs *can* cause system instability, but that doesn't mean that they do. You don't have to go crazy here spending hours researching what each little DLL file does and what program it belongs to. However, if, after reading this section, you believe that you recently installed a new component with an unsigned driver and now you've noticed some system problems, consider searching for and installing a new driver for that device. In addition, if you have several unsigned printer files and you no longer own the printer, see what you can do about uninstalling that software (see Chapter 4). Use this tool as a basis to find out what is unsigned. Consider uninstalling third-party applications that aren't signed and/or reinstalling signed copies of system files.

In this particular list, we can see easily that one of our most recently downloaded and installed tray controls, Trayer.exe, is not signed. Although it hasn't caused any problems, we'll most likely uninstall it. (It could be that the application is signed but the wrong version was downloaded. These are problems we often find on client computers!) You can find out what the many items in this list are simply by typing them into a Web search engine. For instance, typing in *ctregrun.exe* immediately brings up Creative Labs's registration reminder. This can obviously be deleted or uninstalled. Check out **www.greatis.com/regrun3useless.htm** for a long list of useless files similar to this one.

TIP: *If you've found software for hardware in this list, you may have also found a problem device. You can disable problem devices in Device Manager, although you might have to choose Show Hidden Devices from the View menu and then disable the device under the Non-Plug And Play Drivers list. You can also use Device Manager to update drivers; this will be introduced shortly.*

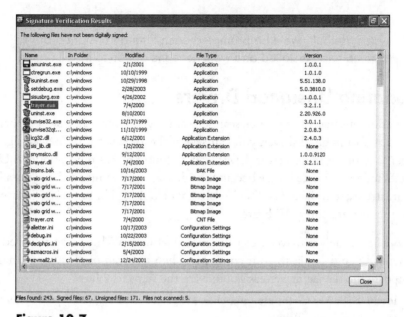

Figure 10-7

Sort files by type, and look for third-party applications that you can uninstall.

Maintenance Sidebar: Set Driver Signing Properties

You can tell Windows to be more careful about installing unsigned drivers from the System Properties dialog box. Open the Control Panel and Performance And Maintenance (if using the XP theme) and click on System. Click the Hardware tab and click Driver Signing. The Driver Signing Options dialog box is shown in Figure 10-8.

Figure 10-8

Configure driver signing options.

> We prefer the Warn setting. With this selected and made the
> system default, we'll be prompted each time an unsigned driver
> is going to be installed and we'll have the option to install or not.

Updating Unsigned Drivers

If you find out that your printer, scanner, camera, or some other piece of hardware has an unsigned driver, you can search the Internet for a newer, signed one. Many times, these newer drivers can be found by running Windows Update. Windows Update is nice because the drivers are downloaded and installed automatically, so it should be the first place you look. Other times you'll have to visit the manufacturer's Web site.

If you find a newer driver from the manufacturer's Web site, you'll need to download it and save it to your computer. Then, you can use Device Manager to update the device driver easily. Here are the steps to follow:

1. Right-click My Computer and click Properties. You can also open System from the Control Panel.

2. In the System Properties dialog box, click the Hardware tab and click Device Manager. (If you notice any items with a red X or a yellow exclamation point, that particular piece of equipment has problems with either the driver or the hardware itself. Double-click on the item to see what the problem is.)

3. Expand the hardware trees, and locate the item you want to update. Double-click it to open the Properties dialog box for that particular item.

4. To update a driver, click the Driver tab, and click Update Driver. Browse to the location of the saved, updated driver and follow the prompts to install it.

TIP: If the new driver doesn't work as planned, use Device Driver Rollback.

In addition to installing a newer driver, you can also disable a device from Device Manager. If you are positive a specific device is lousing up the system and causing performance problems, disable it for a while and see if the problem goes away.

Error Checking

Your hard disk won't run optimally if there are bad sectors on it. Sectors are where data is stored, and if any sectors are damaged and you try to write data to them, you're going to run into problems. To scan for bad sectors on the hard drive, use the error-checking tool in My Computer:

1. Close all running programs, and from the Start menu, click Open My Computer.

2. Right-click the disk you want to check for errors and click Properties.

3. Click the Tools menu, and under Error-Checking, click Check Now.

4. In the Check Disk dialog box, shown in Figure 10-9, check Automatically Fix File System Errors and Scan For And Attempt Recovery Of Bad Sectors. Click Start.

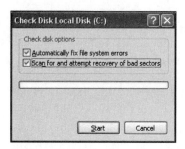

Figure 10-9
Let Windows perform error checking of your hard drive and file system.

5. You'll most likely be prompted to restart Windows and let the error checking run on reboot. Click Yes to reboot, and then click OK.

After the computer boots up, the CHKDSK utility will run. Wait while Windows finds and fixes the hard disk problems. This might take a while, and your computer will be unavailable during this process.

Summing Up

The main idea behind optimizing the hard drive is to get XP to boot faster, to get it to run faster, and to enhance the general performance of the computer. Some things that can make the boot process faster include cleaning up the Startup folder, modifying the BIOS so the floppy disk isn't accessed for startup files, logging on automatically, and disabling any boot delay currently configured.

Once booted, your computer's performance can be enhanced by using NTFS, being aware of system errors and fixing them, detecting errors caused by unsigned device drivers or incompatible hardware, and finding physical problems with the hard drive itself. By repairing existing problems and configuring XP to run efficiently, you can improve performance dramatically.

Installing Upgrades for Your System

Degunking Checklist:

√ Use Windows Update to get up-to-date and stay up-to-date.

√ Enhance performance and security with the latest security patches, critical updates, Windows updates, and driver updates.

√ Learn what updates you can do without.

√ Keep your computer safe and sound with the latest service packs.

√ Enhance the capabilities of your computer by upgrading from Windows XP Home to Windows XP Professional.

√ Enhance media output and performance by upgrading to Media Player 9 and Movie Maker 2.

√ Use instant messaging more efficiently (and have more fun) using MSN 6.1.

You can get more out of your computer—including better performance, better security, and enhanced media capabilities—in a number of ways. You know already that you can clean up the computer, do routine maintenance, stop unnecessary programs and services from running, and tweak XP to your heart's content. But it's also important to maintain and increase the security of your computer by staying up-to-date with Windows Update by configuring it to work automatically.

With Windows Update, you can enhance performance and security by downloading and installing critical patches, updated drivers, and operating system updates. Service packs are critical, too, and it's extremely important to download and install them when they're available. Of course, not all updates apply to all computers or configurations, so in this chapter, you'll also learn how to distinguish between what you do need and what you don't in the way of updates. By understanding the difference, you can keep your computer as gunk free as possible.

In addition to updates, you can also get *upgrades.* If you run Windows XP Home Edition, you can access XP's business-level features by upgrading from XP Home to XP Professional. No matter what edition of XP you run, though, you can enhance performance of some specific components by upgrading your software. You can also enhance performance for applications like Movie Maker or Windows Media Player by upgrading them to their newer versions. If you use Movie Maker or Media Player, these free upgrades are must-haves. (If you don't use these features at all, don't gunk up your computer by installing them!)

Use Windows Update to Stay Up-to-Date

Windows Update is the easiest and most efficient way to keep your computer safe and sound and up-to-date. Windows Update is Microsoft's way of making available all of the security patches, fixes, driver updates, software updates, and other important items that your computer needs to stay in good working order. It's extremely important that you either visit Windows Update regularly or configure XP to visit on its own, in the background.

Keeping your computer updated with security patches, service packs, and critical updates is crucial to maintaining a well-running, high-performance, and secure computing environment because without these patches and fixes, your computer is vulnerable to all of the newly found security holes that hackers and attackers have an open door to. These rogues can access your computer remotely (if they know how) and do damage in a number of ways. While some folks are a bit suspicious of the monitoring and downloading process, as you'll learn later, the information collected from your computer is not information that could personally identify you, your e-mail address, or your surfing habits (among other things).

Several types of updates are provided under the following categories: Critical Update And Service Packs, Windows XP, and Driver Updates. Figure 11-1 shows the Windows Update Web site and the updates available for one of our computers. This Web site is available at **http://windowsupdate.Microsoft.com,** and we'll show you how to use it shortly. You'll notice that this system has been kept up-to-date; there are only five Windows XP updates, and many of them are not needed.

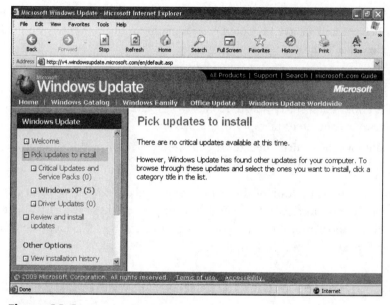

Figure 11-1
The Windows Update Web site is a valuable resource.

In the following sections, you'll learn the various ways to get updates, why they are important, and how to decide if the updates are necessary or not. You'll learn how the updates enhance the security of your computer and why critical updates must be installed if you expect your computer to continue to run smoothly and without problems. You'll also learn how to purchase service packs if you have a slow Internet connection and downloading them would take too long. Finally, you'll learn why critical updates are so important and why they should be installed whenever they are offered.

Updates Enhance the Security of Your Computer

Critical updates are often created to resolve known issues with the operating system. These known issues generally have to do with security holes and vulnerabilities recently discovered. If left unpatched, these vulnerabilities will leave you open to hackers, viruses, worms, and other security threats. These, in turn, can seriously gunk up your computer.

Listed next are a few security vulnerabilities that critical updates have addressed, patched and/or repaired, and if you haven't installed the updates that address these, you're still open to the security risks they cover. Installing these critical updates closes the newly found security holes:

- Without the Cumulative Patch for IE6 SP1 (KB828750), you could visit a Web site and an attacker could run programs on the computer you used to view that Web site.

- Without the security update KB828035, an attacker could compromise the security of your computer by gaining control of it remotely.

- Without the security update KB824105, an attacker could see information in your computer's memory over a network.

- Without the security update KB823718, an attacker could compromise your system and execute code on it.

And these are only four of the many, many updates that have been released! Hopefully this causes you to see just how important these security updates are and how important it is to stay up-to-date. Now that we've convinced you, let's move forward and get those updates.

Get Updates Automatically or Manually

Although you could visit the Windows Update Web site weekly to check for new updates and install them manually, it's much easier to simply configure Windows XP to get them automatically (and in the background) while you're online. If you're online a lot, you should configure Windows Update to automatically check for updates and then notify you if and when updates are available. Then, you can see what updates there are and decide if you need them or not. If you need them, you can install them.

It seems logical that using the automatic settings to download updates would slow down your machine, especially if the updates are downloaded during the day and at the same time that you're trying to download a new screensaver! However, XP's Help And Support files state that the updates will be downloaded in the background and will not interfere with or slow down network activities such as Internet browsing. If you'd like, though (or if you believe you notice slower response time while Windows Update does its thing), you can easily instruct Windows to search for updates late at night (or some other time) when your computer isn't being used. This will let you get the maximum benefit of automatic updates while at the same time avoid any (perceived or real) delays due to the system resources they require.

If you aren't online very much, having XP get the updates automatically won't work for you and you'll have to make it a point to go online once a week or so and check yourself. Staying updated is a fairly common problem for those who use laptops and travel a lot, those with slow Internet connections, or those who simply don't go online very much. Automatic updates might be disabled if you are in a corporate environment, too, and you might simply want to get the updates manually if you have an aversion to things being automatically downloaded to your computer. Whatever the case, staying updated is important, and there's a setting for you.

GunkBuster's Notebook: Yeah, But Is Windows Update Secure?

There's no reason to be concerned about security and Windows Update. Although Windows Update must scan your computer to provide you with the appropriate files, patches, and security updates, it does not collect your name, address, e-mail address, or any other form of personally identifiable information. The information collected is only used during the period of time that you are visiting the Web site, and it is not saved." (This is taken directly from the Windows Update Privacy Statement.)

If you are concerned about what is collected when your computer is scanned, the information it acquires is listed here:

- Operating-system version number

- Internet Explorer version number

- Version numbers of other software

- Plug and Play ID numbers of hardware devices

- Region and language setting

- Product ID and Product Key (As with other information collected, the Product ID and Product Key are not retained beyond the end of the update session, but if the Produce ID is *not valid*, that information *is* retained.)

In addition, the site and transmissions are protected and well maintained, so there's no need to be worried about hackers, viruses, worms, or getting the wrong updates. You can imagine the uproar if the Windows Update site was not secure! So, if you're using a legal copy of Windows (which you should be), if you log on to the Internet frequently, and if you want to get your updates automatically, configuring automatic updates is definitely the way to go.

Get Updates Automatically

Our computers are configured to get updates automatically, and we think it's the best option. Here's how to set it up (or disable it):

1. Right-click the My Computer icon on the Desktop or the Start menu and choose Properties.

2. Click the Automatic Updates tab. This is shown in Figure 11-2.

3. Check Keep My Computer Up To Date. With this setting enabled, Windows Update software may be automatically updated prior to applying any other updates. (Uncheck this option to disable Automatic Updates.)

4. Read through the three settings options. You can be notified before any updates are updated and installed, it can be done automatically, or you can

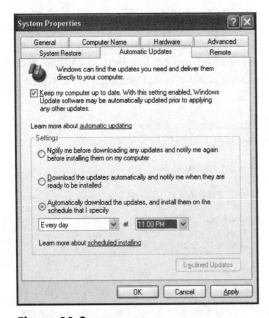

Figure 11-2

Configure Automatic Updates to download and install Windows updates automatically.

schedule when updates should be obtained. Notice in Figure 11-3 that Windows looks for updates at night at 11:00 P.M., so the download won't slow down our Internet connection during the day. Click OK.

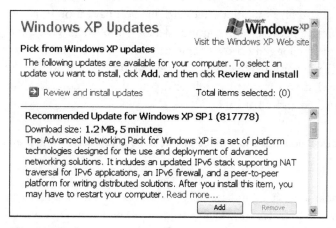

Figure 11-3
Some Windows XP Updates aren't necessary.

Windows will now get the updates automatically, and you'll be better pro-tected and get better performance for it. When using Automatic Updates, you'll be prompted that updates are ready with a pop-up balloon and an icon of the world in the System Tray.

Get Updates Manually

If you need to get Windows updates manually, you don't have to disable Auto-matic Updates unless you just want to. Getting updates manually is easy and you can do it anytime you'd like. To get the updates manually, follow these steps:

1. Click Start, and click Windows Update. You'll be connected to **http:// v4.windowsupdate.Microsoft.com/en/default.asp** if you're in the United States or to your default site in your particular country.

2. Once connected, click Scan For Updates.

The amount of time it takes to get the information depends on the speed of your connection to the Internet. Once the scan is complete, you'll be able to see just how many updates you need and what each update addresses. Read through the following sections to determine what updates you need, and then continue the process to select, download, and install the updates you want.

Critical Updates and Service Packs

Critical updates are just that, critical. You absolutely must download and install them if you want your computer to run efficiently—there's just no getting around it. If you find out after checking that you have 5 or 10 critical updates and/or a service pack, set some time aside, log on to the Internet, and get them manually, or stay logged on overnight and let Windows get them for you. We find that it's much more effective just to let XP do it automatically. You still get to decide what you want to install, and you still have complete control over what is installed and what isn't.

TIP: Install all critical updates and service packs, even if you don't think they apply to you or your system.

Service packs are critical updates. If you find out you need a service pack (SP1 is out now and SP2 will be available mid-2004) and you don't want to wait for it to be downloaded, you can purchase the service pack on disk. Visit **www.microsoft.com/WindowsXP/pro/downloads/servicepacks/sp1/ ordercd.asp** or call 1-800-360-7561 for more information. It's only $9.95 U.S., and each service pack contains the critical updates you're also missing. If you've got $9.95 U.S., this is a great option because you'll always have it in case you switch computers or have to perform a reinstallation.

Other Updates

Other updates that you should consider include Windows XP and driver updates. The Windows XP updates are updates and fixes for the operating system itself and can include fixes for bugs in the system, updates to service packs, and updates to components like Media Player or Movie Maker. Such updates may even include new items as they are available. At the time this book was written, for example, a Windows XP update was available that allows people who do not have a computer running Windows XP Tablet PC Edition to view files that were created in Windows Journal on a Tablet PC. When Windows XP first came out, not nearly as many people had Tablet PCs as they do now; at this juncture, this is a necessary addition to the operating system. (You might have noticed there are Windows XP updates you might not need, like this one for Tablet PC files. Refer to the GunkBuster's Notebook "What Updates Are Really Necessary?" for more information on how to decide what to install.)

We always enjoy running across driver updates with Windows Update. Driver updates will make your computer and attached hardware run better and can include updates for modems, printers, scanners, cameras, BIOS, and any other number of internal or external components. Seeing them on the Windows Update Web site means they're safe, too; so if you have an unsigned driver and are looking for a newer one, look here first! We'd suggest installing all driver updates.

TIP: *You can also increase performance by downloading and installing PowerToys. The best PowerToys I've discovered are detailed in Chapter 14.*

GunkBuster's Notebook: What Updates Are Really Necessary?

As you read the descriptions for some of the available Windows XP updates, you might wonder if all of the updates in this category are really necessary. They aren't, and you'd be right to wonder! You should always read what each Windows XP update contains before installing it. If you are getting the updates manually from the Windows Update Web site, the description of the update is included on the Web site. If you are getting an update automatically, click Details in the Automatic Updates dialog box to see what the update involves. Figure 11-3 shows an example of a Windows XP update. This is one we decided not to install because it involves an advanced networking pack for advanced networking solutions—something we don't think we need because we're not planning on writing any "distributed solutions" anytime soon.

You can make similar decisions. In our latest manual XP Update adventure, we found an update for Windows XP SP 1. We think we'll install that one because it's an update for a service pack, which is a security update. However, we see no reason to install the .NET Framework update; it's for developers, and we're not one. It also takes $2\frac{1}{2}$ hours.

If you need some help deciding what to install and what not to, take a few minutes to read the descriptions for each of them. If the update is written specifically for developers (people who write software) and you aren't a developer, there's no need to install the update. If the update is for the Jet 4.0 database engine and you did not install and do not use it, there's no need for this update. Neither of these is defined as a "Recommended Update" anyway, so we can choose not to install them without any repercussions.

If you read the update and it looks like it applies to you or you'd like to be able to access the specific feature addressed, add and install it. Recently we added and installed the Windows Error Reporting: Recommended Update. This enables us to automatically view responses to Windows error reports. After an error occurs, we can immediately view the fix, workaround, or other information; this is quite helpful. We also installed the Recommended Update Q322011, which enables us to use Preview in the Fax Console. If ever in doubt, install all recommended updates and leave the rest alone.

Upgrade to Windows XP Professional

If you want to get more out of Windows XP and you're using Windows XP Home Edition, you might consider upgrading to Windows XP Professional. There's so much more you can do with Professional, and you'll find that your productivity increases right away. Windows XP has business-level features not available in the Home edition, including the following:

- Remote Desktop: Connect to the office computer (also running Windows XP Professional) and work from home. You'll be able to access all of your data and applications just as if you were sitting in front of the computer at the office.

- Offline Files and Folders: Work on network shares while disconnected from the network server, and then synchronize the files when you go back online. You can work on an airplane, in a hotel, or at home.

- Scalable Processor Support: Use dual processors for even faster performance. You can't use dual processors with XP Home.

- File Encryption: Protect sensitive data with encrypted files.

- Better Security: Use access controls to enhance security to files, applications, and resources.

- Domains: Join a domain, configure group policies, and utilize roaming user profiles. These are all corporate-level perks.

- Multi-lingual: Change the user interface language and get localized dialog boxes, menus, proofing tools, help files, and more. This feature is perfect for the multi-language household or small business.

Upgrading from Home to Professional isn't necessary if you don't need any of these extras. However, if you see one you like in the list and you'd like to try it, you'll have to shell out the $150 U.S. or so that it will likely cost you!

Upgrade the Media Applications

The versions of Windows Media Player and Windows Movie Maker that shipped with your copy of Windows XP are likely not the newest versions available. Windows Media Player 9 and Movie Maker 2 are now available, and the downloads are free! Both enhance their respective applications immensely, and you'll notice a major change right away in performance, ease of use, options, components, graphical interface, and features.

Media Player 9

Media Player 9 offers many enhancements over the Media Player included with Windows XP, and if you download it, you'll see major performance improvements. For starters, Media Player 9 drastically improves media playback with always-on streaming. It also offers a 20% improvement of audio quality, variable speed playback, and the first Smart Jukebox. New additions are automatically added to playlists. You can also rate your favorite songs and personalize your music collection in any number of ways.

Before we spend too much time downloading and installing Media Player 9, let's make sure you don't already have it:

1.   Click Start, point to All Programs, and click Windows Media Player.
2.   Click Help, and click About Windows Media Player. If you have any version prior to 9.0, you need to update.

To update Windows Media Player 9 from inside Windows Media Player, click Help and click Check For Player Updates. Follow the instructions for downloading and installing the new version. (Make sure your computer meets the minimum requirements.) For the most part, the upgrade process is automatic.

Tip: You can install Windows Media Player 9 on other machines, too, including Windows 98, Mac OS X, Windows 95 and NT, and more. You can also download, for free, a player specifically designed for a palm size PC, handheld PC, and similar hardware.

Movie Maker 2

Movie Maker 2 offers many enhancements over the Movie Maker included with Windows XP. For starters, Movie Maker 2 has a much-improved graphical user interface, making capturing and editing film and creating movies much easier than with the previous version. It also provides more wizards, transitions, effects, titles, and AutoMovie—all of which make creating your movie easier and much more fun.

Before we spend time downloading and installing Movie Maker 2, let's make sure you don't already have it:

1. Click Start, point to All Programs, point to Accessories, point to Entertainment, and click Windows Movie Maker.

2. Click Help, and click About Windows Movie Maker. In the About Windows Movie Maker dialog box, note what version is installed. The dialog box shown in Figure 11-4 indicates that Movie Maker 2 is installed.

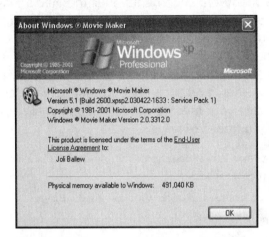

Figure 11-4
See what version of Movie Maker you have.

If you don't have Movie Maker 2, visit **www.Microsoft.com/downloads/**. Type Movie Maker 2 in the Keywords box and press Enter. Browse to the download area and follow the directions for downloading and installing. (Make sure your computer meets the minimum requirements.) For the most part, the process of downloading and installing is automatic.

Upgrade to MSN Messenger 6.1

If you use Windows Messenger to text-message in real time with your friends and family, upgrading to MSN Messenger 6.1 will offer more features than the version of Windows Messenger that came with Windows XP. Although *adding* programs might seem to contradict our whole "degunking" strategy, increasing performance and enhancing ease of use is certainly a major part of making your computer work better.

With MSN Messenger 6.1, you get these improvements:

*   Integrate a Web cam easily.

*   Use new emoticons, backgrounds, and display pictures.

*   Play games with your buddies using the new Messenger launch site.

*   Save conversations.

*   Set alerts for stocks, sales, airfare, shopping, news headlines, weather, and more.

If you're interested, visit **http://messenger.msn.com** for more details and for downloading. Once downloaded, MSN 6.1 acts as a separate program; it is not an upgrade to Windows Messenger. You'll want to tell Windows Messenger you don't want it to start automatically and tell MSN Messenger you want it to start automatically. (You can do that easily from the Tools menu.)

NOTE: *Don't confuse MSN Messenger 6.1 with MSN 8. MSN Messenger 6.1 is a free messaging program and is quite different from MSN 8, an online service that provides features such as parental controls and shared Internet surfing.*

Summing Up

Although degunking generally consists of getting rid of stuff, this chapter focused on improving your system by adding stuff. Windows Update was introduced as an important tool for enhancing security, performance, and overall protection. Critical updates and service packs should always be installed, driver updates are almost always desirable, and Windows XP updates may or may not be needed. Beyond the updates, you learned about upgrades. Windows Professional was introduced, and if you need the business-level features available from XP, you should consider this upgrade.

You also learned that for greatly enhanced performance and ease of use, you should upgrade to Windows Media Player 9 and Movie Maker 2 (if you use these features). MSN Messenger 6.1 offers new productivity tools and more options than Windows Messenger does. Each of these upgrades enhances your computer's performance by offering additional features and better media quality.

The Best Hardware for PC Degunking

Degunking Checklist

√ Purchase and physically install extra RAM (memory) to enhance the performance of your computer.

√ Configure virtual memory settings to fully utilize the memory you have.

√ Add a backup device to perform reliable backups and store them offsite.

√ Add a second (or third) monitor to extend your Desktop and make room for all of your running applications.

√ Physically clean the computer.

√ Purchase a new computer (in case your PC becomes a lost cause) and transfer your files and settings.

T his chapter introduces you to the different types of hardware you can acquire to beef up your system, including RAM and additional monitors. You'll learn how to configure and take care of your existing hardware to get the best possible performance. You'll also learn how having the right hardware can help you with the degunking process. Adding RAM (physical memory) is the way to go if you want faster performance; you'll notice a difference right away. Adding a second monitor can certainly enhance productivity, and installing a backup device can obviously enhance security (if you use it).

Beyond physical hardware though, physically cleaning your machine is a good thing to do occasionally, too; dust and grime can cause problems. You can also tweak how the hard drive stores temporary data when RAM is full by configuring the virtual memory settings. If, however, after all of this you determine that your computer is much too gunked up and you still can't get what you want out of it, you always have the option of purchasing a new one. If that's what you decide to do, you'll want to know all about the Files And Settings Transfer Wizard.

Let's start with the most basic and fundamental way to enhance the performance of your computer—adding memory.

Add Memory

Adding memory is the easiest and fastest way to speed up and improve the response time of your computer. These days, purchasing an extra 128 or 256 MB of RAM won't break the bank. RAM stands for *random access memory*, and it's where XP stores data it needs or thinks it will need to perform a task like print a document, perform a calculation, or receive and open an e-mail. If your computer has 256 MB of RAM or less, you really need to upgrade to at least 512 MB. If you have 512 MB, you'll see a noticeable difference by upgrading as well. If you're into performance, if you play games, or if you do a lot of multitasking between programs, you need to grab as much RAM as you can. My new Sony has three slots that can hold 512 MB each. You might discover you have the same options.

RAM is an important component because it is used for the temporary storage of data and code that you need to perform a task like cropping or recoloring an image, multitasking between programs, and using Copy and Paste. RAM is fast and can be accessed much more quickly than the hard drive. When RAM gets full though, and there's no free space left for storing data temporarily, XP sends data over to the hard drive in an area called a *paging file*. Accessing data from the paging file takes much longer than accessing it from RAM, so if you are low on RAM, you're sure to experience slower response times than you need to.

Physical Installation

So, just how hard is it to purchase and install extra RAM? It isn't difficult at all! These days, you simply figure out what kind of RAM you have, walk into a computer store, and purchase it right off the rack. It used to be much more complicated than this, and you'd have to order directly from the manufacturer or, worse, take your computer to a shop. (Depending on your computer, you might still have to order directly from the manufacturer, but this is fading out quickly.)

The first step involved in adding more RAM is to take a few minutes and determine how much RAM your computer already has. You can do this in a number of different ways, including viewing the My Computer's Properties dialog box or by watching your computer boot up (if this information isn't hidden with a splash page). You can also use a neat little utility called System Information (msinfo32.exe), which can be used to access all kinds of information. Figure 12-1 shows the screen that this utility produces. Notice the trees on the left; each can be expanded to access other information. To view this information, click Start, click Run, and in the Run dialog box, type msinfo32.exe. Click OK.

Once you know how much RAM you have, you can decide if more would be better. In most cases, the answer is yes. There are many types of memory, though, so you'll have to make sure you get the right kind.

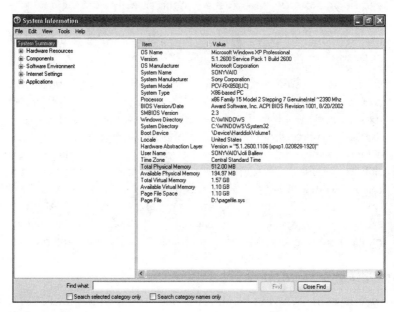

Figure 12-1

Use the System Information utility to find out how much physical RAM is installed, among other things.

Finding the Right Memory for Your Machine

There are lots of kinds of computer memory: SIMMs, DIMMs, PC133, PC2100DDR, PC100, and more. You can't just go out and buy a memory stick; you have to know what kind you need. If you have the information booklet that came with your computer, you can find out what kind of memory you should get by reading the specs page. You can also take the booklet to the store with you and show it to the sales staff. If you purchased a computer from a major manufacturer like Gateway, Hewlett-Packard, Dell, IBM, or Compaq (just to name a few) and you can't find your information booklet, simply call tech support or visit the company's Web site. You'll find the information there.

TIP: *We can't promise this will always work, but in general, typing www.<the company name>.com brings up the company's Web site. For instance, **www.gateway.com**, **www.dell.com**, **www.IBM.com**, and **www.hewlettpackard.com** all link to their respective Web sites. If you can't find the Web sites using this technique, simply search for it on the Web using any Web browser.*

GunkBuster's Notebook: Using the Web to Decipher Your RAM

Many Web sites sell RAM (like **www.crucial.com**). These sites enable you to order the RAM you need directly from the Internet. Just enter into the Web form the type of RAM you want, pony up a credit card number, and wait for it to be delivered. There's no need to even go to the store!

If you aren't sure what kind of memory you need because you own a used computer or simply just don't know, many sites offer a look-up option, where you can type in your computer type and model, motherboard model, and other data to find out. Many sites offer a downloadable tool that will scan your computer and search out the required information. Crucial has a downloadable tool called the Belarc Advisor. We ran it on our system and we were quite impressed. Even if you plan on purchasing your RAM in a store, you can use the automated tools that Web sites like Crucial make available to easily determine the RAM that you will need.

Installation Instructions

Once you have the RAM in hand, you'll need to install it. Your RAM should come with installation instructions, but for the most part, installing RAM is as simple as turning off your computer, unplugging it, locating the slot on the motherboard, and popping in the RAM. Some RAM sticks pop straight in, and some slide in from an angle. Be careful when you install it, though; you don't want to "shock" the board or the RAM stick. Make sure you touch the chassis and that the computer is unplugged before performing any installations. Read the instructions carefully because different memory types install in different ways; however, installing RAM is generally quite simple.

Watch the Boot-Up Process

Once the RAM is installed, you can watch the boot-up process (if your computer doesn't have a splash screen that hides it). Here you'll see the RAM being counted prior to the computer starting. You can also view the new RAM information from My Computer's Properties page or from System Information. You want to make sure your new RAM has been detected properly. If it hasn't, try installing it again, or contact the manufacturer where the memory was obtained for technical support.

Tweak Virtual Memory Settings

When RAM is full, XP sends temporary data and code to an area of the hard drive reserved for such events, and data and code are swapped back and forth as needed. Because it takes longer to access data from the hard drive, you'll obviously want to have as much RAM as you can afford (assuming you are into increasing the performance of your computer)! However, no matter how much RAM you have, the data stored there will eventually be swapped, so you want to make sure that the settings configured for virtual memory are the best they can be.

Virtual memory is the imaginary memory area that makes the computer act like it has more memory (RAM) than it actually does. Virtual memory is implemented using a *paging file* (sometimes referred to as a *swap file),* which is generally located on the C: drive. You can set the size of this file manually if you'd like, or you can accept the defaults. There are two options to change, the initial file size and the maximum file size.

The initial file size box is the area where you provide the number of megabytes for the virtual-memory paging file on the selected drive, and it is where you set the initial (or beginning) size of the file. The maximum size box is the area where you provide the maximum number of megabytes that can be used for the file. The numbers configured here define the size of the paging file. If you want, you can leave your virtual memory settings to whatever Windows suggests, which is about 1.5 times the amount of RAM on the system for the initial size of the file and about 3 times the amount of RAM for the maximum paging file size. However, there are a few tweaks you can make if you desire:

- If you have less than 512 MB of RAM, leave the page file as is, using the default settings.

- If you have lots of RAM, say a gigabyte or more, set the initial page file to about half of the physical RAM and set the maximum size at three times the RAM.

- If you don't have much free hard disk space and upgrading is not feasible, set the initial page file to 2 MB.

- Keep in mind that an extremely large maximum page file does not necessarily increase performance, and may actually hinder it. You don't want to allot too much of the hard drive area to this file.

- Even if you have a gigabyte or so of RAM, don't turn off the page file. Some programs can crash if no virtual memory is available.

If you'd like to tweak the virtual memory settings, here's how you set a custom page file in Windows XP:

1. Right-click My Computer and click Properties.

2. Click the Advanced tab, and under Performance, click Settings.

3. In the Performance Options dialog box, click the Advanced tab.

4. Under Virtual Memory, click Change.

5. Configure the settings as you desire, and click Set. OK your way out of the dialog boxes. See Figure 12-2. If prompted, reboot your computer.

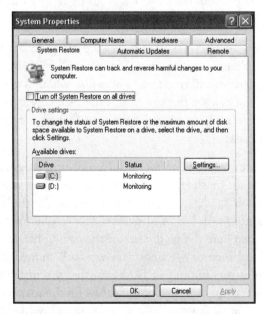

Figure 12-2

Virtual memory settings can be tweaked to enhance performance.

A number of programs are available to help you boost the performance of your machine, including some that will automatically tweak the paging file. Walk into any computer store or search the Internet for *Windows XP performance enhancement software* and you'll find plenty!

TIP: On the Internet, check out www.acceleratedsoftware.net for some great acceleration tools.

Add a Backup Device

To protect yourself from disaster (a blue screen that can't be repaired, a spilled cup of coffee, or a lighting strike, for instance), you'll want to back up your data regularly. While Chapter 15 is all about backing up your files, here, we'd like to talk a little about selecting and adding a physical backup device.

External Hard Drive

A favorite backup device is the external hard drive because we can connect it to a computer, do a backup, connect it to another computer, do another backup, and then unplug it and store it in a safe place until the next full backup is needed. It's important to be able to remove the backup device from the physical area where the computer is, in case of flood, fire, power surge, or other unexpected event. It doesn't do much good to have a backup of all of your important data on a device that can be destroyed by the same cup of coffee you spill on your computer! It's important that the backup can be stored in another area, another room, or even another building.

External hard drives can be purchased from almost any computer store and are generally plug and play. This means that you simply connect the power cord and connect the Universal Serial Bus (USB) or FireWire cable and the hard drive is automatically ready to go. Figure 12-3 shows an example of an installed backup device in Control Panel. In this instance, the backup drive is currently connected to a server in a workgroup and can be accessed as a mapped network drive.

With this backup device available, you can either drag and drop folders such as My Documents or My Pictures, or you can use Windows XP's Backup utility. You'll learn more about that later.

USB CD-R, CD-RW, DVD-R, DVD-RW

The Windows Backup utility can't write to CD or DVD drives that have the capability of being written to, but you can drag and drop files to the recordable

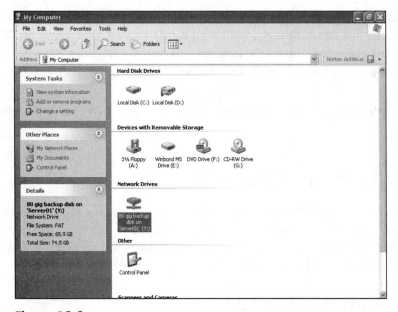

Figure 12-3
Use an external hard drive to safely back up data.

CD device and burn CDs for the purpose of archiving. Archiving old data is necessary so that your hard drive isn't filled up with data you no longer access but want to keep. It's the same theory behind storing (but keeping) your old tax returns. Chances are good you won't need them, but you never know.

TIP: In acronyms such as CD-R, CD-RW, DVD-R, DVD-RW, R means the disk can be written to. RW means the disk is rewriteable, meaning it can be written to again and again.

Installing a USB CD or DVD writer is generally done in the tower and can be quite complicated. Depending on your comfort level, you can either take your hardware to a computer shop or purchase an external rewriteable drive. External drives are generally plug and play, and although a bit more expensive than internal drives, they make great additions. Because they are portable, they can be used on any computer in the home or office (and even your laptop).

Zip Drive

For everyday backups of your latest document, letter, picture, music download, or received files, you can use a Zip drive. Windows Backup Utility can save to a Zip drive, and you can drag and drop files. One of us has a 250 MB Zip drive that can be taken on trips along with a laptop. It's small and can be used to save virtually all the work completed while being away, including pictures. If you have a Zip drive, consider using it as a backup device to save each day's work in between regular full backups. Zip drives are also plug and play.

Other Storage Options

Other options are available for backing up data, including tape drives and newer, portable, USB drives that also double as MP3 players. Tape drives are rather expensive and unwieldy and might not be necessary for the average home user. However, the Creative Nomad fits in the palm of your hand or a pants pocket, can store 128 MB of data (that's like 88 floppy disks), and plugs directly into a USB port. It's plug and play, so it's easy to move data between non-networked computers. As these devices evolve to store more data, they'll make excellent traveling back-up devices.

Figure 12-4 shows the Creative Nomad in the Control Panel, labeled MUVO. This device, as all other removable storage devices, will appear in the Control Panel where they can be accessed and configured.

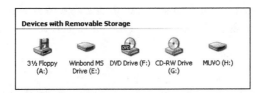

Figure 12-4
Backup devices are getting smaller and smaller. This Creative Nomad can hold 128 MB, but there are similar devices with more storage.

The most important advice we can give is make sure you actually *use* your backup device. Don't put it on your desk to impress the neighbors. Develop a system whereby you back up your data on a regular basis. This is especially important as you become more diligent about removing files and programs as part of your degunking routine. Read Chapter 15 for more information on the Windows Backup Utility, including how to schedule backups to occur automatically.

Add a Second Monitor

If your monitor is all gunked up with running programs and you constantly have to toggle between them, consider adding another monitor. Adding a monitor can be beneficial when you use multiple programs and have to access multiple open windows, such as day trader, programmer, or artist might need.

Windows XP lets you add a monitor (if you have the required hardware) and then *extend* your desktop to it. That means you can add another monitor and open a couple of programs on one and a couple of programs on another. This is a really neat feature that many users don't know about. It can quickly solve the problem of not having enough room on the screen to do what you want to do.

Adding a second monitor is easy if your computer is a newer model. Many newer computers come with display adapters that can already handle two monitors and are compatible with Windows XP. If you are one of the lucky ones, just turn off the computer, plug in the second monitor, and power it up. Then, turn on the computer. Finally, skip to the section "Configuring the Display Settings" later in this chapter to set it up.

Purchasing a New Adapter

If you have a computer that's more than a year old, you'll probably have only one display adapter. If that's the case, you'll need to purchase another display adapter and install it. Not all display adapters are alike, though, so make sure that the adapter you choose is compatible with Windows XP. If it isn't, although you'll probably be able to set up dual monitors, you won't be able to *extend your desktop* to the second one. (The second monitor will just show the same screen as the first.)

In addition to selecting an adapter that is compatible with Windows XP, you need to make sure you have a slot available on the motherboard for it. If you have the information booklet that came with your computer, a tech support line, or access to the company's Web site (if you purchased the computer from a large manufacturer), you might be able to find out if you have any open slots by calling or browsing their site. However, the easiest way to find out is to turn off the computer, unplug it, and open the case. Take a look at the motherboard, and see if there are any empty PCI (Peripheral Component Interconnect) or AGP (Accelerated Graphics Port) slots. You'll have to plug the new display adapter into it, so there has to be one available. PCI slots are long, thin areas that hold cards such as modems and network adapters. They are generally white. AGP slots are generally brown and are shorter than PCI slots. If you are unfamiliar with the inside of a computer, you should consider calling the manufacturer or tech support before going much further.

It doesn't really matter what monitor you use because almost any plug-and-play monitor will do. We have had a few issues with flat screens, though. If you're in doubt, visit Microsoft's Web site and check the hardware compatibility list. You can get lots of information from **www.Microsoft.com/windows/catalog.**

CAUTION: Just because you have an external port on your laptop doesn't mean you can get all of the perks of adding a second monitor. Many laptop display connections only allow you to show the desktop on another monitor; this is different from extending the desktop. If you run into this problem with your laptop, contact the manufacturer and ask for an adapter.

Physical Installation

After you've decided you have an available slot and purchased a new adapter, read the instructions for installing it. Installing a new display adapter generally consists of a few distinct steps:

1. Turn off the computer and unplug it.
2. Open the case and touch the chassis to ground yourself appropriately.
3. Remove the cover that corresponds to the open slot on the back on the computer case, usually held with a single screw.
4. Remove the display adapter from the protective packaging, being careful to touch only the edges.
5. Insert the new adapter into the PCI or AGP slot and use the screw you removed in step 3 to secure it.
6. Close the case, plug in the computer, and power it on.
7. Install any required software.
8. Turn off the computer, plug in the second monitor, and turn the computer back on. Configure the display settings as detailed in the next section.

TIP: If your computer has enough open slots, you can configure up to 10 monitors!

Configuring the Display Settings

Once the additional display card is configured and the monitor is working, you can configure the monitor to show a duplicate of what is on the current monitor, or you can choose to extend the display to the second monitor. Extending the display is the best choice; with this configured, you can move applications over to the second monitor or view a large spreadsheet or image stretched over both.

Follow these steps to configure the display settings:

1. Right-click an empty area of the desktop and click Properties.
2. Select the Settings tab.
3. Click the monitor icon that represents the monitor you want to use in addition to your current monitor.
4. Select Extend My Windows Desktop Onto This Monitor, and click OK.

Now simply drag and drop (from the title bar of your open applications) any application or window you'd like to move to the new monitor and desktop. You're going to love this! Figure 12-5 shows what you'll see in the Display Settings dialog box after you've clicked the Advanced button when two monitors are successfully set up.

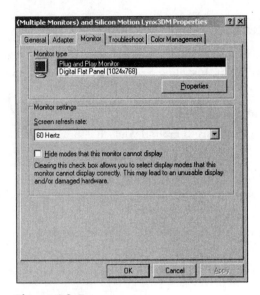

Figure 12-5
A dual-monitor system is shown here.

Physically Clean the Machine

We're not going to say that if you physically clean your machine you'll get better performance, but we will say that if you do, it'll likely last longer than if you never cleaned it. And a big part of the practice of degunking is to extend the life of your machine as much as possible! Maybe the mouse won't hang as often, or you can get a few extra keys to be less sticky, but for the most part, cleaning is a maintenance issue. There are parts of your computer that just collect stuff—your keyboard likely has crumbs in it, your mouse has lint around the ball, your monitor has grime, and the inside of your computer case is filled with dust. If you smoke, if you have cats or dogs, or if children have access to your computer, the problem certainly gets worse. You'll be surprised what you find while working through this section.

CAUTION: Always turn off your PC and all components before cleaning them.

Cleaning Keyboards, Mice, and Monitors

Your keyboards and mice will work a little better if you give them the once-over with a cleanser and remove particles hanging around in there. Monitors will look better if you do some dusting once in a while, and you might be able to use a light cleanser on them as well. If any instructions for cleaning came with your hardware, certainly follow them. For the most part, though, cleaning is a straightforward process.

Perhaps this is going to sound silly, but pick up your keyboard, turn it upside down, and give it a couple of good shakes. What fell out? A few eraser bits, a piece of bread, cat hair, a lost hamster, paper clips, and other odds and ends. This might seem like a primitive way to clean, but it works. Use compressed air to get out those stubborn pieces, and your vacuum cleaner works, too. (You can likely pick up a can of compressed air at your local hardware store.) Now, take a bit of liquid bleach cleanser on a clean, lint-free rag and gently wipe off the keys. Use Q-tips to get into the cracks if necessary, but be careful not to drip any cleaner anywhere. You only want to get enough on the rag to clean the stains; you don't want to immerse the keyboard in cleanser.

If you are cleaning a laptop keyboard, you might be able to pop up the keyboard and get under the keys to really clean the gunk out. If individual keys will pop off your keyboard (many do), you can use a small screwdriver to remove a key to get under where the grime really hides. If you use this technique, make sure you remove only one key at a time and replace it before you pop off another key. Otherwise, you could easily forget where your keys go and you'd end up with a real mess! Laptop keyboards really take a lot of "gunking" abuse because they are often used in environments that aren't always the cleanest, such as airports and hotel rooms.

If you have a generic, roller-ball mouse, flip it over, turn the backing to get inside, and take out the ball. Use a Q-tip and alcohol to carefully clean the ball and the rollers. You might have to reach in there to pull out the gunk that comes off. Make sure the ball and components are dry, and then replace the ball and clean the outside of the mouse with cleanser. (Consider replacing that worn-out mouse pad, too; it can have snags or uneven spots that cause the mouse to hang.) Once you fully clean your mouse like this, you'll be amazed at how well it works.

TIP: The Q-tip and alcohol technique is a common one for cleaning the inside of a printer. Make sure your printer manufacturer agrees before proceeding, though. Oh, and don't forget to see what's hiding under that printer, too!

If you want to clean the outside of the computer case, do so carefully. A small rag with a little dish soap usually works, but you have to be very careful not to drip any cleanser into the case, the disk drives, printer ports, display ports, or USB ports. Getting these components wet could damage or destroy them. The same holds true of the back of the computer case where all of the external hardware plugs in. We wouldn't go near that with anything wet at all. A good dusting with a dry cloth should do.

TIP: Clean scanner beds with window cleaner and wipe until streak-free for better scans.

Finally, clean the monitor based on your manufacturer's instructions. If you have a regular plug-and-play monitor with a glass screen, you can usually clean the screen with a glass cleaner on a clean, lint-free rag. Turn it off first, unplug it, don't spray too much cleaner on the rag, and be sure to clean all of the streaks with a dry towel. If you have an LCD (or flat) screen, use a soft, dry cotton cloth. If that doesn't work, try adding a little rubbing alcohol on the cloth to remove the stubborn stains.

TIP: CD-ROM drives can be cleaned with special CD-ROM cleaners you can purchase from a computer store. This generally involves inserting a disk with a small brush installed on the underside of it that will gently clean the lens.

Degunking Inside the Case

The inside of the computer case contains all of the working parts and should be cleaned at least twice a year to maintain optimal performance. Dust particles, animal hair, and cigarette smoke can get sucked into the computer via the air vents, and before you know it, these contaminants can corrode the circuitry and cause other problems.

Most experts agree that using compressed air is the best way to clean the inside of the computer case, although some prefer a vacuum. Either way, the procedure is basically the same. Here we'll detail the compressed air option:

1. Turn off the computer, unplug it, and carefully open the case. If the case opens on more than one side, open both sides.

2. Position the computer so that when you blow the compressed air into it, the dust will be removed from the case, not just blown around in it. You should also be able to vacuum up what is blown out, so don't blow all of that dust underneath your desk!

3. Hold the compressed air in the upright position and use the air quickly and in short bursts to remove the gunk.

If you're a smoker, have pets, or are in a dusty environment, repeat this procedure four times a year; nonsmokers, those without pets, and those in a clean environment should repeat this procedure twice a year.

Purchase a New Computer

Although I'll stress that this is a measure of last resort only, you might have reached the limits of what degunking can do for you if you have encountered the following situations:

- You've removed all of the extra files and programs from your system but it still takes forever to start up and runs too slowly.

- Your system crashes a lot, you can't figure out why, and you've already tried reinstalling the system with a clean install.

- You find that you need to shut down your computer fairly often and restart it simply to make it run a little better, and calls to tech support don't yield results because the computer has been out of warranty for three years.

- You've tried adding RAM and/or dual monitors but you don't have the slots.

- You've considered adding a CD-RW but find you don't have an extra bay and it's not cost effective to add the drive.

- Your hard drive is too small and not easily upgradeable. The 120 GB external hard drive you want to buy is half as much as a new computer would be.

- Your computer just isn't repairable because you've spilled coffee on it, it's been dropped, or you've shocked the motherboard.

So, what's a degunker to do? You might need to consider a new computer. If you are in this situation, we're not going to tell you what computer to buy, where to buy it, or what kinds of features it should have. What we are going to do is tell you about the pros and cons of transferring your data from your old computer to your new one and, if you decide to do that, exactly how it's done. Setting up a new computer always seems like a big headache and typically needs to be done when you simply don't have the time (like during the holidays or when you're working many hours of overtime). But there are some procedures that you can follow to ease the pain and save you time.

Transferring Data: Pros and Cons

When you get a new computer, you have a couple of choices. You can spend a day or so installing your applications, printers, scanners, cameras, disk drives, and drivers; another day copying your backed-up files, folders, and personal data; and a third day configuring your display settings, Internet connections, network settings, screensavers, Favorites, cookies, and security settings. Or you can spend a day with applications and hardware and use the Files And Settings Transfer Wizard to transfer your personal data and settings automatically.

The upside of the transfer wizard is of course the amount of effort required to set up your new computer. You get to keep your Internet settings, including Favorites and cookies; you get to keep your screensavers, desktop background, and other personal settings; and you get to keep your connections to the Internet and other networks without having to reconfigure them. This saves quite a bit of time. In addition, you can decide exactly what gets transferred. You don't have to transfer the My Pictures folder if you don't want to, and you have similar options with other folders and settings.

The downside to using the wizard is that you should ideally network the computers before you use it, which requires additional hardware like a hub or a null modem cable. If you already have a home network set up, this won't be a problem, but for newbies, this might seem like a lot of work. In addition, you won't get that "new computer" feel. You won't be able to start over, as it were, so if that's important to you, you'll want to consider configuring the new computer manually.

We personally prefer to spend the time configuring the computer and transferring data the long way. Then know exactly what's on it and where it's stored, and there are no possibilities of bringing on residual problems carried over from the previous malfunctioning computer. (If the computer you are moving from is working well, though, and you simply want to create a clone or have purchased a faster, newer computer, the transfer wizard will be perfect.)

Using the Files And Settings Transfer Wizard

Access to the Files And Settings Transfer Wizard is located in the System Tools menu and can be opened by clicking Start, pointing to All Programs, pointing to Accessories, pointing to System Tools, and clicking Files And Settings Transfer Wizard. The wizard opens and offers advice and techniques for connecting your computer and explains what you can transfer. Once connected, click Next. The wizard is quite comprehensive in walking you through the process of transferring data. As shown in Figure 12-6, you can decide what exactly you want to transfer by adding or removing the appropriate folders and settings.

This wizard can be most helpful for those with the appropriate hardware and circumstances. If you are simply purchasing a new computer that will run faster and better than the one you have and you want to transfer your files and settings over, this is certainly the easiest way to go.

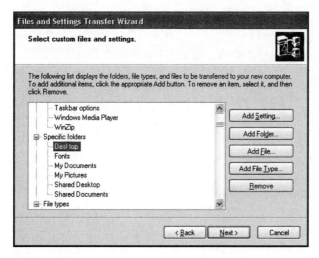

Figure 12-6
Using the Files And Settings Transfer Wizard, you can decide exactly what folders and settings to transfer and what not to.

Summing Up

In this chapter, you learned that enhancing your computer's performance with hardware and physical upgrades can really spark new life into it. You learned that adding memory is the easiest and fastest way to enhance a computer's performance and that an extra 128 MB or 256 MB of RAM can provide a surprising boost. Tweaking virtual memory settings and the page file can help as well. Other hardware tweaks, like adding backup devices and second monitors and physically cleaning the machine, can also boost productivity and performance.

If performance is just about as good as it's going to get, if you have ongoing problems that can't be solved, if the computer blue-screens just as you're really getting the hang of that new video game, or if the computer has 128 MB of RAM and no slots to add extra memory, you might have to consider a new computer. If that's the case, keep in mind that there are tools available to help you make the transition.

PowerToys and Awesome Shareware

Degunking Checklist:

√ Learn what PowerToys offer and how they can help you with your degunking tasks.

√ Learn where to locate PowerToys, download them, and install them.

√ Use the TweakUI PowerToy to customize Windows settings.

√ Use the Virtual Desktop Manager PowerToy to organize your desktop.

√ Use Resize Imager to reduce the size of your graphics files.

√ Locate WUGNET's (Windows Users Group Network) shareware picks. These shareware programs are deemed the highest quality in shareware for Windows.

√ Use shareware favorites including Registry First Aid, Pop-Up Stopper, FolderMatch, and System Mechanic to keep your PC running well.

T his chapter ends the advanced degunking section by offering some advanced power tools for your PC and some awesome shareware. The free power tools are aptly named *PowerToys*. PowerToys can be used to tweak your XP machine, including customizing keyboard keys, configuring a custom background for the Internet Explorer toolbar or the Explorer toolbar, and even using a shortcut to the Group Policy Editor for changing hundreds of additional settings.

The TweakUI PowerToy is an especially nice one to obtain because if offers the ability to change options that are difficult to find and configure or options that simply aren't available. For instance, with TweakUI, you can do the following:

- Define what order grouped items are listed (when button grouping is enabled)
- Configure what the first icon on the desktop should be (My Documents or My Computer)
- Configure what can and can't be added to the Frequently Used Programs section of the Windows XP Start menu.

Having the ability to personalize your computer in this way can help you be more productive, locate things faster, and work more efficiently.

Other PowerToys are available that allow you to resize images with a single click and to toggle between programs more efficiently. There are lots of PowerToys to choose from, but in this chapter we'll only mention the ones we believe will help you enhance performance and/or work faster and smarter.

In addition to PowerToys, we'll introduce you to WUGNET, a users group that tests and picks the top shareware available on the Internet. Each week they feature a different shareware program. Most of the shareware programs are less than $30 U.S. and can be quite useful in enhancing the machine's performance. Many shareware programs can configure settings for best performance by looking at the system configuration, Internet connection, and system resources and configuring those items to work together and at peak performance by applying some tried-and-true tweaks, such as the ones you're learning in this book. Because these programs can create performance boosts, they should be worth trying out.

Use PowerToys for Degunking

PowerToys are for Windows XP users only. They're specially designed for XP machines and they're all free. Although there are numerous PowerToys, we'll only detail the ones we think will benefit you in everyday performance task enhancement.

Downloading and Installing

The PowerToys we'll introduce here will need to be downloaded and installed before you can use them. You'll download each of them from the same Web page: **www.Microsoft.com/windowsXP/pro/downloads/powertoys.asp**. Once at the page, follow these steps to download and install any PowerToy:

1. Locate the PowerToy you want to obtain. Figure 13-1 shows the Alt-Tab Replacement PowerToy.

Figure 13-1

Locate the PowerToy to obtain and click the download link.

2. Click the link and then click Save in the File Download box, as shown in Figure 13-2. The Save As dialog box opens.

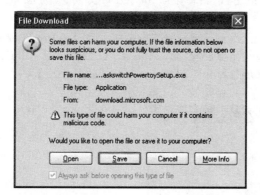

Figure 13-2

Click Save when prompted with a File Download dialog box.

3. If you have a designated folder you use for saving file downloads, browse to it now. If you do not have a designated area for saving downloads from the Internet, in the Save As dialog box, click the My Documents folder. In the My Documents folder area, right-click an empty area, point to New, and click Folder. Name the folder Internet Downloads. (You'll only do this once, and from here on out, you'll save your downloads here.)

4. Click the folder where you want to save the file, and click Save. Figure 13-3 shows what a new Save As dialog box might look like.

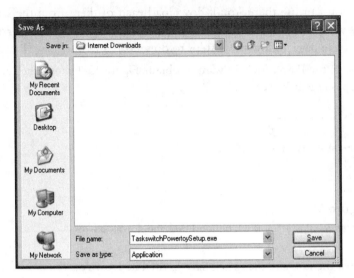

Figure 13-3
Create a folder that can be used to hold your downloaded Internet files.

5. As the download progresses, verify that Close This Dialog Box When Download Completes is not checked in the active download dialog box. When the download has completed, click Open. See Figure 13-4.

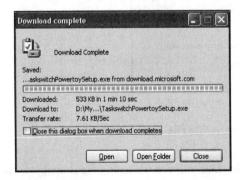

Figure 13-4
The Download dialog box shows the progress of the download and offers an Open command for installing the program.

6. Close any open programs and follow the directions in the wizard for installing the software. Generally the default settings are fine.

7. Locate the new program from the Start menu, All Programs, and PowerToys For Windows XP. (Some programs, like the Alt-Tab Replacement PowerToy or the Virtual Desktop PowerToy, won't show there.)

These steps can be used to download and install almost anything at all from the Internet, even shareware. There might be additional screens, or perhaps an additional Web page to work through, but the process is the same. Locate and choose what you want to download, save it to the hard drive, open the folder, and install it.

Customize Windows Settings with TweakUI

TweakUI is a favorite PowerToy so we've chosen to introduce it first. It gives you access to system settings that are not exposed in the Windows XP default user interface, like mouse settings, Taskbar settings, Desktop settings, and Internet Explorer settings. Figure 13-5 shows the interface, and we've clicked the Taskbar tree. Here, it's easy to disable the balloon tips that pop up in the bottom-right corner of your screen reminding you to do everything from running the Desktop Cleanup Wizard to getting a .NET Passport.

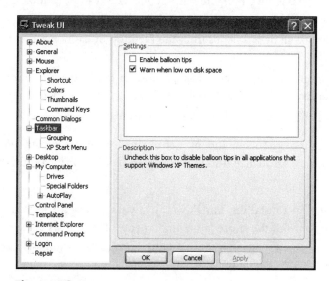

Figure 13-5
Use Tweak UI to configure XP to run exactly how you want it to.

In addition to this marvelous tweak, there are hundreds of other things you can achieve with this software. While we can't possibly list all of them here, we can list our favorites:

- About>Tips: View tips like "Press Win+L to unlock your workstation" and "Ctrl+Shift+Esc will launch Task Manager."

- About>Policy: Run the Group Policy Editor, where hundreds of additional settings can be configured, including titles, bitmaps, and logos for IE's toolbar; password policies for users; local security policies such as requiring (or not) Ctrl+Alt+Del on logon; whether or not to show the last username in the logon screen, and more.

- General: Enable or disable menu and tooltip animation and fading.

- Explorer: Configure what is shown on the Start menu, whether the document list should be cleared on exit, and whether to detect accidental double-clicks.

- Explorer>Thumbnails: Set the image quality of thumbnails.

- Explorer>Command Keys: Configure the keyboard's navigation keys and change what happens when a specific key is pressed.

- Taskbar>Grouping: Configure in what order grouped applications are listed when grouping is used.

- Taskbar>XP Start Menu: Configure what applications can or cannot appear in the Windows XP Start menu as frequently used programs.

- Desktop: Remove all default icons from the Desktop or easily put them back.

- Internet Explorer: Create a custom background for the Internet Explorer toolbar or the Explorer toolbar. This can include a picture or logo as well.

- Logon>AutoLogon: Easily enable or disable automatic logon.

By using TweakUI to its fullest and by getting to know the Group Policy Editor, you can really personalize how XP works and looks. This is a must-have PowerToy.

After downloading and installing this PowerToy, work through the following tweaks to disable some of the more annoying aspects of Windows XP:

1. Click Start, point to All Programs, point to PowerToys For Windows XP, and click TweakUI For Windows XP.

2. Expand the About tree, and click Policy. In the Group Policy Editor pane, click Run Group Policy Editor.

3. In the Group Policy window, expand User Configuration, Administrative Templates, and then Windows Components. Click Start Menu And Taskbar.

4. In the right pane, take a look at the configuration options. Changes made here affect everyone who accesses this computer, even administrators. Consider configuring the following settings: Turn Off Personalize Menu, Turn Off Notification Area Cleanup, Remove Balloon Tips On Start Menu Items, and Remove Clock From The System Notification Area. (Okay, so perhaps it isn't annoying, but it's a cool option.)

5. To enable or disable any setting, double-click and make the appropriate choice. Click OK and exit when complete.

Organize Your Desktop with Virtual Desktop Manager

Microsoft Virtual Desktop Manager (MSVDM) allows you to organize a busy and cluttered Desktop. If you work with many open programs, you can now manage them on four different Desktops. You can switch between the Desktops using buttons on the Taskbar or shortcut keys that you configure. If you always have Outlook Express open, put it on one Desktop. If you always have Internet Explorer open, put it on another Desktop. You can even configure different backgrounds on each Desktop!

Once it's downloaded, Desktop Manager is activated by right-clicking an empty area of the Taskbar, pointing to Toolbars, and clicking Desktop Manager. You can then move a program from one Desktop to another by selecting the Desktop number from the Taskbar and then clicking the program's button on the Taskbar to open it or using Alt+Tab. This provides a really neat way to unclutter your Desktop. Figure 13-6 shows the four Desktops configured, and they are all shown together. The size of the open windows were changed in each so that you can clearly see the four Desktops and their backgrounds. Figure 13-7 shows Desktop #1 chosen and how the others are readily available in the Taskbar.

Here are some rules for working with the Virtual Desktop Manager:

- To configure a Desktop, choose a Desktop number from the Taskbar and then open or start a program to use for it.

- To create a Desktop background for a particular Desktop, right-click the Desktop number in the Taskbar (see Figure 13-7) and choose Configure Desktop Images. From the resulting dialog box, choose an image to use.

- To configure a shortcut key for moving between Desktops, right-click a desktop number in the Taskbar and choose Configure Shortcut Keys. Choose the key combination to get to the various Desktops you have configured.

- To get help at any time, right-click any Desktop number in the Taskbar and click MSVDM Help.

- To choose a Desktop when all four are showing, click the one to use with the mouse.

- To show all four Desktops at once, click the icon to the left of the 1 in the Taskbar. It's called the Preview button.

- To exit Virtual Desktop Manager, right-click the Taskbar, point to Toolbars, and uncheck Desktop Manager.

This software comes with complete help files and can be quite effective once you get the hang of it. It can be used to create a sort of quad-monitor effect, where programs can remain on a single Desktop until needed, thus not taking up space on the current one. It's well worth the download!

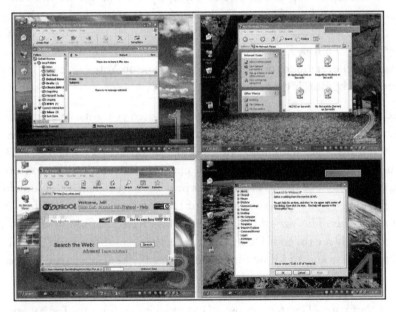

Figure 13-6

Here, four Desktops for the same computer are configured, and each has an open program. To select a Desktop, simply click it once.

Figure 13-7

When a single Desktop is chosen and in use, the Taskbar offers quick access to the others.

Resize Images with the Image Resizer

The two previously mentioned PowerToys offer lots of bells and whistles. The Image Resizer PowerToy, on the other hand, only does one thing, but it can really help you with your degunking work. It allows you to resize images with a single right-click to make them much smaller and reduce the space drain on your hard drive. It is also the perfect tool for resizing images to send to others via e-mail so that you don't gunk up other users' computers by sending out large files such as digital camera pictures.

Once it's downloaded and installed, simply browse to the picture to resize, right-click, and choose Resize Pictures. (If you don't see this option after downloading and installing the application, click Start, click Run, and in the Run dialog box, type regsvr32 shimgvw.dll.) In the Resize Pictures dialog box, choose the picture size you want and click OK. See Figure 13-8 for an example.

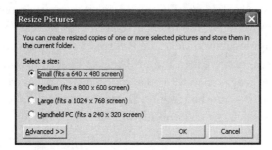

Figure 13-8
The Image Resizer PowerToy lets you resize images with a right-click.

Alt-Tab Replacement

The Alt-Tab Replacement PowerToy is a good one to have if you have lots and lots of open programs and you enjoy using Alt+Tab to toggle between them. With this PowerToy, you simply hold down the Alt key and click the Tab key to move between programs. Icons for the programs are shown in the Alt-Tab Replacement window, and you choose the program to open with the Tab key.

WUGNET'S Shareware Picks

Shareware is software that you pay for and download from the Internet. There is a ton of shareware available. You can find many programs that can help you degunk your PC and improve the performance of Windows. Unfortunately, it's difficult to always know when a shareware program is a good one, short of purchasing and installing it or wading through various posted reviews.

WUGNET, Windows Users Group Network, has taken some of the guesswork out of choosing a shareware program. WUGNET offers its top shareware picks each week and states that they've been thoroughly tested in lots of environments and that they're priced appropriately. Although the list changes often, here are a few of the shareware programs we found (and liked) that can help you with your degunking chores. For the most part, these programs are less than $30 U.S. To see what is available now, visit **www.Microsoft.com/ windowsxp/pro/downloads/wugnet.asp**.

TIP: *If you find a program you'd like to purchase or try out, follow the directions given earlier in this chapter for downloading and installing programs. It's virtually the same process, except sometimes you have to pay!*

Keep Your Registry Clean with Registry First Aid

Gunked up Registries can cause all sorts of problems, including blue screens, crashes, lockups, slow system response, and unexpected errors as we learned in Chapter 9. Since it's nearly impossible to clean the Registry yourself, owning a Registry cleaning tools like Registry Clean Pro or Registry First Aid is almost a necessity. If working in the Registry scares you as much as it scares us, you're going to love this application. It scans the Registry for orphaned file and folder references, left-over files from deleted applications, obsolete Start menu items, invalid fonts, invalid paths, and more and removes them from the Registry. If you haven't ever run a Registry cleaning program, this is an inexpensive way to try it out. In Chapter 9 we used Registry Clean Pro to clean the Registry. We'll now try a different Registry cleaning tool.

To download and install a trial copy of Registry First Aid, and to see what Registry First Aid can do for your system, follow these steps:

1. Visit **www.Microsoft.com/windowsxp/pro/downloads/wugnet.asp,** and locate and click the link to download the free trial copy.

2. Click Open to run the program from its location, and when the download is complete, click Yes in the Setup dialog box to install the program.

3. Once it's installed, launch the application. (Steps 1, 2, and 3 are common steps for downloading and installing any program from the Internet.)

4. When the program starts, click Check The Registry For Errors and click Next.

5. In the page to select what to scan the Registry for, check all options. Click Start, read the information provided, and click OK.

6. When prompted, create a restore point using System Restore (it will open automatically).

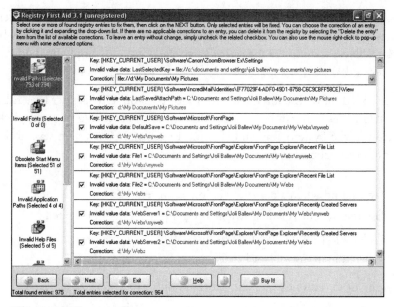

Figure 13-9
Look at all of these Registry errors!

Take a look at the incredible amount of invalid paths (794) shown in Figure 13-9. No wonder this computer barely runs! The program also found obsolete Start menu items (51), invalid application paths (4), invalid Help files (5), invalid shared DLLs (92), autorun programs (2), and unused software entries (17), but it found no invalid fonts.

NOTE: With the trial version, you can only repair 18 entries. For $21 U.S., we thought "What the heck?" and purchased the software. We were extremely impressed with the results, and our computers have never run better.

Get Rid of Annoying Pop-Up Messages with Pop-Up Stopper Professional

Are you sick of those pop-up advertisements you get when you visit Web pages? This kind of gunk can really slow you down when you are trying to read your e-mail and get some important work done, and besides that, it's just plain annoying! There are lots of ways to get rid of them, some free and some not. We use the Pop-Up Stopper Free Edition, but Pop-Up Stopper Professional is also available. Pop-Up Stopper Free Edition is available from **www.panicware.com**, and the Professional Edition is listed on WUGNET's shareware favorites list.

Pop-up stoppers like these block ads with any browser and with all Internet connections. They'll also give you immediate notification if any ad has been blocked. If you want to see the ad (or open the window), simply hold down the Ctrl key and click it again.

Figure 13-10 shows the interface options for the Pop-Up Stopper Free Edition and preferences that can be set. This dialog box is accessible by right-clicking the icon in the System Tray and clicking Preferences. There are several things you can personalize:

- Play a sound when a pop-up window is prevented
- Flash the System Tray icon when a pop-up window is prevented
- Display a pop-up bubble next to the system clock
- Change the mouse cursor briefly

From the other tabs you can also set these options:
- Configure Pop-Up Stopper to start each time Windows starts (or not)
- Purchase the full version
- Get updates

Figure 13-10
Pop Up Stopper Free Edition is a good option for stopping pop-up ads from appearing.

Synchronize Your Folders with FolderMatch

When you make a backup of your data, you copy it and place that copy in a safe place like a separate hard drive, a Zip disk, or a CD. If you work on files at two different computers or physical locations (say, at work and on a laptop), you'll likely have two copies of some data as well. With two copies of the data, there's a good chance that the copies won't always be in sync and contain the same information. Files change often, as do contents of folders. Keeping your duplicate data organized and in sync can require quite a bit of time. To make this task easier, consider purchasing FolderMatch.

FolderMatch can automatically synchronize duplicate files and folders using your choice of comparison types. It's easy enough for the average user to understand, and powerful enough to please even the most sophisticated multitasker. It includes a full-featured duplicate file finder, which is also useful for locating unwanted duplicates of files. This feature can be especially useful when you are degunking your PC by removing all of the extra files. If you need to keep files and folders in sync, consider software such as this.

Keep Your Computer Running Smoothly with System Mechanic

System Mechanic is an incredible application containing 15 tools to keep your computer running smoothly. It can really help it run faster, cleaner, and error free. It can even speed up your Internet connection. At the time this book was written, you could try out System Mechanic for free, which is what we did, and if you like it, you can purchase it. That's quite a deal!

Here are some of the things the System Mechanic checks for and repairs:

- Obsolete or duplicate files
- Invalid Registry keys
- Internet cookies and cache
- Broken shortcuts
- Duplicate files and drivers

In addition, this software allows you to do the following:

- Customize Windows settings
- Customize startup options
- Optimize Windows configuration settings that affect your network and Internet connection speeds

Figure 13-11
System Mechanic is easy to use and repairs lots of common problems.

Figure 13-11 shows the System Mechanic in action.

Summing Up

The purpose of this chapter was to help you degunk, secure, and personalize your computer with PowerToys and shareware available on the Internet. Shareware can enhance both the performance of the computer and how efficiently you work by using computer-powered tried-and-true tools for degunking. PowerToys are free and can be quite useful, and Tweak UI is certainly a favorite for lots of folks. Shareware can also be quite effective in enhancing performance, from applications that synchronize duplicate files to those that clean the Registry.

Improving Security

Degunking Checklist:

√ Discover how secure your computer really is.

√ Protect your computer by purchasing and configuring anti-virus software.

√ Configure Internet options to protect, secure, and keep private information private.

√ Understand good and bad cookies and how to best configure Internet Explorer.

√ Create a Guest account and use it when company arrives.

√ Set local security policies that affect anyone who logs on to your computer.

√ Understand and set up a firewall to improve security.

S ecuring your computer is just as important as enhancing its performance, and that's what we're going to discuss in this chapter. It doesn't do any good to clean up, maintain, and organize your home or garage if you're going to leave the door unlocked for anyone and everyone to drop in without your permission. The same situation is true of your computer. Don't go to all of the trouble of getting it running efficiently, organizing all of its files, and performing scheduled maintenance when you've left a door open to hackers, viruses, worms, and adware or spyware programs, which in turn can really gunk up your machine.

How Secure Is Your Computer?

Microsoft offers a free tool called the MBSA (Microsoft Baseline Security Analyzer) that will check your current security configuration and look for missing critical security updates, common security slipups, and other vulnerabilities. The program will then produce a report with instructions on how to repair the security issues it finds. You can decide after viewing the report if any items need attention. Using this tool is a great way to begin the securing process.

To run this free security check and view a report, make sure you are logged on as an administrator and connected to the Internet. Then follow these steps:

1. Click Start, and open Help And Support. From the Help And Support Center, click Security And Privacy.

2. In the Security And Privacy pane, click Viruses, Passwords, And Safety.

3. In the right pane, under Overviews, Articles, And Tutorials, click Finding Out If Your Computer Is Secure.

4. From the article "Finding Out Whether Your Computer Is Secure," click the link to the MBSA page.

5. Click the link and download and install the application. If prompted by your anti-virus software that a malicious script is present, choose to run the script after the program is installed.

6. When prompted, choose the computer to scan (if more than one are listed). A sample report is shown in Figure 14-1.

As you can see from the partial report shown in Figure 14-1, this computer has an issue with too many administrators, but most of the other security settings are in check. With the report in hand, make the needed repairs, and then continue with this chapter.

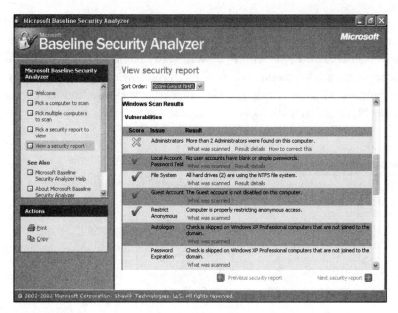

Figure 14-1
Use the MBSA tool to see how secure your computer really is.

Purchase and Configure Anti-Virus Software

Anti-virus software, when kept up-to-date, is the easiest way to protect your computer against Internet risks like viruses and hackers. Anti-virus software is fairly inexpensive, easy to install, and a snap to keep current. If you don't have it now, disconnect from the Internet and run out to the local computer store or stay online and visit your favorite online software vendor and get it right away!

Anti-virus software can protect against lots of different Internet threats, not just viruses and hackers. It can protect against unauthorized connections and privacy threats. It can also repel unwanted cookies and Java applets and scan incoming and outgoing e-mail. Many of these products also include a personal firewall, which can provide even more protection. (We'll talk more about firewalls later in this chapter.) There are lots of anti-virus software manufacturers to choose from, including Symantec, Enteractive, and McAfee. Any of these can be trusted to do a good job at keeping your machine more secure.

Once installed, this software can be configured to suit your needs. Generally, the default settings are fine, but you might want to set the application to look for and download new security definitions every night (instead of the default, which is generally every week) if you want extra security. Also, you might not want to scan each outgoing e-mail for viruses. You can perform full system scans daily, weekly, or monthly and view reports of various activities. Figure 14-2 shows Norton SystemWorks by Symantic.

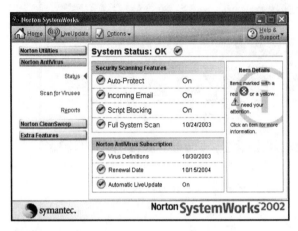

Figure 14-2
Make sure all systems are go when configuring an anti-virus utility. In this example, the system status is OK and the anti-virus subscription information is up-to-date.

As a rule, consider the following configuration choices for your anti-virus software:

* Set the anti-virus program to "auto-protect" and have it start each time you boot the computer. You should leave the application running in the background at all times.

* Show the software icon in the System Tray so that it is easily accessible and alerts can be viewed easily.

* Let your anti-virus program automatically repair any infected files it finds. Quarantine the file if the repair is not successful.

* Perform a complete system scan at least once a week, and perhaps daily (each night) for computers that hold sensitive data.

* Enable script blocking so that malicious scripts (which can be viruses) are not run.

* Scan incoming and outgoing e-mail for viruses.

* Enable protection on any instant messaging systems you use.

* Enable automatic and scheduled downloads of new virus definitions at least

weekly. If you have a continuous connection to the Internet, configure definitions to be downloaded daily.

- Enable protection from spyware and adware, if provided as an option.

- When configuring e-mail protection, configure the application to automatically delete files that contain known viruses. (See Chapter 8 for more information on e-mail security.)

With all of these precautions in place, you should be pretty well protected against viruses, hackers, and general Internet threats. But you can do more. In the next section, we'll take security a step further by configuring Internet options.

Configure Internet Options

You have complete control over how secure your Web surfing is, how much of your private information is given to Web sites, and what content can and can't be viewed on your computer. You can even configure custom security zones to personalize the security options that you've selected.

In the following sections, you'll learn about security zones, how to configure trusted Web sites, and how to restrict what happens when you visit untrusted sites. You'll also learn how to keep your private information private, as well as the pros and cons of using strict privacy settings (including restricting cookies).

Configure Security Zones

The zones are shown in the Security tab. You can view information on each one by clicking it. Let's take a look at the zones you can configure and the ones that are set up by default. Here are the steps to follow:

1. Open Internet Explorer, click the Tools menu, and click Internet Options.

2. From the Internet Options dialog box, click the Security tab as shown in Figure 14-3.

3. Select an Internet zone to view its properties.

TIP: Figure 14-3 shows a Security tab with the defaults chosen. If you've made custom changes to this page, yours will look a little different. If that's the case, simply click Default Level (grayed out here) to see the defaults.

Internet Zone

By default, all Web sites fall into the Internet zone, and the security level for the zone is Medium. (The other zones require you to choose sites manually and

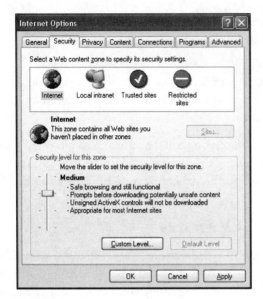

Figure 14-3
The four security zones: Internet, Local Intranet, Trusted Sites, and Restricted Sites.

place them in the zone yourself.) Medium security offers safe browsing while still being quite functional. With this setting, you will get a prompt before anything potentially harmful is downloaded. Medium security is appropriate for most users and Internet sites. You can change the security level for the Internet zone by simply moving the security slider up or down. When you move the slider, the information about the zone's security precautions changes.

Additional Zones

In addition to the Internet zone, there are three other zones: Local Intranet, Trusted Sites, and Restricted Sites. When you use these zones, you must manually place Web sites in them. Once a Web site has been placed in a zone, the site takes on the security measures for that zone.

In the Local Intranet zone, for instance, the default security level is Medium-Low. That's because any site you manually place in this zone should be a site on your local intranet; it should be a trusted and secure Web site maintained by your company.

In the Trusted Sites zone, the default security level is Low. This setting and zone are only appropriate for sites you absolutely trust, like your own. Low security provides minimal safeguards; for example, no prompts appear when ActiveX content is downloaded and run on your machine. Because all ActiveX content is run, it is only appropriate for sites you absolutely trust.

Finally, the Restricted Sites zone has a security setting of High. Place Web sites here that you do not trust. A security level of High reduces functionality, but you'll at least be safe while visiting!

Here's how to add a Web site to any of these zones:

1. Open Internet Explorer, click Tools, and click Internet Options.

2. Click the Security tab and select any zone other than the Internet zone.

3. Click Sites.

4. In the Sites dialog box, type in the Web address of the zone to add and click Add. Note that the URL for trusted sites will have to start with https://, a verification that the site is indeed secure. Figure 14-4 shows an example of adding a Web site to the Trusted Sites zone. When finished, click OK twice.

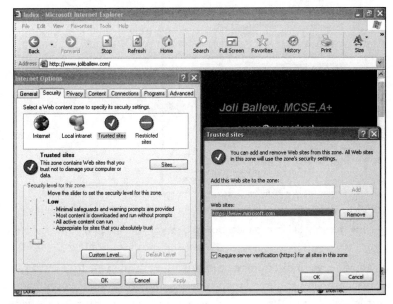

Figure 14-4
When adding a site to the Trusted Sites zone, the prefix of the URL must begin with https://.

Custom Zones

You probably noticed in Figure 14-3 that a Custom Level button is provided in the Internet Options dialog box under the Security tab. Clicking Custom Level here allows you to tweak the default security settings for a particular zone. For instance, if you want to use the Internet zone and the Medium security settings but you'd like to disable the option to have Desktop items installed (instead of the default of being prompted before they are installed), you can configure just that single option using custom settings. Here's how:

1. Open Internet Explorer, click Tools, and click Internet Options.

2. Click the Security tab.

3. Choose a zone to change—for instance, the Internet zone.

4. Click Custom Level.

5. In the Security Settings dialog box, shown in Figure 14-5, make changes as desired. You can use the Reset button to undo the changes if you decide to later.

6. Click OK twice.

Figure 14-5
The Security Settings dialog box allows you to configure custom security settings.

As an aside, we'll discourage configuring your own custom settings. If you run across a problem and need tech support, perhaps a problem with access or with performance on a Web page, the solution can be difficult to uncover. This is especially true if you configured custom settings a year ago and the computer is only now developing problems.

Privacy Options

When you surf the Internet, Web sites you visit will pick up little tidbits of information from you, including information about your computer configuration, what version of Windows Media Player you use, your Internet connection speed, and maybe even your purchasing history at that site, your favorite topics, your favorite screen colors, or other items. While this might seem like it's on the edge of being intrusive and potentially harmful (or downright illegal), it isn't.

Before you panic, keep in mind that if you have the proper security settings and anti-virus software in place, a Web site can't uncover personal information about you unless you supply it yourself. The majority of information collected at Web sites without your knowledge is harmless data about your preferences when you visit. This information, called a *cookie,* is stored on your computer in a text file in the Cookies folder. Each time you visit, the Web site can give you more personalized treatment because of the cookie. Cookies can be used to remember your computer configuration (you use Windows XP, for instance) or a password you created at their site from which the cookie is sent, just to give you a couple of examples.

Information You Give Out

Unlike the generally harmless cookies that Web sites send out and use to make surfing more customized, lots of additional information is provided to Web sites unwittingly. Consider this: you purchase something online, and during the transaction you give out your phone number, address, full name, credit card numbers, passwords, and more. If you create a user account and/or password, you also provide the Web site with permission to collect information about you and your surfing habits while you are visiting that particular site. If you've configured any of the "My" pages from MSN, Yahoo!, or other service, these companies might know even more, but no more than you've told them. Have you created a customized home page at Yahoo! or a similar site? If you have, you might have also configured a "personal profile" and gladly provided information about your age, sex, hobbies, income, and even marital status. That information is public!

The point here is that any information you supply will be collected, stored, and used by the creators of the Web site. You need to be careful about handing out information at sites you don't trust. You should read the agreements you so eagerly accept when creating a password or sign on name. With that bit of warning out of the way, and knowing that we can't control what information *you* give at Web sites, we can show you how to control what anonymous and/or personal information is collected from you without your knowledge or consent.

Understand Your Options

You have control over what cookies are placed on your computer. Open up the Privacy settings as follows, and let's have a look:

1. Open Internet Explorer, click Tools, and click Internet Options.
2. Click the Privacy tab.

3. If Default is not grayed out, click it, and configure the settings to Medium by sliding the security slider. See Figure 14-6.

4. Read the explanation for Medium security. If you'd like more secure Privacy settings, move the slider up; less secure, move it down.

Figure 14-6
The Medium Privacy setting is a good choice for most users.

As with zones, you can configure custom settings by clicking the Advanced button. You can also override default cookie handling for a particular Web site by clicking the Edit button. As with zones, we'll say that for the most part, Medium (or Medium High) is the best choice for Privacy settings. Too low of a setting can make personal information vulnerable; too high and your Web surfing will be extremely limited. You will find that you must have cookies enabled to enter many sites, so enabling cookies is generally a good idea.

GunkBuster's Notebook: More About Cookies

Recapping: Cookies are little bits of data stored as text documents that Web sites place on your computer when you visit. First-party cookies come from the site itself, and third-party cookies come from advertisers and other third-party vendors. Cookies are generally harmless, as long as you keep a Medium or higher level of security. Cookies are what allow Web sites like **www.amazon.com** to know that you enjoy gardening books and don't want to see books on motorcycles, or enable you to log on to a Web site without always having to type a password.

You can view and delete the cookies that have been placed on your computer by using Windows Explorer to locate Local Disk:\Documents And Settings\All Users\<*your user name*>\Cookies. Figure 14-7 shows my Cookies folder. If you look closely at the names of the files, you'll see cookies from PayPal, PC World, and Yahoo!, among others. In our minds, these are harmless or are items we set up ourselves.

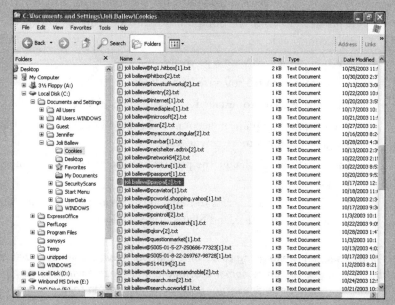

Figure 14-7

This is an example of what a Cookies folder looks like.

You can also delete the cookies stored on your machine from inside Internet Explorer by following these steps:

1. Click Tools, click Internet Options, and click the General tab.

2. Click Delete Cookies to remove all of the cookies stored on your machine.

This would be a good idea if you are selling or loaning the computer to someone or if others share your computer and online accounts.

Create a Guest Account

If you're planning on having guests anytime soon who will want access to a computer for checking e-mail, surfing the Web, printing, or writing letters home, you'll want to enable a Guest account. A Guest account is the perfect way to give visitors the Internet access they need while still keeping the computer and your personal files safe and secure. The Guest account should be configured to show on the Welcome screen so that guests have easy access to it.

Once configured, the Guest account has the following properties:

- It provides access to the computer for anyone who does not specifically have an account on it.
- It is not configured with a password.
- Guests cannot install software or hardware.
- Guests have access to installed hardware and software.
- Guests cannot upgrade an account to Limited User or Administrator or join any group that has more privileges.
- The Guest cannot change the picture or make permanent changes to the computer.
- The Guest will have access to items in the Shared Documents, Shared Pictures, Shared Music, and Shared Videos folders.

TIP: For this section, we're going to assume that you have a computer that is not a member of a larger, corporate domain. Computers in these environments typically have restrictions on accounts such as this. This section is written for stand-alone computers or computers in a workgroup.

Enable and Configure a Guest Account

Once you've decided you need a Guest account, it's extremely easy to enable the default one. When your guests leave, though, you should disable the account immediately. An enabled Guest account is considered a liability and is not a good, long-term security configuration.

To enable and configure the Guest account, follow these steps:

1. Open the Control Panel, and open User Accounts.
2. Click the Guest account icon.
3. On the User Accounts page labeled Do You Want To Turn On The Guest Account, click Turn On The Guest Account.
4. Back at the User Accounts Page, click Change The Way Users Log On Or Off.

5. Verify that Use The Welcome Screen is checked. Click Apply Options.

6. Make sure to log off each time you are finished with the computer. When a guest accesses the computer, they'll go through the Welcome screen to log on.

Figure 14-8 shows the result of enabling the Guest account and the Welcome screen, logging off, and allowing a guest access to the computer. Remember, guests cannot harm the computer by installing applications or hardware, and they will not have access to your private files.

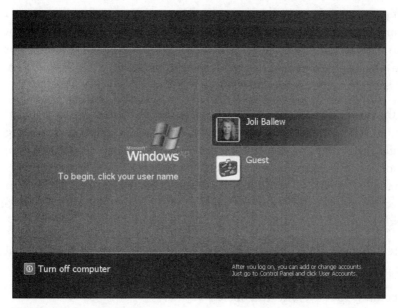

Figure 14-8

Enable the Guest account when company arrives and needs access to a computer.

A Look at Administrative Tools

Administrative Tools in Windows XP Professional allow you to take even more control of your computer. These components allow you to set computer-wide local security policies that affect all users of the computer and contain computer management tools that enable you to monitor system events, create and manage shared resources, start and stop services, view device configurations, and more. Other administrative tools are available as well, but for the most part, these two features, setting computer-wide security policies and monitoring the computer, are the ones you'll use most often. Administrative Tools make good degunking partners because they allow you to set local user policies to prevent other users of the computer from doing harm. You can set rules for passwords and logon attempts to heighten the security of the computer. You can also view events like failed logon attempts. Any tool that gives you more control over your computer, who accesses it, and what they can do while at the computer is a great security asset.

Local Security Policies

A big part of degunking is securing your computer from new gunk, and whether that gunk comes from outsiders or from people you know, you need to have complete control over who can access what and how they can access it. Local security policies can be configured to secure your computer from the people who have access to it, including the night staff, additional users, or coworkers. You'd be surprised just how much damage someone can do in a short period of time, whether it's intentional or not.

In this section, we'll introduce you to some of the less-complicated policy settings and tools that can be applied through a local security policy change. By configuring these policies, you can prevent malicious access of your computer by locking the computer after a specific number of failed logon attempts, you can require users of the computer to use complicated passwords so they cannot be easily guessed, and you can require users to press Ctrl+Alt+Del to log on (just to name a few options).

Listed next are some of the more common security changes you can make. In the next section, you'll learn how and where to apply them.

Account Policies>Password Policies:

- Enforce Password History: Used to determine how many days a password can be remembered in the password history. This is best left at 0 days, thus requiring each user to type in their password each time they log on. The default is 0. For maximum security, set a password and use it each time.

- Maximum Password Age: Used to determine how many days a password can remain active until it expires and must be changed. The default is that the password never expires; however, this might need to be changed if other people have access to the computer and have time to try to guess a password. I set mine to expire every 15 days.

- Minimum Password Age: Used to determine how many days a password must be kept before it can be changed. The default is 0 days, meaning the password can be changed immediately and at any time. This default is recommended.

- Minimum Password Length: Used to configure how many characters must be in a password. The default is 0, but a password containing at least 7 characters is much more secure.

- Password Must Meet Complexity Requirements: Disabled by default, this setting allows you to require complex passwords containing uppercase and lowercase letters, numbers, and symbols.

Account Policies>Account Lockout Policy:

- Account Lockout Threshold: Used to configure how many logon attempts can be made before the account is locked. By default, no lockout threshold is set. For extra security, change this setting to 3 or 5 tries and configure the Account Lockout Duration setting.

- Account Lockout Duration: Used to configure how long an account will be locked out if the account lockout threshold has been met. If an account lockout threshold has been set, the default is 30 minutes.

- Reset Account Lockout Counter After: Used to configure how soon the Account Lockout Threshold counter will be reset after it is locked. Similar to the Account Lockout Duration setting, the default is 30 minutes. After 30 minutes, the user can try to log on again.

Local Policies>Security Options:

- Accounts: Rename Guest Account: Allows an administrator to change the Guest account name.

- Devices: Unsigned Driver Installation Driver Behavior: Determines whether unsigned drivers can be installed. To prevent unsigned drivers from ever being installed, choose the Do Not Allow Installation choice. The Warn But Allow Installation option is the default.

- Interactive Logon: Message Text For Users Attempting To Log On: Allows an administrator to configure a message that each user, upon logon, will need to read.

- Interactive Logon: Do Not Require Ctrl+Alt+Del: Allows you to define whether this key combination is required of users who log on. By default, it is not required.

Making Basic Security Policy Changes

If you share a computer with another person, or if your computer can be accessed by others, either at night or when you are away from your office, you should consider configuring some of the local security polices listed in the previous section to protect the computer and your users. Here's how:

1. Open the Control Panel, and if you are using Category view, click Performance And Maintenance. Click Administrative Tools.

2. Open Local Security Policy. Expand Account Policies and click Password Policy, as shown in Figure 14-9.

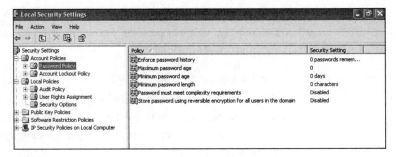

Figure 14-9
Expand Account Policies and click Password Policy to configure password settings.

3. Double-click any password policy to change. Figure 14-10 shows the Maximum Password Age Properties dialog box. Notice it's been changed from the default of 0 to 15 days. Click OK.

4. Repeat these steps to set Account Lockout Policies or Security Options.

Figure 14-10
Double-click any item to configure its settings.

You can be sure with these settings that your computer is more secure and protected than ever. When you are finished configuring the settings, simply close the Local Security Settings window. Your changes will be automatically saved.

Computer Management

Degunking requires that you have access to computer management tools such as Device Manager and Disk Defragmenter, as well as the Properties dialog boxes for the hardware installed on your computer. The Computer Manage-

ment console puts these items in a single place for easy access. Besides these
degunking tools, though, the Computer Management console, like the Local
Security Policy console, offers lots of advanced options for administrators. For
instance, an administrator can use the Event Viewer to view security audits,
which can inform an administrator of failed logon attempts and other security
issues, system failures such as failed printing requests, failed connection requests, and similar errors and warnings. The Users folder shows all of the users
configured for the computer and their properties (which can be changed from
this console). You can also access Device Manager, view properties for removable storage devices, run Disk Defragmenter, and manage the hard disks on
your computer, all from this single console. Figure 14-11 shows this console
with a failed logon attempt security audit selected. Double-clicking the item
offers additional information about the message.

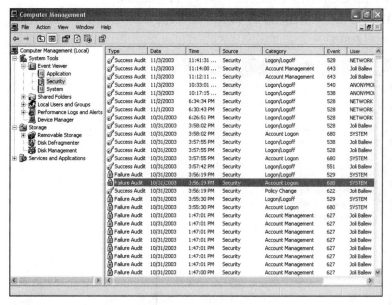

Figure 14-11
The Computer Management Console can be used for a variety of tasks, including
viewing failed logon attempts.

The best way to become familiar with the Computer Management console is
to browse through its options. Many will look familiar, including Disk
Defragmenter, Device Manager, and Services:

1. Open the Control Panel, and if you are using Category view, click Perfor-
    mance And Maintenance. Click Administrative Tools.

2. Open Computer Management.

3. To view Event Viewer, Shared Folders, Local Users And Groups, Performance Logs And Alerts, and Device Manager, expand the System Tools tree in the left pane, and then expand and/or click any item in the list to access it.

4. Figure 14-11 shows how to access the Security log; access the Application and System logs similarly. Double-click any item to view more information about it.

5. Expand Local Users And Groups and the Users folder to view the users who have access to your computer. Double-click any users you've created to change the options and requirements for that user. In Figure 14-12, notice that I can change Jennifer's password requirements or disable the account. I can also view what group she is a member of (Member Of tab) and add her to another group or remove her from any group she is a member of quite easily.

6. Click Device Manager under the System Tools console to view the console and make changes to the computer's configuration.

7. Expand the Storage tree to view Disk Defragmenter or the Disk Management consoles.

Figure 14-12
At this screen, we can change another user's password requirements or disable the account.

If you become interested in setting up users and groups, configuring performance logs and computer alerts, or working with shared folders among computers on a workgroup, there are lots of help files on the subject. Simply click Help, and click Help Topics. In the Help window, choose Computer Management.

Firewalls

Firewalls are important products that will help keep your computer degunked of unwanted files. They protect computers and networks from Internet risks, just as deadbolts on a door protect your home from intruders. Just as you would secure your home with locks and a security system, you should also secure your computer with a firewall *and* anti-virus software.

Firewalls, even the most basic ones, offer lots of protection from trespassers and keep your computer free of many unwanted files. Firewalls come in all shapes and sizes, but a determined hacker can still break in. With that in mind, you should configure your system to thwart attacks by making it as difficult as possible for an intruder to get in and access personal data. There are several ways to do this, including using Windows XP's Internet Connection Firewall or purchasing a third-party hardware or software firewall.

Windows XP's Internet Connection Firewall

Windows XP comes with a host firewall that you can enable called Internet Connection Firewall (ICF). ICF protects you pretty well from what can come into your system from the Internet. It's called a host firewall because it is created for use on a single computer (the host), like a desktop system or laptop. For the home user, Windows XP's ICF might suffice if you also have up-to-date anti-virus software, but keep in mind that it only offers the most basic protection.

Do this to enable ICF:

1. Click Start, point to Connect To, right-click your Internet connection (or open Network connections, and then right-click your Internet connection), and choose Properties.

2. Click the Advanced tab, shown in Figure 14-13.

3. Under Internet Connection Firewall, check Protect My Computer And Network By Limiting Or Preventing Access To This Computer From The Internet. Click OK.

TIP: ICF should be enabled on any Internet connection that is shared with other computers and any connection that is used on any computer to directly connect to the Internet. ICF should not be enabled on any connection/computer that does not directly connect to the Internet.

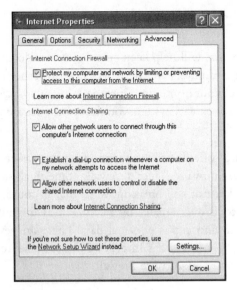

Figure 14-13
Enable ICF.

As mentioned earlier, ICF combined with up-to-date anti-virus software protects the computer pretty well. This might be all you need for a single computer or laptop that connects to the Internet, but complete security isn't necessarily guaranteed.

If you want more protection or have sensitive and valuable data, extra protection is certainly available. A few of the most popular third-party host firewalls include ZoneAlarm and Norton. These offer additional security features, including protecting your privacy, protecting against determined hackers, and other options not found in ICF. You can never go wrong purchasing a third-party firewall for extra protection, so if you can afford it, you should buy it! These products are extremely affordable and well worth the expense and peace of mind.

Home Office and Business Firewalls

Business networks require more protection than a home computer because they generally have larger, internal networks and valuable data that must be protected. Because of this, businesses may use a second type of firewall called a *network firewall*. Network firewalls can be hardware or software based and can range from fairly inexpensive to extremely expensive. One common large-business firewall is Microsoft's ISA Server, which watches traffic that enters and leaves the intranet and looks for uninvited or malicious data. Another popular firewall for businesses is the intrusion detection firewall that identifies attack patterns and uses routers to stop the connection to the source before harm can be done. These advanced firewalls offer protection that is far superior to the simple host-based firewalls such as ICF. You can get plenty of information about these different firewalls—their capabilities, pricing, and configuration— from your local computer store and from Windows XP's help files.

Get the Best Security for the Buck

One sure way to gunk up your computer is to allow a virus or worm to attack it! You want to have the most reliable software and system configuration possible, but how can you do that on a budget? If you have a single home computer that connects directly to the Internet and is not networked, you can probably get by fairly securely and cheaply using Windows XP's ICF and a good anti-virus software program. If your anti-virus software program also comes with a firewall, you're in business! Zone Alarm's Firewall is only around $40 U.S., a good investment. If you have two or three computers on a home network that uses Internet Connection Sharing, the same is true. Those who have small, home-based networks and businesses with lots of sensitive data and e-mail clients and require a more secure configuration should consider a hardware firewall. The firewall protects the network, while additional third-party host-based firewalls can be installed to further protect each computer. Hardware protection generally includes a router with firewall capabilities. Popular hardware firewalls include Linksys Routers and SMC Routers. Your local computer store likely carries at least a few of these hardware and software firewall options.

Summing Up

Improving security is a multilevel task and can be time consuming and expensive. However, an unprotected computer can get gunked up beyond belief by a single virus attack. In fact, you might not be able to recover without reinstalling. As detailed in this chapter, you must enhance security to avoid getting gunked up in the first place!

In this chapter you learned to first repair any obvious holes in security using a security analyzer like Microsoft's MBSA tool. With the most basic security flaws repaired, you absolutely must purchase, install, configure, and keep up-to-date your anti-virus software. Following that, Internet options can be configured to customize and/or configure zones and privacy options.

Administrative actions for securing the computer include enabling a Guest account when company arrives from out of town, setting local security policies for computers with multiple users or those that are left in unsecured environments like unlocked offices, and configuring a firewall. There are many different types of firewalls, including Windows XP's ICF and third-party hardware and software options.

Backing Up Precious Files

Degunking Checklist:

√ Use the Backup utility to back up important files and folders.

√ Learn what to back up and how often.

√ Store backups in a safe place.

√ Configure a scheduled task to run the Backup utility for added flexibility.

√ Learn how to use the Restore utility in case of emergency.

√ Burn to a CD-R as a backup option.

√ Manually drag and drop files to a CD as a backup option.

One of the most important tasks for a computer user to remember to do is to back up data regularly. And as you become more diligent about degunking your PC on a regular basis by using some of the degunking maintenance tasks outlined in this book, you'll need a good backup strategy. After all, degunking your PC properly involves deleting documents and programs as well as moving files around on a regular basis. If you have a regular backup strategy in place, you'll feel more confident about getting rid of files and programs because you'll be able to restore them if you later decide that you need them. The worst kind of degunker you can be is the "packrat degunker," which is the person who is afraid to throw anything away because they think that something valuable might be lost. Usually, this fear comes from having a lousy backup strategy!

Backing up data is especially important these days because we store everything—family videos, pictures, music, important documents, faxes, important records—all on a single hard drive. Imagine how much data could be destroyed by a single hard drive crash. A hard drive crash can be like a house fire or flood; every important picture, video, file, and fax would be lost.

In this chapter, you'll learn all about backing up data: scheduling a task and backing up automatically, configuring and using the Backup utility, and restoring when a crash occurs. You'll also learn what to back up, how often, and how to store your backups. In addition to using the Backup utility, you can back up files by manually dragging and dropping them to another drive, including a CD-R drive.

Perform Backups with the Backup Utility

You'll be a better degunker if you're comfortable with your backups. You'll know that you can restore from backups if you delete anything you decide you want to keep later. The Windows XP Backup utility offers an easy way to back up your data regularly. As you'll learn later in this chapter, you can combine it with the Scheduled Tasks utility to run backups automatically. The Backup utility can be run and configured via a wizard, but my suggestion is that you run it in Advanced Mode because this mode offers so many more choices. In the following sections, we'll work with the Backup utility in various modes and discuss how to use it and what should be backed up and how often, and I'll give you some strategies for storing your backups.

Getting Started

Using the Backup utility does not require you to have any special equipment, but it does require you to have some place to save the backup file. This can be a second hard drive or backup device like a Zip disk, or it can be on your own hard drive. If you use your own hard drive to save the backup, you'll need a CD burner to copy that backup file to a CD for safekeeping. With that in mind, the first step in configuring (and getting to know) the Backup utility is to open it in Advanced Mode:

1. Click Start, point to All Programs, point to Accessories, point to System Tools, and click Backup. (You won't have the Backup option if you run XP Home Edition. If that's the case, you'll have to use another backup option detailed in this chapter, such as dragging and dropping.)

2. If the Welcome To The Backup Or Restore Wizard opens, as shown in Figure 15-1, you're good to go. If the utility opens in Wizard Mode, click the link to start Advanced Mode.

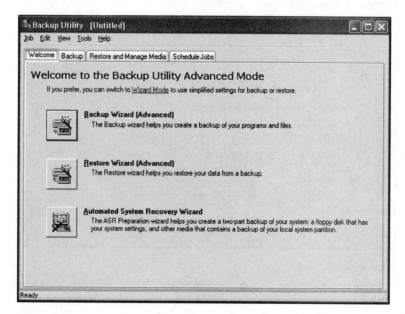

Figure 15-1
Open the Backup utility in Advanced Mode.

3. Click the Backup tab, and on the Job menu, click New.

4. In the Backup Destination area, you can either save the backup as a file or to a tape device (if one is available). File is selected by default, and if no tape device exists, no options will be given.

5. Refer to the next few sections to decide what type of backup to perform and how to select the required folders. Once the folders are selected, you can either set advanced options (also detailed) or simply start the backup.

Creating a Simple Backup

So what's the next step and how do you decide what to back up? The answer to that is not a simple one. If you only want to do a minimal backup of your important data, you can click (not check) the drive that holds the data in the left pane and then simply check the appropriate folders in the right pane. Figure 15-2 shows an example of a simple backup of files and folders. In this example, only the My Documents, My Music, My Pictures, My Videos, and My Webs folders will be backed up.

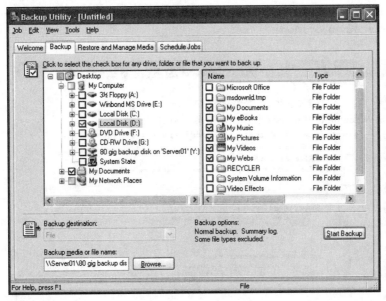

Figure 15-2

A simple backup can be created by checking only folders that contain data to back up.

Once the appropriate folders are chosen, click the Browse button to locate the backup device (an external hard drive, tape drive, Zip disk, or other removable media) or choose to save the backup as a file; then click Start Backup. You can't save a backup to a CD-R, CD-RW, or DVD-R, though, so don't even bother trying to choose any of those devices! (If you want to archive backups to a CD-R, you can always save the backup to your hard drive as a file and then copy that file to the CD. You'll learn how to do that in the section "Copy to CD as a Backup Option" later in this chapter.)

This "simple" type of backup is by no means a complete backup of the system and does not include important data like the system state, the Registry, drivers, and fonts. It also probably won't include downloaded files or programs, your Favorites list, cookies, and other important settings. To get a more complete backup requires a different approach.

Creating a Thorough Backup

To create a more thorough backup, we'll use the Advanced Backup Wizard. This wizard makes it fairly easy to define what exactly you want to back up and includes options to back up the system state.

NOTE: When you back up the system state, you back up the boot files, system files, the Registry, and other important data.

To use the Advanced Backup Wizard to back up anything or everything on your computer, including the system state and Registry, follow these steps:

1. Click Start, point to All Programs, point to Accessories, point to System Tools, and click Backup.

2. If the Welcome To The Backup Or Restore Wizard opens in Advanced Mode, as shown in Figure 15-1, you're good to go. If the utility opens in Wizard Mode, click the link to start Advanced Mode.

3. From the Welcome tab, click the Backup Wizard (Advanced) button.

4. If prompted, click No to clear any previously configured backups, and in the Welcome To The Backup Wizard page, click Next.

5. In the What To Back Up page, you can choose from Back Up Everything On This Computer; Back Up Only Selected Files, Drives, Or Network Data; or Only Back Up the System State Data. If you select the second choice, you'll be prompted to choose folders, as shown in Figure 15-2, before you can continue. If you choose either of the other two choices, the Backup Wizard will continue as described in step 6.

6. In the Backup, Type, Destination, And Name page, choose the backup type (File or Tape Device), browse to a place to save your backup, and type a name for the backup as shown in Figure 15-3. Click Next.

7. In the Completing The Backup Wizard page, verify that the information is correct and click Back to change anything that is not. To complete the wizard and begin the backup, click Finish. To set advanced options, click the Advanced button and work through the remaining pages. The Advanced button allows you to select a backup type, which is detailed in the following

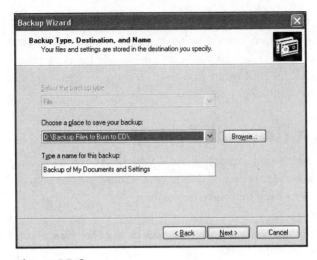

Figure 15-3
Browse to the location to save the backup and name it appropriately.

section. You can also decide if you want to append the data to an existing backup or not and whether to perform the backup now or later. Figure 15-4 shows a backup of the system state in progress.

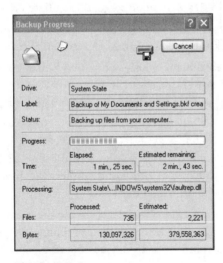

Figure 15-4
Backing up the system state doesn't take very long.

GunkBuster's Notebook: Perform Backups Before Deleting, Installing, Moving, and Experimenting

You know you should create a system restore point prior to performing a risky task like installing a downloaded application from a third party or unreputable Web site, installing software from a file-sharing Internet site, performing virus removal tasks, or installing an unsigned driver. But you might not be aware that you should also perform a backup.

Although System Restore can often restore you computer successfully if something happens, sometimes it can't. (You'll learn more about the System Restore utility in Chapter 16.) This is especially true if a procedure such as removing a virus, editing the Registry, or installing some third-party software that has questionable code goes awry. You'll need a good, solid backup to recover from that. Create a backup before doing anything risky, including the following:

- Installing software you've downloaded from the Internet

- Editing the Registry

- Making changes to the BIOS

- Installing an upgrade

- Creating a dual-boot system

- Using partition-moving software to make major changes to the hard disk's configuration

- Performing a virus removal procedure

- Joining a file sharing Internet group

Use Different Types of Backups

There are several types of backups you can create, and you'll need to understand each type so that you can regularly create a good set of backups that are both efficient and effective. As mentioned in step 7 in the previous example, clicking the Advanced button offers additional options for creating the backup. The options for choosing a backup type are available from either the simple wizard interface or the advanced one, as well as from the Backup tab (after you've clicked Start Backup).

The five types of backups available include normal, copy, incremental, differential, and daily. Depending on the backup type you choose, you can also opt to append the data to the previous backup or overwrite the existing data. To decide what type of backup you should choose, read the following descriptions:

- Normal: You'll generally choose this option the first time you create a backup file. This type of backup is the default. Your selected files are copied and marked as backed up.

- Incremental: With this type of backup, only files created or changed since the last normal or incremental backup are copied and marked as backed up.

- Differential: With this option, only the files that have changed since the last normal or incremental backup are copied, but they are not marked as backed up.

- Copy: All selected files are copied but not marked as being backed up. This is useful if you want to back up files between normal or incremental backups but don't want to affect those normal or incremental backups.

- Daily: All selected files that have been modified the day the daily backup is scheduled or run are copied. The backed up files are not marked as backed up and thus do not affect other backups.

Combining backups and restoring from multiple backups and multiple backup tapes can get a little complicated. You have to fully understand exactly what each backup does and how it is used to restore a computer.

Recommendations for the Home User

Just in case you get gunked up with a virus or make a mistake while editing the BIOS or Registry, make sure you have good, solid backups. For the home user, we'll suggest creating a normal backup of the system state and a normal backup of the My Documents, My Pictures, My Music, and other data folders and then storing those backups on a CD or a separate hard drive. You might also back up the Fonts folder, other personal folders, the Unzipped folder (if you have one), and even a few program folders. You can then combine those normal backups with daily backups if so inclined. In addition, you should create a normal, full backup in case of an extreme emergency. Both can be used with the Restore utility, and you can decide which one to use depending on the situation at hand.

How Often to Back Up

You should develop a backup schedule based on how much data you can stand to lose. We perform a daily backup, but we make quite a few changes every day to the data stored on our hard drives and we consider our data quite valuable. We perform normal backups once a week. If, however, you only log on twice a week to send a few e-mails, there's certainly no need to create a backup schedule like this one. Table 15-1 briefly outlines common backup strategies.

Table 15-1:   Back Up Regularly

If you are a...	Perform a normal (daily) backup ...	Perform a full backup ...
Casual user who only turns on the computer twice a week to e-mail a friend	Once every two weeks or anytime anything is created that cannot be lost	Twice a year
Home user and access the computer daily	Two or three times a week or anytime anything is created that cannot be lost	Four times a year
Home user and digital media enthusiast or if you work from home	Once a day, at the end of each day	Once a week or twice a month
Home user and run a home-based business	Once a day, at the end of each day	Once a week

Regardless of how much you use your computer, you should have at least one full backup at least a couple of times a year. You should perform normal backups combined with daily backups as you deem necessary. We think, for most people, backing up important (and changed) documents at least once a week is a good habit to get into.

About Storing the Backups

A spilled soda that lands on your computer and then spills over onto your backup device will destroy both, so placing your external hard drive (with your backups on it) on top of your tower doesn't make much sense. In the same vein, a lightning strike that gets by your surge protector will likely destroy anything that's plugged into it, so even having the backup device in the same room can offer up problems.

Consider creating a backup on an external drive and then burning that file to a CD-R once a month or so. Then you can store the CD in another room, in a safe deposit box, or at another location for safekeeping. You might also back up to an external drive and then unplug and remove it to protect it from power surges, viruses, spilled coffee, or other catastrophes. Data stored on computers has certainly become *that* valuable; pictures, videos, and some data simply can't be replaced or re-created.

TIP: *Treat your backups as you would your most precious photos or videos. You want to keep them in a safe place where flood, fire, or theft won't be a threat.*

Scheduling a Backup Using the Backup Utility

Although you can use the Scheduled Tasks utility, as you'll learn later in this chapter, to remind you to back up your data daily, weekly, or monthly, you can also schedule a backup using the Backup utility itself. Using the Backup utility is more comprehensive and a better choice because you can change the backup type, what's backed up, and where it's stored for each job you create while creating the scheduled task.

Here's how create a scheduled job using the Backup utility:

1. Open Backup in Advanced Mode as detailed earlier.
2. Click the Schedule Jobs tab and choose a day to create the backup job, as shown in Figure 15-5.

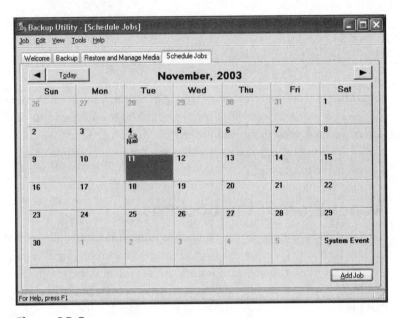

Figure 15-5
Schedule a backup job using the Backup utility.

3. Click Add Job, and click Next in the Welcome To The Backup Wizard page.
4. Continue working through the wizard to create the job as detailed earlier.

You certainly can't have too many backups or back up too often. Configure backups to run at least weekly, store the backups in a secure location, and use the Restore utility if a restoration of data is necessary.

Schedule Backups with the Windows Scheduled Tasks Utility

The Scheduled Tasks utility in Windows XP allows you to schedule almost any task to run automatically whenever you choose so that you don't have to remember to perform the tasks yourself. Scheduled tasks can include running a program like Outlook Express every morning at 8 A.M., running the Backup utility every other day at 5 P.M., running Disk Cleanup once a week at midnight, or having Windows Media Player open each night at 9 P.M. so that you can listen to music or Internet radio when you go to bed. You might even configure System Restore to create a restore point every Sunday afternoon, just before the workweek starts. The tasks can be fun, useful, or necessary, but the task must involve a program, script, or document that is either in the Scheduled Task list or can be browsed to. Scheduled tasks, once configured, run in the background.

You might already have some scheduled tasks configured if you've set your anti-virus program to check for updates or to scan your computer daily or weekly. Figure 15-6 shows a sample Schedule Tasks window, which can be opened in the Control Panel (under Performance And Maintenance if you use Category view).

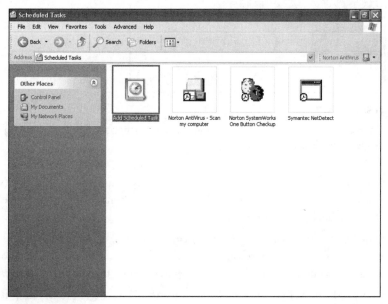

Figure 15-6
The Scheduled Tasks folder might already have some tasks configured by third-party programs.

Configuring a Scheduled Task

Configuring a scheduled task is as easy as clicking Add Scheduled Task (shown in Figure 15-6) and following the prompts from the Scheduled Tasks Wizard. In this example, we'll schedule the Backup utility to run automatically as often as you desire, but you can configure just about any program or task to run by browsing to it instead of the Backup utility we'll schedule here.

To schedule the Backup utility to run automatically on a specific schedule, follow these steps:

1. Open the Control Panel, and if you use Category view, click Performance And Maintenance. Click Scheduled Tasks.

2. Read the first page of the Scheduled Task Wizard and click Next.

3. In the second page of the Scheduled Task Wizard, click Backup as shown in Figure 15-7. Click Next.

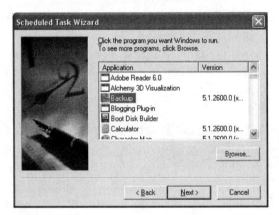

Figure 15-7

Choose the program or application you want to schedule. If it isn't showing in this list, click Browse to locate it.

4. Continuing with the Scheduled Task Wizard, type a name for the task (you can keep Backup if you like), and choose how often to run the task. We'll choose Weekly. Click Next.

5. Schedule the time (and day if applicable) for this task to run. For backups, disk cleanups, and other maintenance tasks, choose a time when no one will be using the computer but when the computer will be turned on. Click Next.

6. Many tasks must be run using an administrator's account, and Backup is one of them. Enter the name of an administrator as well as the password. Confirm the password and click Next.

7. Check Open Advanced Properties For This Task When I Click Finish. Click Finish.

8. In the task's Properties box (Backup is shown in Figure 15-8), type in comments on the Task tab, verify the schedule on the Schedule tab, and configure any advanced settings on the Settings tab. Advanced settings can include starting the task only if the computer is idle, whether the computer should be awakened to perform this task, and more. Generally the defaults are fine. Click OK.

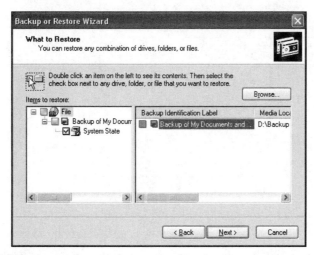

Figure 15-8
Each task's Properties dialog box offers advanced options for configuring the task.

With the Backup utility configured to run, you'll need to configure it so Windows will know what you want to back up and to where. System Restore is next.

TIP: *Make sure the scheduled task is run under an administrator's account and that it also has a password assigned. If you have problems with the task running as scheduled, check this first by right-clicking the task in Scheduled Task and clicking Properties.*

Using the Restore Utility

If you've decided you need to restore data because it has become corrupt, because you accidentally deleted it, or because you purchased a new computer and want to transfer the backed-up files to it, you can do so easily with the Restore utility in Backup. You can also use the Restore utility if you've so seriously gunked up your computer that you've had to reinstall everything!

Restore can be run in Wizard Mode or Advanced Mode. Restoring in Wizard Mode is the easiest, and the wizard even goes to the trouble of locating the saved backups for you! Figure 15-9 shows an example of how the restoration option works.

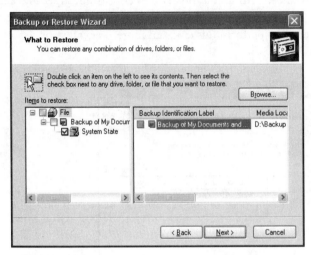

Figure 15-9
Restoring is easy with Backup and the Wizard Mode.

TIP: Don't restore system state to a new computer. Your system state and Registry files are unique to your computer.

Follow these steps to restore from backup:

1. Open Backup and choose the Wizard Mode. Although you can use Advanced Mode or the Restore tab, this is easiest. Click Next to begin.

2. When prompted at the Backup Or Restore page, choose Restore Files And Settings. Click Next.

3. In the What To Restore page shown in Figure 15-9, locate the backup to restore with and click Next.

4. In the Completing The Backup Or Restore Wizard page, click Advanced. You can chose to restore the files to their original location, an alternate location, or a single folder. Click Next.

5. In the How To Restore page, choose how to restore the files. You can choose Leave Existing Files (Recommended), Replace Existing Files If They Are Older Than The Backup Files, or Replace Existing Files. In most instances, the first option is recommended. Click Next.

6. In the Advanced Restore Options page, leave the defaults and click Next. Click Finish to begin the restoration.

TIP: *When restoring to a new computer, you might choose to alter the default settings and restore the files to a single folder. This way you can place the files you've restored into the exact folders you'd like them to go in.*

Restoring is a great way to put things back where they were before the computer got really gunked up. Restoring allows you to put back into place data such as valuable pictures, music, movies, and documents as well as the system state, fonts, and even permissions, audit entries, and ownership settings.

Copy to CD as a Backup Option

Archiving unneeded data is a great way to keep your computer gunk-free. If you only have a few specific folders to back up, if you don't have a device to save a backup to, or if you have created a backup file that you'd like to burn to a CD for archiving, you can use the CD Writing Wizard to burn a backup CD via Windows XP. CDs make great archiving tools and allow you to keep copies of important data in a separate location easily. As you know, the Backup utility can't be used to burn directly to a CD-R.

We'll show you two ways to use CD-R. In the first example, we'll show you how to create a backup file and save it to your hard drive and then how to copy that backup file to a CD-R. This is the perfect backup arrangement for those who do not have a backup device such as an external hard drive, tape device, or Zip disk but who do have a CD-R drive. In the second example, we'll show you how to drag and drop any folder using Windows Explorer, bypassing the Backup utility altogether.

Here's how to burn a backup to a CD:

1. Open the Backup utility and use the simple wizard, the advanced wizard, or the manual backup option to select the files to back up. In this example, we've chosen the simple wizard, and we've chosen to back up My Documents And Settings. Note where you are saving the files; you'll browse to them next.

2. Once the backup is complete, browse to the folder holding the files. Figure 15-10 shows a backup we've created and saved to the hard drive D:. Hover the mouse over the folder to select it, and notice the option to copy this file in the left pane.

3. Choose Copy This File from the File And Folder Tasks pane, and put a CD-R disk in the CD drive.

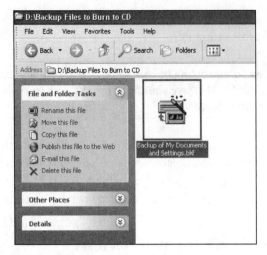

Figure 15-10
Copy a backup to a CD-R by browsing to it first and then choosing Copy This File.

4. From the Copy Items dialog box, browse to the location of the CD drive and click Copy. See Figure 15-11.

Figure 15-11
Browse to the CD-R drive and choose Copy.

5. Wait while the files copy, and when the CD is ready, browse to it and choose Write These Files To CD from the CD Writing Tasks pane, shown in **Figure 15-12.**

6. Name the CD and click Next in the CD Writing Wizard.

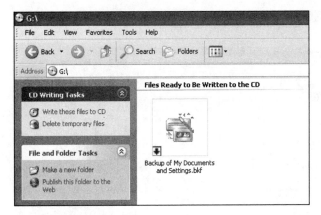

Figure 15-12
Write files to the CD once they're copied.

You'll probably find this option a quick and easy way to get around not having a backup device. Unfortunately, you might also find that your CDs won't hold all of the data you'd like to back up, especially if you're trying to back up your entire system. If that's the case, you'll either have to create the backup manually, being careful to choose a limited number of files to burn for each CD, or manually drag and drop the folders you want to copy to the CD, keeping track of how much you're putting in there along the way.

To drag and drop files and folders and copy the data to a CD-R, follow these steps:

1. Place a CD-R disk in the appropriate drive.

2. Open My Computer and select the CD-R drive. Position the window so that it takes up only half the screen.

3. Right-click the Start button, and choose Explore. Browse to the folder to copy, and then right-click and drag it to the CD-R folder.

4. Once the folder has copied, hover the mouse over it to see its size. As you can see in Figure 15-13, the Cookies folder is only 34.3 KB. The CD can hold 702 MB, so there's plenty of room for this folder and then some. Continue adding files and folders to copy until the disk is 95% full.

5. When you are ready to write the files to the CD, click Write These Files To CD in the CD Writing Tasks pane.

Whatever way you decide to go, backing up is certainly a necessity and worth the time it takes to perform the task. It doesn't have to be anything elaborate; just a simple backup of your pictures and documents will generally suffice. Choose a backup program that you can live with, and then stick with it!

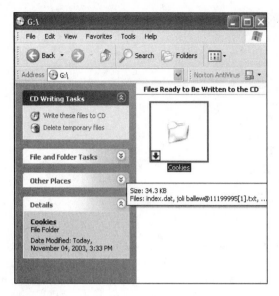

Figure 15-13

You can manually drag folders to copy and keep track of their size by hovering the mouse over the items to copy.

Summing Up

Good backups promote good degunking habits. If you know you have a backup of your important data, you're more likely to experiment with the degunking techniques introduced in this book. Besides that, though, it's important to keep up-to-date backups for the pictures, videos, Webs, and other data stored on your computer because losing all of this data could be potentially devastating. Windows XP comes with a Backup utility just for this purpose and offers several different types of backups. Besides backing up manually, you can schedule backups using Scheduled Tasks or you can configure Backup to run at specific intervals. Once the backups are created, you should store them in a safe place in case they are ever needed.

Last Resort Degunking Techniques

Degunking Checklist:

√ Check your system for incompatible hardware and uninstall these devices using the Windows XP CD-ROM.

√ Solve problems with drivers by installing new drivers and using the Device Driver Rollback utility when necessary.

√ Configure and prepare System Restore in case it's ever needed.

√ Recover from a computer problem or minor crash using System Restore.

√ Use the Repair option on the Windows XP CD-ROM to repair your computer.

√ Upgrade to Windows XP if Repair can't be used.

√ If you decide to reinstall and format your drive, gather all the critical information on settings, configurations, and applications.

√ Perform a clean installation only if you really, really have to.

D egunking does have its limits. At some point, you might experience problems with your computer that become so bad that degunking and normal troubleshooting won't work. Don't panic just yet because we still might be able to help you. Perhaps you installed a new driver recently and your computer bluescreens, or you deleted some necessary files and your computer now produces errors on boot-up. You also might discover that your computer mysteriously shuts down while running applications or it simply won't get past the loading of system files during the boot process. If errors like these occur, you can employ some specific techniques for getting your computer working properly again.

In this final chapter, you'll learn how to solve some common (but tricky) problems by locating incompatible hardware and using the Device Driver Rollback and System Restore utilities, two excellent programs for correcting serious errors. You'll also learn how to replace missing files needed for booting and for starting Windows XP by using the Windows XP CD's Repair option. Finally, you'll learn how to upgrade to Windows XP if you can't access the Repair option and how and when to perform a clean installation of Windows XP. Installing a new version of XP is certainly a last resort; however, if all the other degunking strategies you learned in this book no longer work for you, the smartest thing to do is to install a clean version of XP.

Locate Incompatible Hardware

You might at first feel helpless if you are having recurring and unexplainable problems with your computer, such as those listed here:

- Your system crashes randomly.
- Programs that you use regularly lock up without warning.
- Your computer freezes up when performing tasks like printing files.
- A new device you've recently connected to your computer, such as a scanner or a printer, is causing your computer to lock up and exhibit other strange behavior.

You've probably tried a number of things to solve one or more of these problems, including asking everyone you know who knows anything at all about Windows. You've also probably tried to play detective and duplicate the cause of the problems. Often in situations like this, the problems might not be with your computer or the operating system files. They might be created by the hardware that you've added to your computer.

Before panicking and reinstalling the entire system, you should run a compatibility check. If such a check finds anything that's not compatible, it'll tell you right away. Uninstalling the problem device or locating a new driver for it might solve all of your problems.

Here's how to check system compatibility:

1. Put the Windows XP CD in the CD-ROM drive. It should start automatically. If you don't have an XP CD, you might try the disk that came with your computer. If you can't find your XP CD or if you don't have one, you're out of luck here.

TIP: *If you know your product ID number (also called your Product key) but can't find your own XP CD, you can borrow a CD from a friend or colleague. This only works if you can produce your own product ID, though.*

---

2. From the choices on the What Do You Want To Do? page, select Check System Compatibility. On the next page, select Check My System Automatically.

3. If prompted, choose to let XP get updated system files from Microsoft's Web site.

4. Once the process is complete, you'll receive a report about any incompatible hardware or software.

The compatibility report offers quite a bit of information if incompatible hardware or software is found. For instance, it will list the name of the incompatible device or program and allow you to view details regarding it. Figure 16-1 shows a system compatibility report, and Figure 16-2 shows the information received when Details is clicked. Notice in Figure 16-1 that an installed printer is listed.

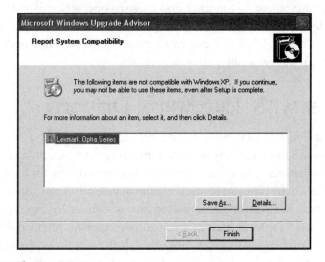

Figure 16-1
A system compatibility report lists incompatible software and hardware.

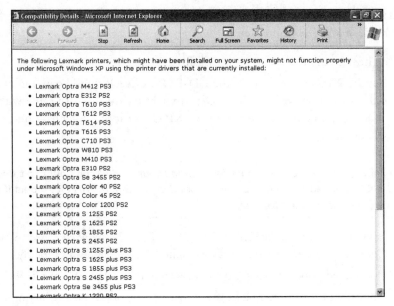

Figure 16-2
Clicking Details in the Report System Compatibility dialog box offers additional information.

If you find out that you have some hardware that is not compatible with Windows XP, read the details to see what can be done to remedy the situation. As shown in Figure 16-2, drivers are a common issue. Therefore, you'll generally search for a newer driver first. If you can't find a signed one, seriously consider uninstalling the device and removing it from your system. From my personal experience, an incompatible device can cause major problems, but once it's removed, the system will generally perform normally.

Fix Problems with Hardware Drivers

If you've ever installed a newer driver for a piece of hardware like a camera, printer, or modem and then had problems after installing it, you know firsthand how dangerous bad drivers can be. Installing an incorrect driver for a device doesn't just affect the hardware you're installing the device for. It can also wreak havoc on the entire system, causing unexpected blue screens or having applications shut down for no apparent reason. If you suspect a newly installed driver has caused a system problem, you can remove that driver and replace it with a different one. You can also use the rollback feature of Windows and instruct your system to use an older version of a driver. We'll show you how to do this in the next section.

To solve a driver-related problem, follow these steps:

1. Isolate the hardware device that is causing problems for your computer. This can be a little tricky if you have recently installed more than one hardware device, such as a camera and a scanner. If this is the case, disconnect all of the hardware devices that you have installed recently and then connect each device, one at a time, and test to see if you can find the device that is causing problems for your system.

2. Once you find the problem device, you should reinstall the hardware driver for it. Use the installation disk that came with the hardware device and follow the instructions carefully. It is possible that device driver files become corrupted and simply reinstalling a driver can solve your problem.

3. If you have an Internet connection, you may want to visit the Web site of the company that produces the device you are reinstalling the driver for. Many companies offer driver updates for free, and their Web sites are likely to have the most recent drivers. Find the driver you need, download it, and install it.

4. After you successfully install the new driver, reboot your computer to ensure that the new driver gets initialized properly.

TIP: *When trying to diagnose your driver problems, don't forget to use the Web. If you are having a problem with a hardware device, it's likely many other users are having the same problem. Companies who produce hardware devices often post troubleshooting sections on their Web sites to make it easier for you to play detective and solve tricky problems.*

Return to Older Versions of Drivers Using the Device Driver Rollback Utility

If you are having a problem with a hardware device that you have been using for a while and have installed different drivers for it, you can easily use the Device Driver Rollback utility to return to an older version of the driver. When hardware manufacturers issue new versions of their drivers, usually the new drivers will help fix problems that have been detected in the past by users. In some situations, new drivers will unfortunately create problems that didn't exist before. If this happens, your best bet is to use an older version of the driver. This is easy to do because Windows provides a built-in feature for managing driver versions.

To use Device Driver Rollback, follow these steps:

1. Right-click My Computer and click Properties.

2. Click the Hardware tab, and then click Device Manager.

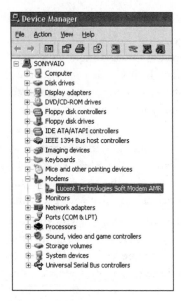

Figure 16-3
Use Device Manager to locate the device that has a problematic driver.

3. Locate in the device tree, shown in Figure 16-3, the device whose driver needs to be rolled back. (This new driver was installed because it came up during a driver update test as a compatible driver. However, because problems ensued, rolling back the driver is the best choice.)

4. Double-click the device, and in the device's Properties dialog box, click the Driver tab. Figure 16-4 shows this tab and the available options.

5. Click Roll Back Driver, and click Yes to roll back to the previous driver.

If, after rolling back the driver, you are prompted to restart the computer, do so. If a problem occurs with the rolled-back driver, run Device Driver Rollback again. If problems still occur, consider System Restore, detailed in the next section.

TIP: As you can see from Figure 16-4, you can also update or uninstall the driver from this dialog box.

Return Your System to an Earlier State with System Restore

One special trick that many Windows XP users aren't aware of is that they can restore their computer to the state it was in prior to the present state. Why is this important? Let's say that over the past two weeks you hooked up a few new

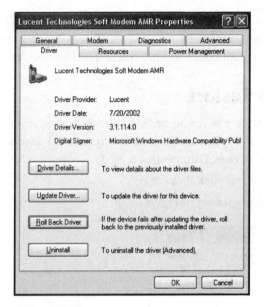

Figure 16-4
The Driver tab offers several options.

hardware devices, installed hardware drivers, and loaded up a few new applications. After this was done, your computer really started to act up. You tried some of the critical degunking tasks outlined in this book—such as installing new drivers and removing gunk off of your hard drive—but your machine still won't run as it did a few weeks back. With the help of a seemingly magical tool called System Restore, you can return your computer to the state it was in before you made all of your changes. The best part is that you can restore your computer without losing any recently added items like documents, Internet Favorites, e-mail messages, or your Internet History files. If this sounds like the next best thing since time travel, you're right!

TIP: *The System Restore feature provides a good approach for backing up important system-level data, such as the Registry. We recommend that you use this feature before you consider making any changes to the Registry. This technique is covered in Chapter 9.*

In order for the System Restore utility to be able to perform its magic, you must make sure that it is first enabled. (It is likely enabled on your system by default.) Once enabled, it operates by creating what are called *restore points.* These restore points keep track of the different states of your computer over time as you make changes. You can think of them as bookmarks. Depending on how much space is reserved for System Restore, you can have up to three weeks worth of restore points available, and they are created almost daily. While this data takes up some space on your hard drive and uses some system resources, it is vital to recovery. You should configure and use the System Restore feature.

Configure System Restore

Take a look at how System Restore is configured on your computer, and verify that it is running, so that you can be sure to have the maximum amount of protection against computer glitches, failures, and errors:

1. Right-click My Computer and click Properties.

2. Click the System Restore tab, shown in Figure 16-5.

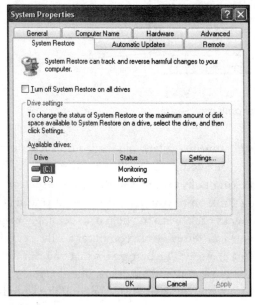

Figure 16-5

Verify that System Restore is enabled and is monitoring all of the drives on your computer.

3. Verify that Turn Off System Restore On All Drives is not checked and that all available drives are being monitored. System Restore won't work if you have less than 200 MB of free space on your computer's hard drive.

4. Click a drive, and click Settings. In the Settings dialog box, verify that ample space is provided for System Restore to store its data. I keep mine at about 1000 MB, but I have a huge hard drive. You'll have to decide how much space you'd like to share: 10–12 percent of the hard drive's available space is fine, but depending on the size of your hard drive, this could mean 7000 or 8000 MB of space. At least keep 1500 MB of space reserved for System Restore to allow for optimal protection. Click OK.

5. Check any additional drives for System Restore settings. Click OK to exit.

Now, if you ever need to restore your computer to an earlier time—say, before you installed that last driver, last downloaded Internet application, last screensaver, or last piece of hardware that blew out the system—you can do so quite easily.

Create Restore Points Manually

Restore points are created automatically by System Restore whenever the program is enabled, once a day or so. They're also created when you install specific applications and programs. Windows XP creates them when you install unsigned device drivers, when you install automatic updates, and when you use the restore operation. Anytime you use System Restore, the restoration process is absolutely reversible. However, if you know that you are planning on doing something risky or something that might make your computer unstable (such as installing that screensaver you're so fond of), you can create a restore point manually.

Creating a restore point manually is incredibly easy:

1. Click Start, point to All Programs, point to Accessories, point to System Tools, and click System Restore. The initial System Restore page is shown in Figure 16-6.

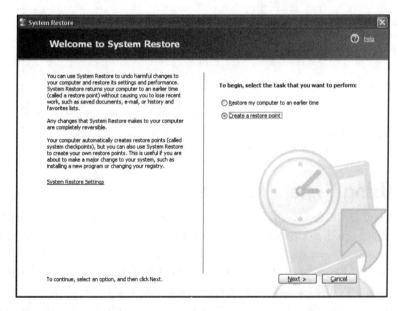

Figure 16-6

System Restore can be used to restore the computer to an earlier time, but it can also be used to create a restore point manually.

2. Select Create A Restore Point and click Next.

3. In the Create A Restore Point page, type a description of the restore point. Click Create.

4. The new restore point will be created. Click Home in the Restore Point Created page.

5. To see the new restore point, back at the Welcome To System Restore page, click Restore My Computer To An Earlier Time and click Next.

The new restore point will be selected and visible, as seen in Figure 16-7. You can now use this restore point if your risky installation doesn't go well.

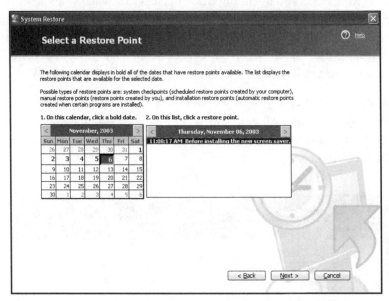

Figure 16-7
Check out the new restore point.

Using System Restore

If you've decided you need to use System Restore, it's just about as easy as rebooting, and if you aren't happy with the results, you can switch back. System Restore creates its own restore point before it uses one you've selected, so you're safe using it whenever you feel it's necessary. The restore process will restore your computer to an earlier time, any that you choose, and the computer will act like it did on that date. This is the perfect way to solve minor problems with applications gone bad, downloads gone wacky, or drivers gone crazy. It can also be used if you are suddenly having difficulty diagnosing computer problems, problems with applications, or problems with hardware. Simply use System Restore to return to a date when the computer was working properly.

Here's how to use System Restore:

1. Click Start, point to All Programs, point to Accessories, point to System Tools, and click System Restore.

2. Select Restore My Computer To An Earlier Time and click Next.

3. Select a restore point. Restore points are marked with a dark blue font. Locate the restore point; use the arrow to return to a previous month if necessary. Click Next.

4. Click Next in the Confirm Restore Point Selection to begin the process. The computer will reboot, and you'll be prompted on startup that System Restore is reversible.

System Restore is the first thing you should try before running more time-consuming tasks like the Repair option or upgrading using the Windows XP CD. These are also better choices than performing a clean installation.

Repair XP with the XP CD-ROM

Before using the Repair option with the Windows XP CD, you should have tried the following:

* Employed the critical degunking techniques outlined in this book
* Downloaded and installed the latest and critical Windows updates
* Used Device Driver Rollback to switch back to earlier versions of device drivers for your hardware
* Attempted to solve your current computer problem with System Restore by restoring your system to an earlier state

If you are still having problems with your PC, you can try to solve your problem with the repair option on the Windows XP CD. The repair option is a powerful tool and can fix startup problems, problems with system files, and more, all automatically.

CAUTION: *We highly recommend that you try the repair option before you install a new version of Windows XP. Always remember that installing a new version of XP should be your last resort.*

To repair your system with the Windows XP CD-ROM, make sure you have a valid product key before starting. You can locate the product key from the Windows XP CD's packaging materials.

What If I Don't Have an XP CD?

If you purchased a computer that did not come with a Windows XP CD and you want to use the Repair option, you are probably out of luck. Perhaps you purchased the computer secondhand and it didn't come with a disk, or your new computer came with a restore CD instead of a Windows XP CD. Either way, you can't use the Repair option if you don't have the disk! (If you've broken or lost your disk and have a valid product ID, you can get a replacement from Microsoft.)

Unfortunately the missing disk phenomenon happens to a lot of buyers, and the restore CDs that many people receive with their computers will only reformat the drive and revert the computer back to the state it was in the day you purchased it. If this has happened to you, the installation files might be stored on your computer or restoration CDs. We'd suggest calling the computer manufacturer's technical support line to inquire. If worse comes to worse, and it probably will if you only received a restore CD, you might want to purchase an XP CD from your local computer store or online dealer.

If none of these solutions works, do a complete backup of all of your files, settings, and system state; use the Restore CD to reformat the computer; and then use the Backup And Restore utility to restore your data to the newly installed computer.

TIP: To protest the missing CD phenomenon, make sure you insist your next computer comes with a real XP CD. If all computer buyers insisted, we'd all have the CDs we need!

How to Boot to the CD

If you use the repair option, your computer will have to be configured to boot to the CD. Chances are good it already is configured that way, so before you go messing around in the BIOS, pop in the Windows CD and reboot the computer. If you see an option during boot-up telling you to "Press any key to boot to the CD" or something similar, follow the instructions to do so. If you do not see that option and you cannot boot to the CD, you'll have to make a change in the computer's BIOS.

Changing the BIOS

Entering the BIOS requires you to press the right key combination or the correct function key at the right time during boot-up, and it isn't always that easy. Computer manufacturers would rather you not fiddle around in there, and they don't make it that easy to find. If you don't know your key combination and it isn't listed at boot-up, try pressing the F1, F2, F3, or similar key at the splash screen. If that doesn't work, you might have to visit the Web site of your computer maker and search through its knowledge base.

Once you can access the BIOS, browse through the pages using the arrow keys and locate the page that offers a listing of the boot-up sequence. Use the arrow keys and follow the instructions listed to change the boot sequence to include the CD-ROM drive as the first option. Exit the BIOS saving the changes, and continue on to the next section.

Repair XP Without Doing a Clean Install

You can repair XP without doing a clean installation. This option is the first one you should try if you've been having serious problems with startup errors, boot errors, or hard-to-diagnose problems that no other degunking technique has been able to solve. Here's how to perform a repair:

1. Put the Windows XP CD in the CD-ROM drive and reboot the computer.

2. When prompted to boot to the CD, perform the required steps. Generally this is achieved by pressing any key during the boot process.

3. Wait while Setup loads the files. At the Welcome To Setup screen, press Enter to select the option To Set Up Windows XP Now.

4. Press F8 to agree to the terms. At the next screen, use the arrow keys to select the partition that contains XP's current files.

5. Press R on the keyboard to start the repair process.

CAUTION: Do not press Esc because this will start a clean installation of Windows XP and will format the drive.

---

6. Wait while the drive or drives are examined and follow the prompts as you work through the repair task.

7. The computer will reboot. Do *not* choose to boot to the CD again; the process will simply start over. Let Windows reboot on its own.

8. When prompted, set up Regional and Language settings and type in the product key located on the XP packaging.

9. After the installation is complete, work through the activation pages.

We've found that the repair option works really well in solving operating system problems, and on boot-up, errors are usually gone and the system is fully functional. With a repair, you don't lose any existing files, data, applications, or settings, so it's one of your best options as a troubleshooting technique.

Upgrade to Windows XP

If you can't boot to the CD, you won't be able to use the Repair option. If this is the case, you can perform a repair by reinstalling Windows XP using the Upgrade option. Upgrading preserves your installed programs, data files, and computer settings and does not format the hard drive as a clean install would.

TIP: The Upgrade option does the same thing the Repair option does but generally takes 60 to 90 minutes, in comparison to the 40 minutes or so a repair takes.

If you can't configure your computer to boot to the Windows XP CD but you'd like to use the repair option, you'll have to work through the process this way:

1. With the computer running, put the Windows XP CD in the CD-ROM drive.
2. At the Welcome screen, choose Install Windows XP.
3. In the Windows Setup dialog box, choose Upgrade and click Next.
4. Accept the license agreement and click Next.
5. Type in the activation code and work though the setup process.
6. After installation is complete, finish by working through the activation screens.

Performing an upgrade or a repair installation will fix many common problems with the operating system because it recopies the operating system files and puts everything back in the proper place. Performing an upgrade does not cause you to lose any data, pictures, music, or e-mails and is a good way to get a gunked-up system running again.

Do a Clean Install But Only If You Really Have to

If you've given up all hope of repairing your computer on your own, if tech support has told you that reinstalling is the only option, or if you are going to sell your computer (or give it to someone) and want to erase all of the data on it, you should perform a clean installation of Windows XP. But beware! A clean installation will format your drive, which means all of the data you have saved on the computer will be erased. You'll want to make careful backups of everything you've created before moving forward.

GunkBuster's Notebook: When to Perform a Clean Installation

Performing a clean install of the operating system should be a last-ditch effort to save the computer from the trash heap. Your computer needs to be so severely gunked up that you simply can't stand to look at it, or it needs to be so unresponsive that it hangs up regularly and causes loss of data (and headaches). You can do a clean install for good reasons too, though, like when you're selling the computer to someone else to buy a new one! Here are a few telltale signs you need to reinstall clean:

- You want to sell the computer.
- The computer hangs when printing documents.
- You get DLL errors on boot-up that an upgrade or repair doesn't solve.
- The computer blue-screens or hangs more than once a week.
- The computer is severely slow, even though it has a fast processor and plenty of RAM.
- You've tried all of the degunking tasks in this book.
- You're beginning to hate your computer.

Gather Your Critical Information

Since the computer's drive will be reformatted, you'll want to take special precautions in not only backing up all of your data to a disk or CD, but also in writing down the settings for your ISP, the phone number you dial, your broadband configuration, network settings, and other critical information. You'll also need to gather up all of the applications you use, including their product or activation keys. There are other things you should make a note of too: printers, cameras, scanner drivers, software you've purchased from the Internet, downloads that you don't have on disk, and screensavers you dearly love.

Before you begin, sit down and make a list of everything you can think of that will need to be reinstalled and see if you can locate them either in your desk or on your computer. If they're on the computer's hard drive, locate the program folder and burn a CD of the files.

Although this is not a complete list of things you should locate and/or back up, Table 16-1 will help you get started. For a more complete list, refer to the form in Appendix A.

Table 16-1:   **Clean Installation Checklist**

Items to Acquire and Back Up	Check Here Once Acquired
System folders, including My Documents, My Pictures, My Music, My Webs, and My Videos	
Any personal folders you've created	
Program files for downloaded applications that you do not have on disk	
Anti-virus disks and activation codes	
The Windows XP product key	
Service packs on disk if you have them	
ISP phone numbers and settings	
E-mail account information	
E-mail address book	
Hardware drivers and software disks	
Computer name and workgroup name	

You can acquire some of this information by browsing through the settings for your Internet connection, viewing Outlook or Outlook Express settings for accounts and options, and viewing the Properties dialog boxes for codes and activation keys. Other information such as product activation keys can be retrieved from a disk's packaging materials or from e-mails you received when you purchased the software. Figure 16-8 shows an example of where to find

Figure 16-8

There are a lot of things to remember to back up or write down before performing a clean installation, including your e-mail account settings.

information about incoming and outgoing e-mail server settings. (In Outlook Express, click Tools, click Accounts, and click Properties.)

With the required information in hand, reinstalling Windows XP is pretty easy:

1. Put the Windows XP CD in the CD-ROM drive and reboot the computer.

2. When prompted to boot to the CD, perform the required steps. Generally this is achieved by pressing any key during the boot process.

3. Wait while Setup loads the files, and at the Welcome To Setup screen, press Enter to select the option To Set Up Windows XP Now.

4. Press F8 to agree to the terms, and at the next screen, use the arrow keys to select the partition that contains XP's current files. Make a note of the partitions and their size.

5. Read the directions for deleting or creating partitions. Either tell XP to install over the existing partition that holds the system files, or delete and re-create the partitions as desired.

6. Continue with the installation, setting the regional settings, time and date, network configuration (if necessary), and any additional settings, as required.

7. When the installation completes, work through the activation process. Once you've done so, you'll be ready to reinstall each of your programs.

Reinstall Everything

With a clean slate, you can really do things right! As you copy and import your backed-up data, make sure to put it in the right place the first time! As you reinstall hardware, make sure not to install any unsigned drivers. Reboot between each installation to verify no problems occur because of it.

As you reinstall applications, make sure to activate them immediately so problems can be solved immediately.

If you do decide to install something risky, like an unsigned driver, third-party screensaver, or incompatible device, do so slowly. Install the device and its unsigned driver on Monday, and wait until Wednesday or so to see if the computer acts as it should.

A freshly installed computer should not have issues unless you cause them. If you discover a few days after installing that cheap Web cam that the computer is sluggish, generates blue screens, or has similar problems, uninstall it, remove it from your system, and then use System Restore to return to your system's state before it was installed for extra protection.

Maintain the Computer

Finally, remember to use Disk Cleanup and Disk Defragmenter to keep your computer clean. Remember to perform simple maintenance tasks like emptying temporary files once in a while and deleting cookies that can build up on your computer. Above all, keep your anti-virus and firewall software updated. You can have a nice, smooth, fast, and efficient computer; you just have to know how to treat it right!

Summing Up

Sometimes, problems occur that are so bad, specific actions are necessary, like using Device Driver Rollback or System Restore, reinstalling Windows using a repair or an upgrade, or performing a clean installation. Windows XP makes it pretty easy to do these things, and often only a single System Restore is needed to get your computer working flawlessly again. When troubleshooting, work through the techniques described in this chapter in the order given, and save performing a clean installation as a last resort.

Appendix A

Performing a Clean Windows Install

In Chapter 16 we discussed when you may need to perform a clean install of Windows XP. Because a clean install will format your drive, all of the data that you have saved on your computer will be erased. You will also lose all your configuration settings for items such as e-mail, Internet connection properties, network properties, applications, and so on. To help you compile all of the settings and information you will need after you perform a clean install, we've created the form provided in this appendix. We suggest that you use the form as a checklist to save all of your personal data and gather all of your critical settings and write them down.

You will need to gather up all of the applications you use, including their product or activation keys. Don't forget to compile the registration numbers for products that you installed directly from the Web, such as FTP clients or other utilities. The hardware drivers that you use to support devices such as printers, digital cameras, scanners, PCMCIA cards, Wi-Fi hardware, and so on are also very important. It's likely that you have these drivers stored on the CDs that came with the devices you installed. If you installed newer drivers from the Internet, make sure that you backup copies of these drivers. You should also make sure that you backup your e-mail files so that you have copies of your personal inbox and outbox e-mails.

If you follow the guidelines suggested here, you will have a good record of all of your settings, along with the data that you need to save. This will help save you much time and aggravation when you need to perform a clean install. One of the most difficult and time-consuming aspects of re-installing Windows involves re-configuring your PC so that it will operate just as it did before you did the re-install. The settings and data that you compile before you start the re-installation process will save you from having to perform a lot of detective work after the fact.

Settings Needed for Reinstalling Windows

Personal Data to Save:

My Documents: ☐

My Pictures: ☐

My Music: ☐

My Webs: ☐

My Videos: ☐

Any personal folders you've created (check all hard drives):

Hard Drive Configuration:

FAT 32 or NTFS: _____

Drive configuration/format (C: drive only or C: and D: drive): _____

_____

Internet Connection Properties:

Phone number dialed: _____

Dialing options: _____

Security settings: _____

Custom settings (if used): _____

TCP/IP protocol properties: _____

Type of dial up server: _____

Any special ISP settings: _____

FTP addresses and passwords (if used): _____

E-mail Settings and Data:

Account names: _____

User information (name and password): _____

Server URL for any http servers: _____

Incoming and outgoing POP3 and SMTP servers: _____

Connection settings: _____

Advanced settings:

E-mail address book: _____

Saved e-mail messages: _____

Network Configuration Settings:

Workgroup or domain name: _____

Computer name: _____

Passwords: _____

Local area network authentication settings: _____

Application Disks and Activation/Product Keys:

Operating system: _____

Microsoft Office (if used): _____

Internet browser (if applicable): _____

Disks needed to install hard drives (if applicable): _____

Antivirus programs: _____

Firewall program (if applicable): _____

Other application software: _____

_____

_____

_____

_____

Other utility software: _____

_____

_____

_____

_____

Drivers and Software:

Printers: _____

Scanners: _____

Cameras: _____

Other hardware: _____

Other:

Third-party software downloaded to the computer but not stored on disk: _____

All of your data using the Backup utility and burned to CD: _____

Service Packs (if applicable): _____

Tips on Locating Personal Data and Configuration Settings

Most of the personal data components that you'll need to save (and later re-store) when re-installing Windows are relatively easy to locate. You just need to spend a little time and think about all of the folders that you have created on your hard drive(s). Here are a few tips to help you gather your data:

1. Hard Drive Partitions. Review how your hard drive is partitioned and formatted. For example, do you have a single drive (C:) or more than one drive (C: and D:)?

2. E-mail. Look in the directory where your e-mail program (Outlook or AOL, for example) is stored to locate the e-mail client's main data files. It's important that you backup the files that store your actual e-mails and your address book, if you use one.

3. Applications. If you have special applications that store data in the folder where the program itself is stored, make sure you view these folders and backup any critical data files. If you use older applications, you'll find that that they often store their main data file in the default directory where the program is stored. For example, a program such as Quicken would probably store its main data file in the directory C:\Programs\Quicken.

The configuration settings that your computer uses are a little trickier to locate, but with a little detective work you can find them. You can acquire some of the information you need by browsing through the settings for your Internet connection, viewing Outlook or Outlook Express settings for accounts and options, and viewing the Properties dialog boxes for codes and activation keys. Other information, such as product activation keys, can be retrieved from a disk's packaging materials or from e-mails you received when you purchased the software. Here are some specific tips to help you locate the settings that are more difficult to find:

Locating Hard Drive Configuration Settings

To determine how your hard drive is set up:

1. Double click on My Computer from the Desktop. The My Computer window will then be displayed.

2. Scan the window to locate the Hard Disk Drives section. You should see at least one disk drive listed. Note the number of drives that are available.

3. Click on one of the drives to select it (select the C: drive if present), right click, and select the Properties option from the menu that appears. This will display the dialog box shown in Figure A-1.

4. Look for the label "File system." This section will tell you how your drive is formatted. You should see the text "FAT 32" or "NTFS" to indicate if your drive is formatted as FAT or NTFS. This information is important because you'll likely want to keep the format of your drive the same when you re-install Windows.

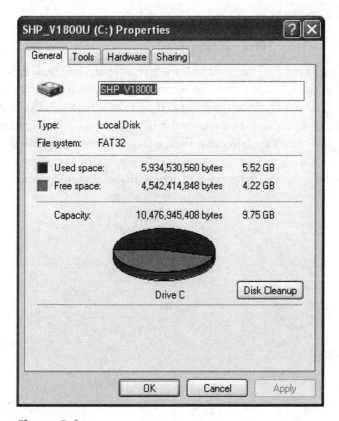

Figure A-1

Viewing the properties of your hard drive to determine its configuration settings.

Locating Your Internet Settings

The Internet settings you need to record (and later restore) will depend on whether you connect to the Internet by a dial-up modem or a high-speed ISP connection. If you use a dial-up modem, you'll need to save the phone number(s) and passwords that you use to connect. If you have an ISP connection, you can locate the settings by following these steps:

1. Click on the Start menu and select Settings and then Control Panel.

2. From the Control Panel window, double click the Internet Options icon.

3. Click the Connections tab that is displayed in the Internet Settings window.

4. Select the internet connection you use and click the Settings button. You will then see a screen showing your connection settings.

Locating Registration Information for Software You Download

If you have software that you've downloaded, registered, and installed, you likely won't have installation CDs with the registration information for the software. When you re-install Windows, you'll need to re-download and re-install this software. The easy way to locate your registration information is to run the software and try to locate the Help menu for the program. Most programs provide an About option that displays information about the program, including your name and registration number. This is the information that you should record.

Recovering from a Corrupted Registry

Believe it or not, just as we were putting the finishing touches on this book, one of us encountered a problem with the Windows XP Registry. This problem kept the computer from booting. In Chapter 9, we explored the Registry in some detail and showed you how to clean and tweak the Registry. This degunking task should help to keep your machine running well, but if you ever encounter a problem with the Registry, you could suffer from the same fate that happened to one of us.

In this appendix, we'll outline a course of action to recover from a Registry problem that keeps your computer from booting. With a little bit of knowledge and patience, you can quickly recover from such a problem and get your computer back up and running.

Using Microsoft Support for Help

If you encounter a problem with your Registry that prevents your computer from booting, the first thing to do is check with Microsoft support services. They provide an excellent service that helps registered Windows users fix critical problems, such as booting problems with the Registry. Don't feel that you have to be a hero and fix your own Registry problems. As you learned in Chapter 9, the Registry is very complicated and requires specialized knowledge to repair, especially if the Registry is corrupted to the point where your computer will not boot.

The information that Microsoft provides for fixing a corrupted Registry can be found on a Web site that Microsoft provides for customer support: **http://search.support.microsoft.com/kb/c.asp?fr=0&SD=GN&LN=EN-US**

When you get to this site, search for article number 307545, "How to Recover from a Corrupted Registry That Prevents Windows XP from Starting."

How to Know When You Have a Registry Boot Problem

While working at home one day or traveling on a flight for a business trip, you might boot up your computer, only to discover the following error message that tells you Windows can't start:

Windows XP could not start because the following file is missing or corrupt:

\WINDOWS\SYSTEM32\CONFIG\SYSTEM

The error message might also contain information about a specific Registry key or hive that is damaged.

Fixing Your Corrupted Registry

Although the Registry involves a set of various files, as we leaned in Chapter 9, there are five critical files that will likely need attention if your computer won't boot due to a Registry problem:

- System
- Software
- Sam
- Security
- Default

Each of these files is stored in the directory C:\Windows\System32\Config. To fix a corrupted Registry problem, you basically need to replace each of these files. But if you replace one of these files, you must replace them all— that's the law—of the Registry.

Replacing the Registry files might sound simple, but there are a few catches. First, because your computer won't boot, you can't simply get on the computer and replace the files. The second catch is that even if your computer could boot under Windows, you can't simply copy over the files because Windows is always accessing the Registry files while it is running. (For more information about how the Windows Registry operates, see Chapter 9.)

Fortunately, Windows provides a tool called the Recovery Console (good name, right?) that you can use to access your system and replace the corrupt Registry files with default repair versions. You can do this because the Recovery Console doesn't need to run under the full Windows operating system. You'll then be able to boot up Windows and access your archived copies of the Registry files that were created by the System Restore feature, which is built into Windows XP. (The System Restore feature was covered in Chapter 16.) Once you locate the proper files, you can rename them so that you can later use them and move them to the proper directory.

For the third major task, you can use the Recovery Console again to move the Registry files to the C:\Windows\System32\Config\ directory so that Windows can access them. Finally, you can re-boot Windows and, if you did everything correctly, your PC should be restored.

NOTE: *In the remaining sections of this appendix we'll show you how to briefly perform the Registry recovery tasks just outlined. Because Microsoft provides very good technical information on this process, we suggest you either call Microsoft for technical support or obtain the Microsoft Knowledge Base Article introduced at the beginning of this appendix.*

Task 1: Use Recovery Console to Set Up Replacement Registry Files

One little-known secret is that Windows stores replacement or "repair" copies on your computer of the five Registry files that you can use to get your PC to boot. So for our first step, we will use the Recovery Console to locate these files and move copies into the C:\Windows\System32\Config directory. Keep in mind that these Registry files are only "repair" files and they won't fully restore your computer to run as it did, with all of your settings, before you encountered problems. To perform this task, follow these steps:

1. Locate your Windows XP Setup CD-ROM.

NOTE: *If you don't have an XP Setup CD-ROM, you won't be able to run the Recovery Console. If you have a computer that came with XP installed and thus the Setup CD-ROM was not provided, you may need to purchase a copy of the Windows Upgrade CD. (Often many computers that have Windows XP Home edition installed do not ship with Setup CD-ROMs.) The advantage of purchasing this CD-ROM is that you will then become a registered Windows user and you can call Microsoft support for help. You may not be happy about spending additional money, but this is a relatively inexpensive way to go if* *you have a system crash and the Upgrade CD-ROM can get you up and running again. It also ensures that you can get ongoing support from Microsoft in the future.*

2. Boot up from the XP Setup CD-ROM. (The detailed instructions for doing this are presented in Chapter 16.)

3. Run the Recovery Console, which provides you with a command-line prompt. (This prompt will look similar to the prompt you see when you use DOS.)

4. Make a temporary directory by typing in this command:

md temp

Make sure to press Enter after each command you type in.

5. Next, you'll need to make backup copies of the existing Registry files. You do this by issuing each command shown next for each of the five Registry files:

copy c:\windows\system32\config\system c:\windows\temp\system.bak

copy c:\windows\system32\config\software c:\windows\temp\software.bak

copy c:\windows\system32\config\sam c:\windows\temp\sam.bak

copy c:\windows\system32\config\security c:\windows\temp\security.bak

copy c:\windows\system32\config\default c:\windows\temp\default.bak

Remember to press Enter after each command.

6. Delete the Registry files using these commands:

delete c:\windows\system32\config\system

delete c:\windows\system32\config\software

delete c:\windows\system32\config\sam

delete c:\windows\system32\config\security

delete c:\windows\system32\config\default

7. Copy the "repair" Registry files to the directory where they need to be so Windows can boot:

copy c:\windows\repair\system c:\windows\system32\config\system
copy c:\windows\repair\software c:\windows\system32\config\software

copy c:\windows\repair\sam c:\windows\system32\config\sam

copy c:\windows\repair\security c:\windows\system32\config\security

copy c:\windows\repair\default c:\windows\system32\config\default

8. Quit the Recovery Console by typing in exit. Your computer should re-boot automatically.

Task 2: Locate Replacement Registry Files

Task 1 allows you to boot Windows temporarily so that you can now get in there and locate your archived Registry files, which you will use to replace the repair files. This is an essential task because the repair files you just set up do not contain all of your Registry settings, such as the configuration settings for your applications, desktop settings, and so on. In fact, your computer might look a little different to you right now—but don't panic!

NOTE: *You must log in as an administrator to perform the steps presented in this section. You might also need to boot your computer in "Safe" mode. The easiest way to do this is to continue to press the F8 key while your computer is booting. This should display a screen of boot options. Select the Safe Mode option and continue with the boot process.*

Follow these steps to locate and rename the archived Registry files:

1. Start Windows Explorer.

2. Select Tools and then click Folder Options.

3. Click the View tab to display the file and folder settings.

4. Using the setting window, select the Show hidden files and folders option and deselect the Hide protected operating system files (Recommended) option as shown in Figure B-1. This step is necessary to unhide the system level files and folders that you will need to locate.

5. When the dialog box is displayed confirming that you want to unhide files and folders, click Yes. Click OK to close the Folder Options dialog box.

6. From your Desktop, locate the hard drive where Windows is installed (likely the C: drive), and double click on the drive to obtain the list of folders stored on the drive. Open the System Volume Information folder. You should see a screen like the one shown in Figure B-2.

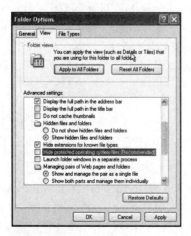

Figure B-1

Selecting the options to unhide files and folders.

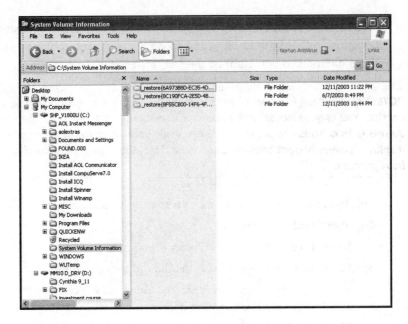

Figure B-2

Viewing the System Volume Information folder.

7. In this folder, you should notice a set of folders that start with the label "_restore ..."These folders represent the different restore points or "snapshots" that have been saved on your computer. Open the folder that has the latest date and time. Don't open the one with the current date and date, if present.

8. Open one of the restore points folders you see (look for the name "RP...") and then open the folder named Snapshot. This folder, as shown in Figure B-3, contains the actual Registry files you'll need to copy and move.

9. Look for the files labeled, REGISTRY_MACHINE_SECURITY, REGISTRY_MACHINE_SAM, REGISTRY_MACHINE_SOFTWARE, REGISTRY_MACHINE_SYSTEM, and REGISTRY_USER_.DEFAULT, and copy them.

10. Paste copies of these files in the directory C:\Windows\Temp.

11. Rename the files copied as SECURITY, SAM, SOFTWARE, SYSTEM, and DEFAULT.

This is far as we can now go with these files because Windows is currently running and accessing the versions of the Registry files that are stored in the C:\Windows\System32\Config directory. We can now use the Recovery Console again to delete the temporary repair files and replace them with the versions that we just obtained from the Snapshot folder.

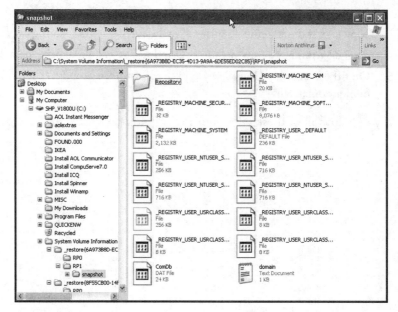

Figure B-3

Locating the Registry files in the Snapshot folder.

Task 3: Use Recovery Console to Set Up Archived Registry Files

Your repair Registry files have done their job, so it's now time to replace them with the real Registry files. We'll use the Recovery Console to move over the files that are now stored in the Temp directory we created. To perform this task, follow these steps:

1. Boot up from the XP CD-ROM.

2. After you boot from the CD-ROM, run the Recovery Console.

3. Delete the Registry files stored in the C:\Windows\System32\Config directory:

   del c:\windows\system32\config\system

   del c:\windows\system32\config\software

   del c:\windows\system32\config\sam

   del c:\windows\system32\config\security

   del c:\windows\system32\config\default

4. Next, you'll need to move over the archived Registry files from the Temp directory. You do this by issuing this set of commands:

   copy c:\windows\temp\system c:\windows\system32\config\system

   copy c:\windows\temp\software c:\windows\system32\config\software

> copy c:\windows\temp\sam c:\windows\system32\config\sam
>
> copy c:\windows\temp\security c:\windows\system32\config\security
>
> copy c:\windows\temp\default c:\windows\system32\config\default

5. Quit the Recovery Console by typing in exit. Your computer should reboot automatically.

If you follow all of these steps your PC should now be fixed.

Appendix C

Troubleshooting Your PC with Degunking Techniques

If your PC is currently gunked up and you are having specific problems that are slowing you down or keeping your PC from running, we can show you how to apply some degunking techniques to solve the most common problems you are likely to encounter. This appendix will help you if your time is limited and you can't take the time to degunk your entire PC by following our twelve-step degunking program (see Chapter 2). The Degunking Sheet we presented in the first part of the book can also help you perform different degunking tasks, depending on the amount of time you have.

To get the most out of this appendix, we suggest that you first identify the problem (or locate the one listed in this appendix that is most similar to your problem) and then perform the corrective action we recommend. You'll be surprised at the number of problems that you can fix by referring to this list and simply performing the right degunking tasks. After you solve a specific problem, put a little time aside later to more fully degunk your PC. For example, if you encounter the problem of not being able to save a document file because your hard drive is full, and then you fix the problem by deleting a few large files, we suggest that you later return to this area and perform the degunking tasks covered in Chapter 3. That way you can get rid of a lot of files and keep the "full disk" problem from occurring again. Our experience shows that if you encounter a problem, it will likely continue unless you put some type of maintenance plan in place.

Operating System Problems

Problem: Your PC boots slowly, or the boot process sometimes stalls and you need to re-start your machine.

Windows may be having difficulty loading one of its system-related files, or you may have too many programs that are trying to be loaded into the System Tray at boot-up. To speed up the boot process, we recommend:

1. Remove some of the programs that get loaded when Windows starts (see Page 79).

2. Clean the Registry using a Registry cleaning utility (see Page 149).

Problem: You recently installed new applications or made changes to the Windows Registry and your PC is having difficulty booting or is running very poorly.

It's likely that something has occurred while you were installing new programs or making changes to the Registry. Rather than try to find the actual problems, which can be really difficult, we recommend that you use the System Restore feature to return your system to an earlier state (see Page 266).

Problem: Your computer won't boot and you receive an error message that you have a corrupt or missing file in the directory C:\Windows\System32\Config.

One of your Registry files may be missing or corrupted. You can fix a problem such as this by following the instructions provided in Appendix B.

Problem: Your computer freezes up when performing tasks like printing files, or you notice that your computer crashes randomly.

Problems like this could be created by the hardware that you've added to your computer. You should run a compatibility check of your hardware and drivers to see if there are any problems (see Page 262).

Problem: You are having serious problems with startup errors, boot errors, or hard-to-diagnose problems that no other degunking technique has been able to solve.

You can still possibly repair Windows XP without having to do a clean install by using the XP Setup CD-ROM (see Page 271).

Problem: You get an "error report" message, and your system asks you if you want to send the report to Microsoft.

Microsoft likes to track system errors so that they can better help their customers. By clicking OK and sending the report to Microsoft, you can possibly help other users down the road. You don't need to worry about any security or privacy issues because of sending the report to Microsoft.

File Management/Hard Drive Problems

Problem: Other users who have used your PC have left files and folders on it that you want to get rid of, and you aren't sure how to access those files and folders.

You'll need to log into your computer as the Administrator and then use the Control Panel to see which users have accounts on your computer. You can then use a Control Panel component called User Accounts to delete an account and the associated files (see Page 41).

Problem: You use multiple computers and you are having difficulty synchronizing your files and folders.

The best way to synchronize your files and folders is to use a third-party utility such as FolderMatch (see Page 219).

Problem: You have too many temporary files on your computer, and you are concerned about how to find all of them so you can delete them.

You can locate and delete most of the temporary files on your PC by using Disk Cleanup, the utility that is provided by Windows XP (see Page 38). You can also delete other temporary files that Disk Cleanup doesn't find by applying some smart searching operations (see Page 39).

Problem: Your hard drive is just about out of free space and you are having trouble running your applications.

You need to first manually delete as many personal files and folders as you can (see Chapter 3). Then you need to uninstall all the programs you no longer use (see Chapter 4). When all of the unnecessary files and programs have been removed, empty the Recycle Bin (see Page 70). To finish your work, you should run the Disk Defragmenter utility (see Page 73). After you complete these steps, you should check your hard drive to make sure that you have created enough free space.

Application Problems

Problem: While using an application such as Word or Excel, you receive an error message indicating that a file you are working on can't be saved because your hard drive is full.

You need to quickly free up some space on your hard drive. We suggest you:

1. Look in your default folder for old files you don't need (see Page 24). Pay particular attention to large files.

2. Remove all of the temporary files on your system (see Page 37).

3. Once you are able to save your data from the application, we suggest you close all of your applications and perform the other file cleaning tasks presented in Chapter 3. Make sure you run the Disk Cleanup utility (see Page 38).

Problem: An application freezes, and you can't close it or work with it.

If the application freezes often, there may be a problem with how the application was installed. In such a case, we recommend you remove the application and re-install it:

1. Remove the application by utilizing the application's uninstall options (see Page 46). If the application does not have an uninstall option, you should remove it using the Control Panel (see Page 47).

2. Once the application has been uninstalled, you can re-install it using any setup software that you have. If you are uninstalling and then reinstalling an application that you have previously downloaded from the Internet, make sure you first take note of the application's registration information before you un-install it.

Problem: It takes forever to load an application.

If you encounter this problem, the application could be installed incorrectly or the setup information about the application could be stored incorrectly in the Registry. To solve such a problem:

1. Try cleaning the Registry using a Registry cleaning utility (see Page 149).

2. If cleaning the Registry does not improve the problem, remove and then re-install the application using the techniques presented for the previous problem.

Problem: You can't find applications you need on the All Programs menu.

You can easily add an application to the Start menu so that it shows up in the All Programs list by following the steps presented on Page 87.

Problem: An old program that you used with a Windows 98 computer installs but it doesn't work right.

If you find that an older program that worked fine on your Windows 98 machine doesn't run so well on your Windows XP machine, you can tell Windows to run it in Program Compatibility Mode (see Page 55).

E-Mail and Web Browsing Problems

Problem: When you try to send an e-mail, it just sits in your Outbox and doesn't go anywhere, or it takes forever to send a two-line e-mail.

Your e-mail system might be so overloaded with saved e-mails that it can't send out or receive e-mails. To fix this problem, you should clean up your e-mail gunk by following the instructions in Chapter 8.

Problem: You have only one e-mail address, and you are getting so much spam that you are having difficulty getting to important e-mail.

You should set up different e-mail accounts to reduce the spam you receive (see page 98). You should also set up a spam filtering utility to help reduce the spam you receive (see Page 108).

Problem: You send e-mail messages to some of your friends or business associates but they don't receive them.

You may be including items in your e-mails that are triggering other people's spam filters (see Page 118).

Problem: Your e-mail program takes an exceptionally long time to start up.

It's likely that your combined set of e-mail inboxes and outboxes have gotten too large. You should follow the instructions in Chapter 8 to clean up your mailboxes. Pay special attention to the task of eliminating the attachments that might be gunking up your mailboxes (see Page 128).

Problem: When you visit Web sites, you get deluged with annoying pop-up messages.

Windows doesn't currently have a global built-in setting for controlling pop-up messages, but you can use a third-party utility such as Pop-Up Stopper Professional to block the pop-up messages (see Page 217).

Problem: You can't save images from the Internet using the Save As command.

You can solve this problem by cleaning out your temporary Internet files (see Page 40).

Problem: You can't load a Web page because your system indicates cookies aren't enabled.

Configure your browser to allow cookies to be used (see Page 229).

Problem: While using your browser to access the Web, you get errors indicating that you are in a restricted zone and you can't view the Web page.

Your browser is limiting your access to the Web because of the security and privacy settings that have been configured. To reconfigure the privacy and security settings, see Page 225.

Security Problems

Problem: You think that intruders have been getting into your computer and possibly accessing your data or leaving unwanted files.

You should install a firewall (or make sure one is installed already) on your PC. You can set up the Windows XP Internet Connection Firewall (ICF), which is a free firewall that comes with Windows XP (see Page 239). If you feel you need additional security, you can set up a third-party firewall (see Page 240).

Problem: Your anti-virus program doesn't run automatically any more.

Keeping your anti-virus program running and up-to-date is crucial because you don't want viruses to sneak onto your machine. If your anti-virus program is no longer running automatically, your registration might have expired. Many anti-virus programs are set up to run for a specific amount of time. You also should check to make sure that your ant-virus program is set up in the System Tray so that it will load when you start Windows (see Page 79). Additional anti-virus configuration information is provided on Page 223.

Problem: You're concerned that your kids are accessing adult-only Web sites or other sites you don't want them to visit.

You can easily set up Internet security zones by using your Web browser (see Page 225).

Problem: You're concerned that Web sites are gathering too much information about you when you visit these sites.

You can control the amount of information that Web sites gather from your computer by using Windows' privacy settings (see Page 228).

Hardware and Peripheral Problems

Problem: You don't have enough memory to run an application, run multiple applications at the same time, or open an attachment.

You'll need to add additional memory to your PC. You can do this by following the instructions presented in Chapter 12. If you are not sure of the type of memory to add to your PC, there are a few ways to determine the type and amount of memory you'll need (see Page 192).

Problem: You've recently installed a new hardware device - such as a digital camera, printer, or scanner - and your computer is running poorly or crashing when you use the hardware device.

You may have a bad or incorrect driver installed. If you suspect a newly installed driver is causing a system problem, you can remove that driver and replace it with a new one (see Page 264).

Problem: You are having trouble typing on your keyboard because some of the keys keep sticking.

You can really improve the performance of your keyboard by cleaning it with compressed air (see Page 201).

Index

100-message e-mail rule, adhering to, 123

A

Administrative Tools, Windows XP, 233–238
Advanced Backup Wizard, 247
Alt-Tab Replacement PowerToy, understanding, 215
Antivirus software
  configuration guidelines for, 224–225
  purchasing and configuring, 223–225
Archiving, 257
AutoHide
  System Tray program icons, removing, 82–83
  Taskbar, locking the with, 84
Autosort feature, using, 123–124

B

Backup devices, adding, 195–197
Backup e-mail addresses
  setting up, 99–100
  understanding, 98–99
Backup tab, 249
Backup utility, 244–252
  Advanced mode, 244
  opening in Advanced mode, 245–246
  scheduling backups with, 252
  scheduling to run, 254–255
  simple backups, 246–247
  system state backups, 247–248
Backups. *See also* Backup utility
  copying to CD, 257–260
  creating simple backups, 246–247
  creating thorough backups, 247–248

for home users, 250
importance of, 20
manually creating, 259–260
restoring from, 256–257
schedule for, 250–251
scheduling with Backup utility, 252
storage space for, 245
storing, 251
of system state, 247–248
types of, 249–250
Basic input/output system (BIOS), changing, 272–273
Boot delay, avoiding configuring, 164
Boot files, backing up, 256
Boot process
  boot delay, avoiding configuring, 164
  cleaning, 163–168
  floppy drive search during, skipping, 163–164
  logging on automatically, 164–165
  System Configuration Utility, using, 165–168
Business office firewalls, using, 240–241

C

Cascading folders, transforming into My Documents folder, 155–156
CD recordable devices, types of, 195–196
CD Writing Wizard, burning backups with, 257–258
CDs
  backing up to, 251
  copying to, 257–260
Classic Start Menu, customizing, 87–88
Clean installations

checklist for, 275–276
in Windows XP, performing, 274–278
Clean start, performing, 20
Compatibility reports, understanding
system, 263–264
Compressed files, displaying in alternate
colors, 156
Computer cases, degunking inside,
202–203
Computer Management console
becoming familiar with, 237–238
understanding, 236–238
Computer memory
adding, 190–195
correct/compatible, finding, 192
installation success, ensuring, 193
installing, 191–193
Computers
housekeeping 101, 3, 24–42
how to physically clean, 200–203
Recycle Bin, restarting before emptying,
71–72
repairing problems with, 3
usage analysis, 15–16
Control Panel, removing programs using,
47–48
Cookies
defining, 230–231
deleting, 231
disabling and accepting, 10
Copy backups, 250
Critical Updates And Service Packs,
acquiring security enhancements for, 182
Custom zones, configuring, 227–228

D

Daily backups, 250
Data
backing up, 275–277
storing, 65–67
transferring, 203–204
Data archiving, 257
Data files, disorganization of, 8–9
Data storage
on CD recordable devices, 195–196
on DVD recordable devices, 195–196
on external hard drives, 195
on other storage options, 197
on tape drives, 197
on zip drives, 196–197
Default folders

cleaning up, 24–31
creating, 66–67
organizing, 64–70
personalizing, 68–70
Degunking
12-step program of, 20–21
procedures for, 18–19
strategies for, understanding, 14–20
Desktop
cleaning up, 17, 89–94
Cleanup Wizard, running on, 92–93
default icons, adding and removing,
90–91
folders, creating, 91
folders, removing, 92
icons, removing, 157–158
organizing, 89–90
overrun, 6–7
personalizing, 89–94
program shortcuts, creating on, 91
program shortcuts, removing from, 92
Recycle Bin, removing from, 91
screensavers, choosing, 93
themes for, choosing, 93–94
Desktop Cleanup Wizard, running, 92–93
Desktop themes, choosing, 93–94
Device Rollback utility, returning to older
versions of drivers using, 265–266
Differential backups, 250
Disk Cleanup utility, using, 72
Disk Defragmenter utility, using, 73–75
Disk space, conserving, 29–30
Display adapters
installing, 199
Windows XP compatible, selecting,
198–199
Disposable e-mail addresses
e-commerce, using for, 107–108
services that manage, list of, 108
setting up, 99–100
understanding, 98–99
Dr. Watson, viewing errors, 168
Drafts folder, managing, 132
Driver updates, importance of, 182–183
Drivers
unsigned, deleting, 168–172
unsigned, setting properties of,
171–172
unsigned, updating, 172
Drwtson32.exe, running, 168
DVD recordable devices, types of, 195–196

E

E-mail
100-message rule, adhering to, 123
attachments, managing, 128–130
Autosort feature, using, 123–124
checklist for cleaning, 130–131
degunking, 17
deleting, 124
files, cleaning up, 40
folder hierarchy, creating and organizing, 124–128
folder list, keeping it to one screen, 125–126
housekeeping pointers, 131–137
keeping, holding, or deleting, 122–123
nesting folders in, 127–128
time-delimited, storing, 126
E-mail addresses
choosing, 98–101
newsgroups or discussion boards, obfuscating on, 106–107
posting on Web, 105
types of, 98
unsubscribing from spam lists, 104
using, 104–108
E-mail clients
alternative, using, 103–104
choosing, 101–104
Outlook, gunking up, 101–102
POPFile and, configuring, 113–114
Eudora V6, defeating spam beacons using, 104
External drives, backing up to, 251

F

File management, understanding, 16–17
File shredder
functions of, 135–137
using, 135–137
File signature verification, using, 169–172
Files
disorganization of, 4
duplicate, locating, 37
e-mail, cleaning up, 40
Internet, cleaning up, 40
temporary, deleting, 37–40
unsigned, deleting, 168–172
unused, deleting, 34–36

unused user, deleting, 41–42
zipped, deleting, 36
Files And Folders Task pane, using in Windows XP, 70
Files And Settings Transfer Wizard, using, 204–205
Firewalls
as affordable security, 241
business office, 240–241
home office, 240–241
Internet Connection Firewall, 239–241
purpose of, 239
understanding, 239–241
Floppy drives, skipping search for, 163–164
Folder hierarchy
nested folders in, using, 127–128
one screen, 125–126
one-screen, creating and organizing, 124–128
for time-delimited e-mail, 126
FolderMatch shareware, synchronizing duplicate files with, 219
Folders
desktop, creating on, 91
desktop, removing from, 92
moving data into, 70
options of, exploring, 94–96
renaming, copying, and deleting, 69

G

Games, enhancing capabilities of, 56–57
Guest accounts
creating, 232–233
enabling and configuring, 232–233
properties of, 232
GunkBuster's Notebook
"A Little About Installed Programs," 45
"Be Careful What You Delete," 31–32
"Centralizing Storage of Install Suites," 51–52
"Changing the Default Location of Your My Documents Folder," 69
"Creating Default Folders for Multiple Partitioned Hard Drives," 66–67
"Editing Values in the Registry," 153–155
"Finding Performance Utilities on the Internet," 167–168
"Managing Sent Items Folder," 126–127

"More about Cookies," 230–230
"Perform Backups Before Deleting,
    Installing, Moving, and
    Experimenting," 249
"Saving Space by Spotting Duplicate
    MP3s," 29–30
"Spring Cleaning on Your E-Mail,"
    130–131
"Using the Web to Decipher Your
    RAM," 192
"What Updates Are Really
    Necessary," 183
"When to Perform a Clean
    Installation," 275
"Yeah, But Is Windows Update
    Secure," 179–180
Gunking agents
    cookies, 10
    data files, 8–9
    desktop, overrun with, 6–7
    files, 4
    hard drives, overrun with, 7–8
    menu systems, overrun with, 5–6
    software programs, 5
    spam, 4–5
    Spyware, 9–10
    temporary files, 4
    Web favorites, 9

H

Hard drives
    disorganized, 7–8
    errors on, checking for, 172–173
    external, adding, 195
    main, cleaning up, 31–37
    optimizing, 18
    partitions, resizing, 161–162
    sectors on, checking, 172–173
    segmented, 7
    space, 7–8
Hardware
    incompatible, locating, 262–264
    system compatibility of, checking,
        262–264
Hardware drivers
    fixing problems with, 264–266
    older versions of, returning to, 265–266
Hardware programs, removing, 54–55
Hidden files, displaying with Windows
    Explorer, 157

HKEY_CLASSES_ROOT, defining, 144
HKEY_CURRENT_CONFIG, defining, 144
HKEY_CURRENT_USER, defining, 144
HKEY_LOCAL_MACHINE, defining, 144
HKEY_USERS, defining, 144
Home office firewalls, using, 240–241
Home users, backups for, 250

I

Image Resizer PowerToy, resizing images
    with, 215
Incremental backups, 250
Information
    gathering critical, 275–277
    personal, protecting, 228–229
    providing, 229
Install suites, storing, 51–52
Internet Connection Firewall (ICF)
    enabling, 239–240
    Windows XP and, 239–241
Internet privacy options
    configuring, 225–231
    personal information, protecting,
        228–229
    understanding, 228–231
Internet zones, configuring, 225–226

K

Keyboards, how to physically clean,
    201–202

L

Local Intranet zones
    security level of, understanding, 226
    Web sites, adding to, 227
Local Security policies
    configuring, 234–236
    security changes, 234–236
Logons, automatic, 164–165

M

Mail proxies, understanding, 111–113
Mailbases
    duplicate copies of, deleting, 132–133
    finding, 133
Main hard drives. *See also* Hard drives

cleaning up, 31–37
deleting files or programs on, cautiously, 31–32
Media applications, upgrading, 185–186
Media Player 9, upgrading, 185
Menu systems, gunked, 5–6
Mice, how to physically clean, 201–202
Microsoft Baseline Security Analyzer (MBSA), running, 222–223
Microsoft Virtual Desktop Manager (MSVDM)
    desktop, organizing with, 213–214
    guidelines for working with, 213–214
Microsoft Windows
    degunking strategies, 14–20
    limited resources in, managing, 15
    processes of, degunking, 3
    Registry and, 141–142
Monitors
    how to physically clean, 201–202
    second, adding, 197–200
    second, configuring display settings of, 199–200
Movie Maker 2, upgrading, 185–186
MSN Messenger 6.1, upgrading to, 186–187
MSVDM. *See* Microsoft Virtual Desktop Manager (MSVDM)
Multimedia, enhancing capabilities of, 56–57
Multiple partitioned hard drives, creating default folders in, 66–67
My Computer, using error checking tool in, 172–173
My Documents folder
    cascading folders, transforming into, 155–156
    cleaning up, 25
    default location of, changing, 69
My Music folder, cleaning up, 28–30
My Pictures folder, cleaning up, 26
My Videos folder, cleaning up, 27–28

N

New computers
    purchasing, 203–205
    restoring to, 256
    system state, restoring to, 256
Normal backups, 250

NT file system (NTFS)
    converting to, 160–161
    FAT32 and FAT versus, 160
    understanding, 160–161
NTFS. *See* NT file system (NTFS)

O

Outlook
    degunking, 17
    gunking up with spam, 101–102
Outlook Express
    blocked sender entries, removing and locating, 133–135
    degunking, 17
    gunking up with spam, 101–102

P

Partitions, resizing, 161–162
Pegasus Mail V4.1, defeating spam beacons using, 104
Poco Mail 2.6, defeating spam beacons using, 104
Pop-Up Stopper Professional, using, 217–218
POPFile utility
    download location of, 112–113
    e-mail client for, configuring, 113–114
    installing, 113
    magnets in, creating, 116–117
    understanding, 112
    using and training in, 114–116
PowerToys
    Alt-Tab Replacement, understanding, 215
    defining, 208
    for degunking, 208–215
    downloading and installing, 209–211
    Image Resizer, understanding, 215
    Microsoft Virtual Desktop Manager, understanding, 213–215
    Tweak UI, understanding, 211–213
    Windows XP and, 208–215
Primary e-mail addresses
    setting up, 99
    understanding, 98–99
Program Compatibility Mode, configuring, 55–56
Program File folder, exploring, 50–52

Program shortcut icons, exploring properties of, 55
Program shortcuts
  desktop, creating on, 91
  desktop, removing on, 92

Q

Quick Launch toolbar
  adding icons using, 83–84
  using, 78–79

R

Random access memory (RAM)
  adding, 190–195
  finding correct/compatible, 192
  installing, 191–193
Recycle Bin
  emptying, 70–73
  removing from desktop, 91
  reviewing contents of, 72
RegClean, cleaning Registry in Windows
  platforms with , 152–153
REGEDIT versus REGDT32, 142
REGEDT32
  compressed files, displaying alternate
    colors of, 156
  hidden files, displaying, 157
  My Documents folder, turning cascad-
    ing folders into, 155–156
  versus REGEDIT, 142
  Registry, backing up and restoring
    sections of, 145, 148–149
  Registry, tweaking, 153–158
  Registry keys, types of, 144
  understanding, 142–144
Registry
  backing up, 144–149, 247–248
  boot problems, 288-289
  breaking up and restoring full, 146–148
  breaking up and restoring sections of,
    145, 148–149
  cleaning up, 18, 149–153
  inside of, 140–149
  Microsoft Windows and, 141–142
  recovering from a corrupted Registry,
    287–294
  REGEDT32 to view, using, 142–144
  restoring, 144–149
  tweaking, 153–158

Registry Clean Pro
  Registry sections cleaned by, 152
  using, 150–152
Registry First Aid shareware
  downloading and installing, 216–217
  Registry, keeping clean with, 216–217
Restore utility, 255–257
  Advanced Mode, 256
  Wizard Mode, 256
Restricted Sites zones
  security level of, understanding, 227
  Web sites, adding to, 227
Root Directory (C:)
  deleting files from, 32–34
  organizing, 33–34

S

Scheduled Tasks utility, 253–255
Scheduled Tasks window, 253
Scheduled Tasks Wizard, configuring,
  254–255
Screensavers, choosing non-system
  intensive, 93
Sectors, checking hard drive, 172–173
Security
  current configurations, checking,
    222–223
  setting up, 18–19
Security zones
  configuring, 225–228
  types of, 225–228
Service Packs, understanding, 182
Setup folders, cleaning, 162–163
Shared Documents folders, cleaning up,
  30–31
Shareware
  defining, 215
  FolderMatch, 219
  Pop-Up Stopper Professional, 217–218
  Registry First Aid, 216–217
  System Mechanic, 219–220
Software programs
  finding unknown, 50–54
  installing too many, 5
  Registry cleaning, types of, 150–153
  removing unused, 44–50
  removing using Control Panel, 47–48
  tools of cleaning, 150
  understanding, 45
  uninstall commands of, using, 46–47

Spam
  beacons, understanding, 102–103
  dictionary attacks, avoiding, 100–101
  preventing, 4–5
Spam beacons
  defeating with e-mail clients, 104
  managing with e-mail clients, 103–104
  understanding, 102–103
Spam filtering
  within e-mail clients, 110–111
  glossary, using, 109–110
  mail proxies and, relationship be-
    tween, 111–113
  POPFile utility, 112–113
  separate utilities for, 108–117
Spam filters, avoid triggering, 118
Spammer dictionary attacks, avoiding,
  100–101
Spammers Mailing Lists, unsubscribing
  from, 104–105
Spamspiders, understanding, 105–106
Spyware
  removing, 52–54
  understanding, 9–10
Start Menu
  Classic, customizing, 87–88
  cleaning up, 17, 49–50
  personalizing, 85–88
  using, 78
  in Windows XP, adding items to, 87
  in Windows XP, tweaking, 86–87
Startup process, degunking, 162–168
System Configuration utility, using,
  165–168
System files, backing up, 247–248
System Mechanic shareware, using,
  219–220
System performance, enhancing options
  of, 57–59
System Restore, 249
  configuring, 268–269
  Registry, backing up and restoring full,
    146–148
  restore points, manually creating,
    269–270
  tweaking, 59–61
  using, 270–271
  in Windows XP, 266–271
System restore points, 247–248
System settings, improving, 3
System state

  backing up, 247–248
  restoring, 256
System Tray
  managing, 79–83
  program icons, adding to, 80–81
  program icons, hiding inactive, 82–83
  program icons, removing from, 81–82
  using, 78–79T
Tape drives, adding, 197
Taskbar
  AutoHide, grouping items using, 84
  AutoHide, locking using, 84
  cleaning up, 78–85
  components of, 78–79
  personalizing, 78–85
Temporary files, permanency of, 4
Trusted zones
  security level of, understanding, 226
  Web sites, adding to, 227
Tweak UI PowerToy
  capabilities of, 208
  customizing system settings with, 85,
    211–213
  download location of, 85

U

Uninstall commands, using, 46–47
User files, deleting unused accounts from,
  41–42
User preferences, improving, 3
Users, system usage of, 15–16

V

Virtual memory
  defining, 193
  tweaking, 193–195

W

Web crawlers, understanding, 105–106
Web favorites, disorganization of, 9
Windows components
  removing or installing, 48–49
  tweaking, 55–61
Windows Messenger, upgrading to MSN
  Messenger 6.1 from, 186–187
Windows settings, using Tweak UI
  PowerToy for Windows XP, 211–213
Windows updates

acquiring, 178–181
acquiring automatically, 180–181
acquiring manually, 181
Critical Updates And Service Packs,
  importance of, 182
running, 172
security enhancements of, 178
types of, 177
using, 176–184
Windows User Group Network
(WUGNET)
  defining, 208
  purpose of, 216
  shareware picks of, 215–220
Windows XP
  Administrative Tools of, 233–238
  Backup utility, using, 145
  CD-ROM, rebooting to, 272
  CD-ROM, rebooting to change BIOS,
    272–273
  clean install, performing, 274–278
  Dr. Watson in, using, 168
  Files And Folders Task pane in, using,
    70
  Internet Connection Firewall, 239–241
  logging on automatically in, 164–165
  media applications, upgrading to,
    185–186
  monitor, adding a second, 197–198
  My Documents folder, location of, 69
  NT file system and, 160
  page files in, setting custom, 194–195
  performing a clean install, 279-286
  PowerToys and, 208–215
  random access memory and, 190,
    193–195
  Registry in, backing up and restoring,
    144–149
  Registry misconceptions, 145
  Registry tools of, using, 142–144
  reinstalling everything in, 277–278

repairing with CD-ROM, 271–274
repairing without CD-ROM, 272
repairing without performing a clean
  install, 273
settings needed for reinstalling, 280-
  283
Start Menu, adding items to, 87
Start Menu, tweaking, 86–87
System Restore feature, using, 145,
  266–271
tips on locating configuration settings,
  283-286
updates, acquiring, 178–182
using Microsoft support for help, 287-
  288
Upgrade option, reinstalling using,
  274
Windows settings, customizing with
  Tweak UI PowerToy, 211–213
Windows XP Professional, upgrading
  to, 184
Windows XP Professional, upgrading to,
184
WUGNET. *See* Windows User Group
  Network (WUGNET)

Z

Zip drives, adding, 196–197
Zones
  Custom, 227–228
  Internet, 225–226
  Local Intranet, 226–227
  Restricted Site, 227
  Security, 225–228
  Trusted, 226–227